Fusion
LEADERSHIP

Fusion LEADERSHIP

UNLOCKING THE SUBTLE FORCES THAT CHANGE PEOPLE AND ORGANIZATIONS

Richard L. Daft / Robert H. Lengel

Berrett-Koehler Publishers, Inc.
San Francisco

Berrett-Koehler Publishers, Inc.
450 Sansome Street, Suite 1200
San Francisco, CA 94111-3320
Tel: (415) 288-0260   Fax: (415) 362-2512

ORDERING INFORMATION

Individual sales. Berrett-Koehler publications are available through most bookstores. They can also be ordered direct from Berrett-Koehler at the address above.

Quantity sales. Special discounts are available on quantity purchases by corporations, associations, and others. For details, contact the "Special Sales Department" at the Berrett-Koehler address above.

Orders for college textbook/course adoption use. Please contact Berrett-Koehler Publishers at the address above.

Orders by U.S. trade bookstores and wholesalers. Please contact Publishers Group West, 4065 Hollis Street, Box 8843, Emeryville, CA 94662. Tel: (510) 658-3453; 1-800-788-3123. Fax: (510) 658-1834.

Printed in the United States of America

 Printed on acid-free and recycled paper that is composed of 50% recycled fiber, including 10% postconsumer waste.

Library of Congress Cataloging-in-Publication Data

Daft, Richard L.
     Fusion leadership : unleashing the subtle forces that change
people and organizations / Richard L. Daft and Robert H. Lengel.
        p.   cm.
     Includes bibliographical references and index.
     ISBN 1-57675-023-X (alk. paper)
        1. Leadership. 2. Organizational change. I. Lengel, Robert H.,
     1946–   . II. Title.
     HD57.7.D34   1998
     658.4'092—dc21   97-52979
                                                                 CIP

First Edition

02 01 00 99 98   10 9 8 7 6 5 4 3 2 1

Book Production: Pleasant Run Publishing Services
Composition: Classic Typography

CONTENTS

PART TWO:
UNLOCKING SUBTLE FORCES
THROUGH PERSONAL FUSION

PART THREE: UNLOCKING SUBTLE FORCES THROUGH ORGANIZATIONAL FUSION

ACKNOWLEDGMENTS

We started this book ten years ago. Its publication documents an ongoing conversation we have had between ourselves and with executives, colleagues, fellow inquirers, friends, students, and family, all of whom are wrestling with change, transformation, and leadership in their lives and organizations. As we reflect back on this conversation, we are humbled by the number of voices that contributed significantly to the final product. We especially want to acknowledge the following people:

- Marvin Weisbord and Sandra Janoff, for their training in future search technology, which provided us with deep insight into the power of guided conversation across boundaries.
- Margaret Wheatley and Myron Kellner–Rogers, for their Sundance dialogues.
- Kathy Dannemiller and her associates, particularly Paul and Kathy Tolchinsky, who helped us understand the working details of the whole-scale change process.
- Juanita Brown and David Isaacs, who helped provide a philosophical focus for this book and gave us the concept of "remembering" as a way to connect with the subtle forces.

- Bill Isaacs at Dia-logous, for sharing his theory and expertise in the Foundations of Dialogue.
- Michael Jones and Nancy Margulies, for helping us understand the power of music and art in enhancing reflection and conversation.
- Wayne Bodensteiner, for championing the Center for Professional Excellence at the University of Texas at San Antonio when few people understood what we were trying to do.
- Jim Gaertner, dean of the College of Business, for supporting the center and enabling its growth beyond our expectations.
- Dean Marty Geisel of the Owen Graduate School of Management, Vanderbilt University, for providing support for the Center for Change Leadership and the time and opportunity to work with corporations to refine and field-test our ideas.
- Our academic colleagues who challenged our thinking and supported us. They include Bruce Barry, Alan Craven, Ray Friedman, Barry Gerhart, Vic Heller, Mike Kelly, Rich Oliver, Paul Preston, Jerre Richardson, Bill Spruce, and Greg Stewart.
- Executives from the following organizations, who shaped our thinking by affirming or challenging us in conversations, dialogues, round tables, or fusion projects: J. C. Bradford & Co., Central Parking System, City of San Antonio, SBC Communications, City Public Service, Fort Sam Houston U.S. Army Medical Command, HEB, Jacoby & Meyers, LLP, Northern Telecom, Pratt & Whitney San Antonio, Seaworld of Texas, Six Flags Fiesta Texas, State Farm, Team Leadership Resources, Tristar Corporation, Ultramar Diamond Shamrock, USAA, USAA Federal Savings Bank, and Vanderbilt University Medical Center.
- Chris Atcher, for researching numerous books on myths, stories, and spiritual images, and drafting materials to keep us moving. Also, many of our uncited images and metaphors are drawn from the Buddhist and Hindu literatures, especially the discourses of Sri Sathya Sai Baba, for which we are most grateful.

- Linda Roberts and Rita Carswell, in the Center for Change Leadership, and Kristie Rutherford and Natalie Shaw, program coordinators in the Center for Professional Excellence, for riding with the ups and downs of this fusion leadership project, helping with endless revisions of the manuscript and its graphics, and providing logistical support for our work with companies.

- Our students in M.B.A. and Executive M.B.A. programs, as well as those in corporate programs in leadership and change, for accepting our relentless experimentation. They were exposed to early versions of this manuscript, exercises and activities designed to unlock their subtle forces, and experiments aimed at refining our application of fusion change technologies.

- Participants and facilitators in the dialogue and other groups we have attended, for insights into ourselves and into subtle fusion processes.

- The team at Berrett-Koehler for their excellent work on this project and for trusting and supporting our dream.

- Our wives, Dorothy Marcic and Sandy Lengel, for their devotion and commitment. After reading a magazine article on fusion-fission, Dorothy suggested it might make a good metaphor for the work we were doing. We agree! Sandy lived through every breath of this project, never giving up support despite the many dead ends and surprise resurrections.

This book is truly a fusion of many voices, and to each voice we offer our deepest appreciation.

January 1998

Richard L. Daft
Nashville, Tennessee

Robert H. Lengel
San Antonio, Texas

THE TRANSFORMATION MIRACLE

We began work on this book with the intention of describing the excitement and relevance of new science concepts when they are applied to management. After repeated delays and disagreements, we decided to spend several days together to crystallize our shared vision and to make a start on the writing. We picked historic Santa Fe for our retreat, renting a house near the central plaza so that we could walk, enjoy the weather, and explore the city while doing our work.

We learned so much from our discussions and discoveries in Santa Fe that we changed, and so did the book.

The downtown plaza is a square park edged and crisscrossed by sidewalks. Across the street on the north side of the square, Native American artisans sell jewelry and pottery in front of a museum. Shops and galleries on the other three sides of the square offer craft work and art of all types. The stores on streets radiating from the plaza also contain high-quality goods, including painting and sculpture.

The plaza atmosphere seemed cosmopolitan and diverse. As we walked, we intermingled with second-generation hippies being entertained by a tattooed guitar player, conservative businessmen in suits, Native American vendors selling their wares, sunburned tourists in shorts, cowboys, robed and turbaned devotees of some religious order, teenagers playing kickbag, and a bearded birdman preaching the gospel while feeding the pigeons. This was a city of enduring cultural diversity: Anglo, Hispanic, Native American; gay and straight; traditionally religious and New Age spiritual. Nobel laureates from the Santa Fe Institute could attend a talk by the Dalai Lama.

We soon realized that Santa Fe—"the city different"—celebrates the individual, perhaps more than any community we knew. There is also a unity consciousness wherein people see value in their opposites. We talked with Buddhists, Quakers, and Methodists who welcomed each other. We observed feminists, gay rights activists, and men's groups all coexisting. The value of individual differences was captured in a Tony Hillerman story about a visitor from Africa. The visitor reported that to fit in with New York City's businesspeople, he was expected to wear a suit and tie, yet he was still treated as a foreigner. In Santa Fe, he walked around the city in his native tribal costumes. A few days before a city election, party workers handed him brochures and cards representing their candidates. He was perplexed. Talking with the campaign workers, he was told that they didn't know he was a foreigner. They assumed this exotically dressed man was just another citizen of Santa Fe.

A lasting image was imprinted on our memory in an art gallery we discovered during our wanderings. The gallery displayed a collection of oil paintings of old doors, windows, and entryways, partially opened, set in thick, weather-beaten walls. Most striking was the incredible detail captured on canvas, approaching that of a photograph. A gallery employee explained that the paintings were the collaboration of a husband and wife team. Each takes a turn painting, adding to or changing what the other has done. They paint over each other's work, adding their own impressions, until they agree on a final image. As struggling coauthors, we asked how the artists succeeded, since painting arises from individual creativity. The woman explained that they had developed an intimate sense of mutual trust and respect, and subordinated their individual egos to the picture being created on the canvas. They co-create. The paintings bring together the opposites of realism and impressionistic warmth, merging the two artists' distinct styles. The paintings are fiction and nonfiction in confluence, forming something more than real.

The paintings were powerful for us, because co-creation is what we had tried and failed to achieve. The artists had fused their separate talents into a unified whole. Fusion is what organizations achieve when employees' creative energies contribute to the common goal. Instead of staying behind high walls, people open doors to each other, achieving results beyond what is possible when they remain separate. The simultaneous expression of individuality and collaboration in Santa Fe was a metaphor for what we and many corporations were trying to become.

We also found that during our time in Santa Fe, our relationship changed. We had worked together for years, but didn't really know each other. This time provided opportunities for meandering discussions and disagreement. The difference in our agendas for the book became clear, but we discovered common ground in our shared concerns about marriage, work, stress, management of our leadership centers, and relationships with client companies—strong common ground that had nothing to do with the book.

Perhaps it was no coincidence that our conversations occurred only thirty miles from Los Alamos, where the atomic bomb was given to the world. Splitting the atom released power beyond imagination at that time, and the hydrogen bomb soon followed, with power several times greater. Modern corporate hierarchies depend on a division of labor and systems of control reminiscent of atomic fission, and therewith have produced an abundance of products and services. The hydrogen bomb is fusion-based, meaning that atoms are joined together rather than split apart. In companies, the equivalent process is bonding employees together for empowerment and partnership so that they can achieve an even higher level of performance.

Our own version of fusion occurred during a "front porch" conversation that laid the basis for a book going farther than either of us had imagined. Although we both think of ourselves as individualists, we found ourselves able to set aside our egos and differences, to listen to each other, and to reconcile our conflicting agendas. Understanding each other on a personal level became as important to the project as our knowledge of techniques for changing organizations. It enabled us to paint on one canvas, not two.

We saw that the problems faced by companies we worked with would not be solved with new science concepts alone. A book such as Margaret Wheatley's *Leadership and the New Sciences* provided a powerful new lens through which to understand today's organizations, but equally important are ideas about individuality and personal growth. These ideas are explored in books such as David Whyte's *The Heart Aroused: Poetry and the Preservation of the Soul in Corporate America* and Stephen Covey's *The Seven Habits of Highly Effective People.* It is the fusion of these two elements—the system and the person, the exterior world and the interior world—that makes a company unstoppable. Indeed, they need each other: the self-organizing, empowering company needs whole people who are growing and want to contribute their best to the fast-changing organization.

We also began to see why companies moving from hierarchical control to empowerment have such a difficult time. Organizational structure and systems need to change, but so do the people giving and receiving empowerment. A self-adapting organization asks more from every person. A mindset shift away from separation and toward fusion must occur in everyone, whether leader or follower. This is a different paradigm from the conventional management thinking that relies on separation of individuals by department, division, and level.

PREVIEW OF THE BOOK

The purpose of this book is to describe organizational leadership by reference to principles of fusion (joining together) rather than fission (splitting apart, separating).

Part One (Chapters One and Two) describes how traditional hierarchies have suppressed individual qualities, and how fusion awakens personal subtle forces—for example, mindfulness, courage, and vision—that can transform a company.

Part Two (Chapters Three through Nine) is devoted to the idea of personal fusion. These chapters explain the interior self and challenge you to unlock the subtle forces, each of which we describe in depth.

Part Three (Chapters Ten through Thirteen) explores organizational fusion and describes transformational technologies that can catalyze fundamental change in large organizations.

Throughout the book, we make extensive use of stories, parables, and metaphors. A story is designed to go beyond logical argument to touch the subtle mental, emotional, and spiritual elements within you. Stories and metaphors are gentle in their approach, yet provide greater depth than is normally possible in a book about leadership and change. We invite you to spend time with the parables and stories. Let them soak in. Develop your own interpretation to gain access to the subtle forces within you. Readers who want to move instantly to the bottom line may find this approach unfamiliar but will quickly understand the deeper possibilities within themselves that these stories evoke. Whereas direct exposition (strong force) appeals to the rational mind, stories and metaphors (subtle force) appeal to the spirit within. Watch your reactions to these subtle images as an indication of your own progress toward personal fusion.

End-of-chapter questions and exercises will trigger self-reflection and personal discovery and will thus help you to "remember" the subtle forces. These forces already exist within you. Fusion leadership is not about new skills as much as it is about remembering and unlocking potentials that have been there all along. Self-inquiry will help you remember, in a sense, who you really are, and when you do, you will be able to awaken these potentials in others.

Answering end-of-chapter questions is a first step toward creating fusion within yourself. We encourage you to write answers to the questions and to discuss those answers with others. In our experience, both writing and conversation provide access to a deeper place than does solitary reflection.

In our relationships with executive students, corporate clients, and participants in leadership and change workshops, we are constantly reminded of peoples' desire for something more than is currently being expressed in their work. They yearn for subtle things like meaningfulness, a shared dream, a voice, opportunities to give of themselves, to learn, to venture beyond tradition, to work on what they care about. When we touch these yearnings, personal enthusiasm and energy skyrocket, and organizations reap huge rewards.

This book describes how leaders can make the transition to fusion. The transformation of people and organizations is accomplished through self-inquiry and social science technologies such as *dialogue, future search,* and *whole-scale change,* which redefine the relationship between individuals and organization. On the basis of personal empowerment, autonomy, and a shared future with others, people in traditional structures can discover and embrace their inner potential for leadership.

THE PROMISE OF FUSION

CHAPTER ONE

FUSION LEADERSHIP

Five years ago, the new CEO of a major retail employer in South Texas held a company-wide meeting to explain the challenges to corporate survival in the 1990s. The company had a history of financial success, but competition was cutting into profit margins. In a few years, he warned, the company would be out of business unless costs were reduced, competencies enhanced, and new markets found. He asked for everyone's participation in meeting this challenge. The high operating targets he defined in the speech were a wake-up call, sending chills through a complacent workforce.

Within a year of that meeting, new quality and continuous improvement programs were introduced, and empowerment teams were formed at all levels. Several management gurus were invited to talk to employees.

Today, the employees are frozen in a state of decision paralysis. Communication across hierarchical levels has broken down. Frustration is high. The efforts to empower

*people simply haven't worked. Comments made to us
included:*

"It's not fun to come to work any more."
*"No one wants a dictator, but no one has faith in the
    empowerment process—it didn't work!"*
*"What did we do wrong, and how do we untangle this
    mess?"*
"I don't trust the intentions of top management."
*"I don't have people who I trust enough to empower.
    No one takes responsibility—they want to be told what
    to do."*
"My people are constantly whining and complaining."
"Personally, I don't care anymore."

THE DISAPPOINTING RESULTS OF MANY ORGANIZATIONAL CHANGE EFFORTS

These quotes could have come from managers and employees
in hundreds of companies. This particular retail firm continues to hang on, but performance indicators are still down. Most
managers see the need for constant innovation and improvement and want the help of committed, enthusiastic employees.
Most employees yearn to contribute more of their creativity
and potential. Yet what seems like a perfect alignment of mutual interest in change is met with frustration and failure. Here
are some more examples we have observed:

•   An eight-hundred–person manufacturing firm was
dropped as a supplier by its major customer because employees,
mostly unionized, refused to accept management's dire warn-
ings and attempts to "reengineer" improvements in quality and
efficiency. Management didn't know how to lead employees in
change. *Why couldn't employees see the crisis and adapt to it?*

• In a large medical center, each division of physician specialists kept to itself, reluctantly accommodating needs of patients, other specialties, nurses, and administrators, despite the wave of managed care changes that demanded better coordination and improved customer relationships. Initiatives to change the doctors' mindsets produced little result. *Why were attempts to change doctors' mindsets ineffective?*

• A senior manager in an energy company sent middle managers to a management course. One participant used what he had learned to show the senior manager that one project had no potential for financial return. The senior manager had other priorities and told him to stick to his regular job. This failure in senior leadership was compounded because the middle manager could not muster the vision or courage to lead with an initiative in which he believed. *Why did both people fail as leaders with the courage to change things?*

• At a large insurance company, recent hires with knowledge of current technologies got to work on new projects that further developed their skills. Older employees were relegated to maintenance of the old systems and were thus locked out of career development. They suffered great stress as a result, but HR initiatives to ameliorate the situation met resistance from line managers. *Why couldn't changes in the company accommodate the needs of all employees?*

The inability of managers to lead change seems to be a universal frustration in companies, especially when the desired or necessary change is an increase in the enthusiasm and ingenuity of employees. Top managers often feel that they alone are aware of the threats and complex challenges facing the company. Middle managers frequently feel controlled and unappreciated by the upper echelons and resent the lack of response from the bottom. Lower-level staff may feel oppressed and alienated by the system and may see little hope of using their talents and ingenuity to improve things.[1] Few leaders know how to thaw these mindsets, and few have the courage or vision to try. No matter how many consultants are hired by management or how hard managers push change onto people below, movement is exasperatingly slow.

THE NEED FOR A BROADER VIEW OF CHANGE

It would seem that practically every manager is thinking about, participating in, resisting, or leading organizational change. The examples above illustrate the failure and frustration that occur when managers attempt to initiate change, even in circumstances where there are confluent interests in improvement. Organizations too often struggle and fail at change. Thousands of programs focusing on restructuring, reengineering, quality improvement, technology, empowerment, incentive systems, and downsizing have fallen short of their promise and left skepticism and alienation in their wake.

The problem we address in this book is that management's understanding of change is too narrow. First, managers limit themselves by relying on objective and rational systems for change. Organization charts, control systems, work flows, job descriptions, strategy, and incentive programs are tangible and obvious targets of change. However, focusing on objective systems overlooks the resources for change that exist within people. Second, managers limit themselves by assuming a we-they mentality; they often see themselves as separate from the people and systems to be changed. Staff are perceived as a problem to be fixed. This narrow view has not worked. Real change occurs when managers fuse with other levels and departments and everyone changes together.

In this book, we take a broader view of change that includes the recognition of subtle forces within employees that increase the speed, acceptance, and impact of change initiatives. In our experience, most managers have not learned to facilitate change from their deeper wisdom. The personal potential so critical to leading transformation is held hostage by managers' concern with objective systems. Among the untapped resources within employees are their yearning for meaningful work, their desire to contribute, their dreams, their creative potential, and their courage. These vital human attributes and qualities provide the motivating energy for rapid change. We show that powerful but subtle forces can be unlocked by fusion and directed toward transformation.

OVERCOMING RESISTANCE TO CHANGE THROUGH FUSION LEADERSHIP

To solve the problem of resistance to change, we propose a new kind of leadership, *fusion leadership,* which is based on a set of assumptions about the unlocking of these subtle forces. The leadership processes we will describe are specifically designed to help managers and organizations transcend conventional thinking and break out of the constraints of traditional hierarchies.

This is consistent with the new sciences approach to organizations introduced by Margaret Wheatley and others. Their work provides the conceptual foundation for fusion leadership, for organizing in a way that allows the subtle forces to surface naturally.[2] When that happens, people self-organize, changing themselves and their systems to keep up with changing environments. Change then occurs without either top-down force or bottom-up resistance.

Our understanding of change is based on a broader perspective of what people bring to the organization. We show how to develop personal forces that make every person a leader—someone who will initiate change and take responsibility for its implementation. When large numbers of employees are thus empowered, they create a firestorm of improvement that sweeps away resistance.

LEADERSHIP: FROM FISSION TO FUSION

Physics distinguishes between fission and fusion. The process of *fission,* exemplified in the atomic bomb, creates energy by splitting the nucleus of the atom. It demands vigilant control because of dangerous toxic waste, so the release of fission energy is typically associated with layers of control systems. As atomic energy was harnessed for nonmilitary applications, its impressive power had to be carefully managed.

Fission is our metaphor for the style of management that has evolved over the last century. Mass production and scientific management have been based on division of labor, individual accountability, and formal authority and control. Organizations maintain rigid boundaries between individuals and departments, which compete with one another for resources, promotions, and salary or budget increases. Managers compete with each other. They also see themselves as separate from workers, and vice versa. Responsibility and access to information are narrowly defined. Layers of hierarchy and authority are used for control. People are even subject to an internal split, for they are encouraged to work with their hands, and perhaps their minds, but not with the emotional and spiritual aspects of themselves.

The work of a fission-based organization is efficient and controlled because it harnesses strong organizational forces. In this type of structure, managers and staff experience pressure from those above them in the hierarchy, from bottom-line goals, and from control systems that direct individual behavior to meet the needs of the organization. They are motivated by self-interest to accept such control. An individual gains by maximizing what he takes from the organization and minimizing what he gives. The organization obtains routinized, predictable behavior in return for resource incentives. The machine-like organization runs with little emotion, capitalizing on rational analysis and self-interest. This is a powerful system, which efficiently directs people into desired roles, jobs, and behaviors.

Two drawbacks to this approach are the limitations it places on ingenuity and creativity, and organizational inertia with respect to rapid change. These are serious deficiencies in today's turbulent world, but they can be addressed by recourse to the concept of fusion.

In physics, *fusion* is the opposite of fission. Rather than splitting atoms apart, fusion joins together atomic nuclei—a difficult operation, because each atom has a positive charge that repels others. This obstacle is overcome by the removal of an atom's boundary electrons and the generation of pressure. When fusion occurs, it produces *five times* the energy of fission. Even more remarkable, one gram of fusion material produces the same amount of energy as eight tons of oil, with virtually no waste.

Fusion, too, is a metaphor for a certain style of management. Fusion is about joining, coming together, creating connections and partnerships. It is about reducing barriers by encouraging conversations, information sharing, and joint responsibility across boundaries. Fusion is achieving a sense of unity, coming to perceive others as part of the same whole rather than as separate. It is seeing similarities rather than differences. Fusion implies common ground and a sense of community based on what people share—vision, norms, and outcomes, for example. And for an individual, fusion means not splitting off or ignoring essential parts of one's self. Each individual can be whole, bringing body, mind, heart, and spirit to the workplace. Fusion strives for wholeness in both individuals and organizations.

When working with groups of executives, we often illustrate fusion with a simple exercise. Each person is asked to draw a picture of his or her vision for the company. The executives are then assigned to teams and asked to explain their pictures to each other. Each team is asked to develop a single picture that all team members are willing to accept.

There are three strategies for achieving this single team picture. First, team members may agree that one picture is best, or simply yield to the strongest member's vision. This approach is fast and efficient. It indicates the presence of a strong leader who "knows what's best" for the organization.

A second strategy is to create a composite or collage of all the individual pictures. This is a participation or consensus approach. The resulting team picture is achieved efficiently, but is not a true fusion of interests. The collage has the look of agreement, but team members have not changed themselves to build a shared vision out of their various dreams. The team picture shows fragments of individual images. In other words, fission is at work, because people's visions are kept separate rather than being unified.

The third strategy is true fusion. Executives present their visions and then engage in conversation to reduce the images to their underlying essence. Team members seek to understand each other at a deeper level, where they will form the common ground for the new collective image. Through dialogue, participants modify their visions in response to what they hear from others. The team vision that emerges is different from any of the individual visions, yet it reflects the deeper needs of each member. Separate images have disappeared. The team vision co-evolves via a process of fusion that integrates the voices and hopes of everyone. As the boundaries that initially separated the participants disappear, a commitment to the vision and to organizational change grows rapidly. This small taste of true fusion shows executives the incredible motivating power of creating a shared vision from their deepest hopes and dreams for the company.

Participation, empowerment, consensus, teamwork, and team building are concepts that many organizations want to embrace. Yet these approaches seldom attain true fusion, because individuals maintain separateness and autonomy with respect to important issues such as vision. The result is that change initiatives like those described at the beginning of this chapter fail despite an underlying common interest in change.

A fusion approach can counteract many of the strong pressures that trigger resistance in managers and employees. The power of fusion is that it can release a set of subtle forces from within individuals that have far-reaching impact on organizational empowerment and change.

FROM STRONG FORCES TO SUBTLE FORCES

When leaders choose a fission or a fusion management philosophy, they also choose whether to use organizational strong forces or personal subtle forces to achieve outcomes. What we call *organizational strong forces* are those elements in organizations that act as strong pressures on people's attention. A demanding boss can be a dominant influence on behavior, whether that behavior is designed to please him or to avoid him. A strong force commands attention because of individuals' needs, fears, or desire for acceptance and success. Strong forces in companies include financial results, operating goals, budgets, engineering efficiency, performance evaluations, close supervision, and pay raises. Such forces typically involve control and often reflect a watchdog mentality. They direct people toward making a positive impact on the company's bottom line. Strong forces typically favor the organization's needs over the needs of individuals.

What we call *personal subtle forces* are less obvious and less tangible; they are harder to see, define, and influence. They include passion, ingenuity, vision, enthusiasm, morale, values, and corporate culture. Subtle forces can be suppressed by the directive and heavy-handed organizational strong forces. Subtle forces seem delicate and fragile, but they provide extraordinarily strong motivation and influence when unlocked.

Information, so abundant in today's world, is a subtle force. The meaning of information exists within people and is exchanged among people, but cannot be quantified, seen, or tasted. Information reaching Eastern Europe was as responsible as the West's military might for the fall of the Berlin Wall and the Iron Curtain.

Or consider the end of the nineteenth century, when radio waves were discovered. The idea of harnessing this invisible force for communication was revolutionary. People were aware only of things tangible and concrete. Making use of these invisible waves has provided incalculable benefit to humanity. At this very moment, there are people talking and playing music in the room you are in, although you cannot see or hear them. All you need is a device called a radio or television that will pick up these subtle waves.

Within organizations, unlocking the subtle forces means employing often underutilized parts of human beings, including intellectual, emotional, and spiritual abilities and understandings. When, beyond this, efforts are made to draw together the inner talents of everyone in the organization so that they are working in concert, the effect is even greater. Just as the capacity of a computer system is geometrically increased when computers are networked together, the brain, heart, and soul capacity of the organization can be increased geometrically through fusion-based teamwork, dialogue, and the sharing of information.

Subtle forces are typically invisible and beneath the surface. For example, listening for unexpressed employee or customer issues is a subtle force. So is a vision that binds people together, or courage to stand alone and take independent action. Subtle forces include independent thinking, attention to the big picture, and creativity. Affirming subtle forces encourages people to act from inner knowing as well as from rational analysis, to use their personal courage to serve the organization rather than take from it, to believe in the potential of human beings, and to act in terms of destiny and life purpose. Subtle forces include love of what one does and love of other people.

Often, when the rewards are great, the task is not easy, and this is true of the use of subtle forces. As a famous psychologist writes:

> *Humans no longer have instincts in the animal sense, powerful, unmistakable inner voices which tell them unequivocally what to do, when, where, how and with whom. All that we have left are instinct-remnants. And furthermore, these are weak, subtle, and delicate, very easily drowned out by learning, by cultural expectations, by fear, by disapproval, etc. They are hard to know, rather than easy. Authentic self-hood can be defined in part as being able to hear these impulse voices within oneself, i.e., to know what one really wants or doesn't want, what one is fit for and what one is not fit for.*[3]

The motivating power of personal subtle forces is that people yearn to use them, to be free to express more of their personal creativity, purpose, risk-taking instincts, and enthusiasm. Subtle forces are like the water contained in a reservoir that is pulled toward the ocean when the dam breaks, or like the oil waiting to escape in a gusher when the drill bit reaches deep enough. The yearning is within you and others, even if not obvious to the eye. Fusion leaders look beyond the easy-to-see physical and material world of rules, procedures, measurements, and direct supervision and appreciate people's yearning to express their essence as human beings.

THE SUBTLE FORCES OF FUSION LEADERSHIP

What are specific subtle forces that might be unlocked by fusion? They are drawn from people's basic humanness. The broad historical literature, from Aristotle to Covey, has emphasized that whole human beings operate from body, mind, heart, and spirit.[4] To be a whole person and to make use of all one's capacity requires physical, mental, emotional, and spiritual development. The physical body is visible and tangible and is the container and the expresser of more subtle qualities. The subtle forces are not the body; they are in the mind, heart, and spirit within the body.

In our review of the literature on leadership, and through our consulting and classroom experiences, we have observed many subtle expressions of mind, heart, and spirit.[5] For the purposes of our discussion of fusion leadership, we have identified six subtle forces that embrace the essence of human potential and ingenuity. The subtle aspects of intellect are captured in mindfulness and vision. The subtle forces of emotion are revealed through heart and communication. And the subtle forces of spirit are reflected in courage and integrity. These six forces define the underlying potential for leadership and change.

- *Mindfulness* includes independent thinking, personal creativity, an open mind that welcomes novel and unusual ideas, and thinking outside the box.
- *Vision* is the higher purpose toward which people work that provides meaning and inspiration for their collaborative efforts.

• *Heart* represents caring and compassion, the positive feelings and emotions that underlie connections and relationships in the workplace.

• *Communication* is the act of symbolically influencing others with respect to vision, values, and emotions. Subtle communication also involves listening and discernment.

• *Courage* is the motivation to step outside the traditional boundary and comfort zone, to take risks, to take the lead, to be a nonconformist, to stand up for something, and to be willing to make mistakes as a way to learn and grow.

• *Integrity* is honesty, trust, and service to others, which means going beyond "me, me, me" to give something to the team and the organization.

Each of these subtle forces can be released to provide powerful motivation for leadership and change. These forces can transform organizations, and fusion is the process through which they are unlocked.

EMBRACING THE FUSION APPROACH

The question to be explored in this book is: How can leaders and organizations develop fusion relationships that enable people to express their latent resources of mindfulness, heart, vision, courage, communication, and integrity so that they, too, can lead and achieve rapid, continuous change?

The fusion approach is compared with the fission approach in Exhibit 1.1. Many contemporary organizations still operate under premises of separation, internal competition, individualism, and external pressures to achieve rewards and fulfillment. The conventional fission approach is concerned with control "over" others, clear boundaries, response to higher authority, and giving the best that one's hands and mind have to offer.

Exhibit 1.1
How Is Fusion Different?

Fission Approach   **Fusion Approach**

- Division of labor, separation, split apart, individualism
- Control "over" others
- Clear boundaries for information and responsibilities by levels and functions
- Organizational goals, targets, rules, standards
- Body and mind as performers of tasks

- Joining, coming together, connection, relationship, community
- Control "with" others
- Absence of boundaries, sharing of information and responsibility, unity, wholeness
- Common ground of shared vision, values, norms, outcomes
- Body, mind, heart and spirit as instruments of change

Relies on   **Unlocks**
Organizational Strong Forces   **Personal Subtle Forces**

- Hierarchy of authority
- Bottom line
- Organizational control
- Individual incentives

- Mindfulness
- Vision
- Heart
- Courage
- Integrity
- Communication

Efficient, routinized, stable organization that is resistant to change

Energized, empowered, self-adapting organization

These organizational strong forces can drive people into behavior that fragments organizations and reinforces individual egos with islands of bureaucratic separateness. Organizational approval can become more important than a person's inner wisdom.

The strong forces produce an efficient organization, but overreliance on them creates an organization that is resistant to change, even in a time of chaos and turbulence. In a fission organization, change is pushed downward through the hierarchy and imposed on others, who typically resist, causing problems, delays, frustration, and failure.

By contrast, a fusion approach breathes life into subtle forces within each person that can become the basis for corporate survival and transformation. The fusion approach is about joining, coming together, and creating connections and relationships. It means controlling the organization "with" others, valuing boundarylessness, shared information, and unity.

Through the fusion process of developing shared purpose, vision, and outcomes, a whole set of personal forces is unlocked. These forces bring to the organization the individual creativity of mindfulness, the purposefulness of vision, the enthusiasm of heart, the dissolution of old boundaries through courage, the ability to both influence and discern through communication, and the trustworthiness and service associated with integrity. These are areas of human contribution that lie fallow under the conventional organizational hierarchy. When the subtle forces are brought into creative balance with organizational strong forces, change flows naturally.

We will show how to achieve both the personal and the organizational fusion to unlock and harness subtle forces that will transform people and organizations. Fusion-based organizations can become energized, self-adapting systems that simultaneously maintain efficiency and fluidity with the environment. An organization operating on fusion principles and subtle forces can change faster than its fission-based competitors.

THE FUSION CHALLENGE

Writers and consultants in the new sciences have suggested that managers turn their attention away from mass production models that seek to maintain equilibrium by mimicking the operation of machines. In the fusion perspective, organizations are systems in which people seek identity and purpose in organizing themselves and co-evolving with the environment. But the transition in mindset has been slow. As we noted in the examples at the beginning of this chapter, change toward more adaptable, empowered organizations is not happening extensively, or at least is not happening very fast.

The replacement of craft jobs with machine-like hierarchical structures that limited the expression of individual abilities occurred over several generations after the advent of the modern corporation. Is this direction of evolution inevitable? Or is it possible to reignite fusion and burn away historical layers of dependence on hierarchy and stability?

Fusion is attainable, as we will describe in this book. The overall process of fusion is shown in Exhibit 1.2. The organization and the individual have been separated by traditional boundaries of structure and habit. When hearts and minds of individuals are fused with real needs of the organization and environment, personal subtle forces are unlocked. Real change in culture and mindsets then occurs, creating focused joint action to meet needs of the organization and environment.

The challenge is for leaders to see that traditional organizational structure, with its enforced separation and boundaries, is artificial and designed for an earlier world of mass production. When they do, real change can begin. By recognizing the need for fusion leadership and by empowering subtle human qualities, organizations give themselves a real chance to prosper, no matter how competitive the environment or uncertain the future. But old habits are compelling. Employees will

Exhibit 1.2
Achieving Fusion in an Organization

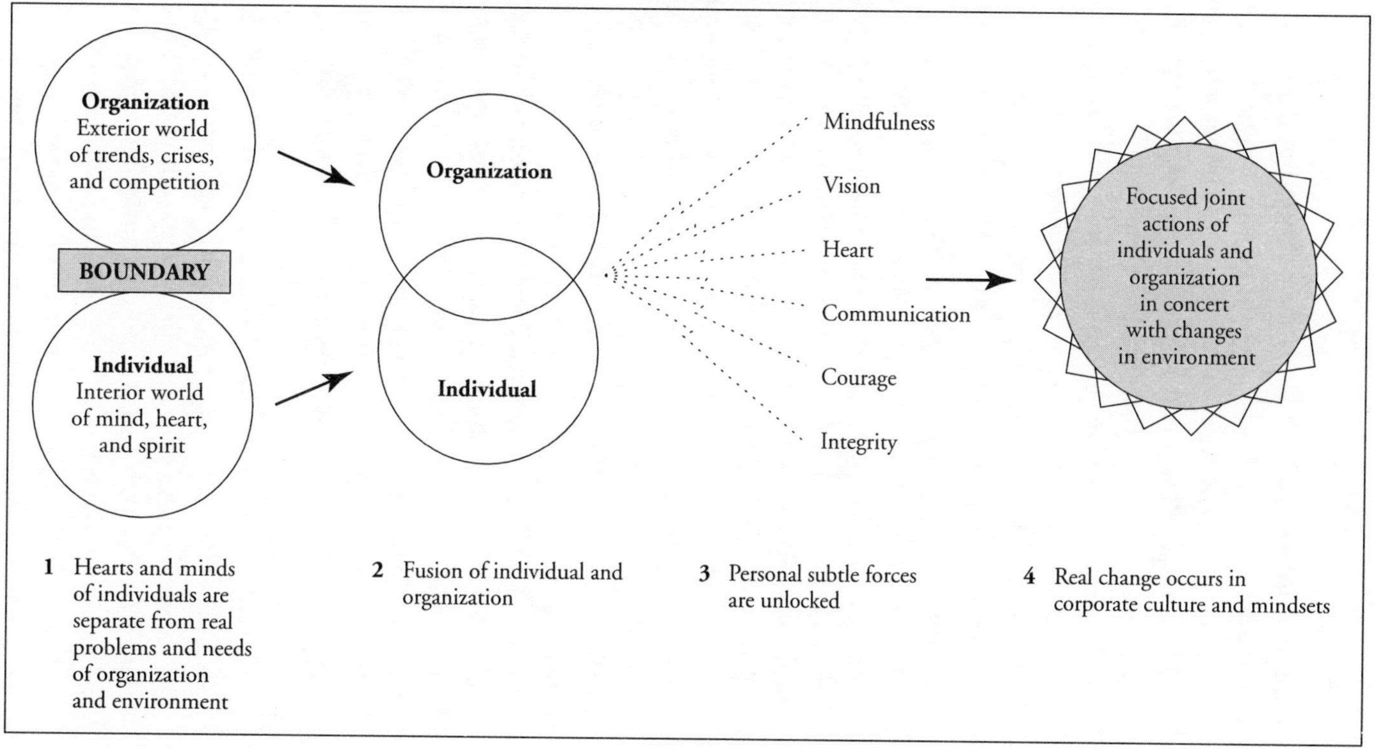

Organization
Exterior world of trends, crises, and competition

BOUNDARY

Individual
Interior world of mind, heart, and spirit

Organization

Individual

Mindfulness

Vision

Heart

Communication

Courage

Integrity

Focused joint actions of individuals and organization in concert with changes in environment

1 Hearts and minds of individuals are separate from real problems and needs of organization and environment

2 Fusion of individual and organization

3 Personal subtle forces are unlocked

4 Real change occurs in corporate culture and mindsets

choose passive resistance if it is the only option they see. The imperative is to enlarge the range of possibilities so that strong and subtle aspects of organization can evolve in natural balance.

One example of successful fusion is the Ciba-Geigy agricultural chemical plant in Cambridge, Ontario.[6] Gerry Rich, the director, inherited a plant going nowhere, with low standards and productivity. He also observed employees who were leaders outside work—in community organizations, Boy Scouts, sports teams—but took no lead on the job. They left their ability to think and lead at the factory gate.

With the help of a consultant, Rich and the workers began a redesign project. People started crossfunctional conversations. A design team was elected, and each member sat on a study group investigating a different part of the plant. Managers became advisers and often rotated through different managerial positions. Old divisions, boundaries, and rivalries disappeared. Some established managers had to rejoin worker teams. A few employees found they just couldn't work in teams or could not let the personal subtle forces emerge, but most welcomed the opportunity for fusion and involvement.

The Ciba-Geigy plant organization now looks like the circles on a dartboard, with production, warehouse functions, and maintenance at the center. Surrounding circles include support groups and managers. Managers truly are advisers, who fuse together previously separated groups and individuals by acting as team facilitators, conflict resolvers, team coordinators, and training program leaders.

The fusion of people and departments has brought about significant change at Ciba-Geigy. Through extended discussions involving the relevant work group, employees are carefully chosen for each task. There is harmony between a person's potential and his or her assigned position. Workers who have awakened their subtle potentials do not need managers. They set schedules, write job descriptions, interview new hires, and manage costs. Layers of bureaucracy have been removed, and the remaining employees have grown enormously, each becoming a leader in his or her own way.

The lesson from Ciba-Geigy is that a conventional organization can use fusion leadership to transform itself, with individuals confounding expectations and becoming leaders. We will provide more examples later in this book.

Personal Fusion and Organizational Fusion

Fusion is the process of bringing parts together into a whole. This can occur for both persons and organizations. *Personal fusion* brings together one's physical and mental abilities with the hidden and often forgotten subtle potentials of mindfulness, vision, heart, courage, communication, and integrity. Most human beings are separated into an exterior and interior sense of self. The exterior or "conditioned" self is concerned with operating in the objective external world. The interior or "essential" self is the arena of inner meaning, potential, truth, and self-expression. This interior self is the source of subtle forces. Personal fusion enables individuals to integrate the interior and exterior so that their emotional, intellectual, and spiritual resources can be used for effective leadership of organizational change.

Organizational fusion is a process for bringing together all parts of the organization, reducing boundaries, and creating a whole system that is fluid, adaptive, and empowering for employees. Organizational fusion is the integration of the individual and the collective, the fusion of "I" with "We." The collective is based on connections, relationships, shared values, mutual understanding, and common ground. The fusion of individuals into a collective "We" can propel changes in structure, strategy, hierarchy, technological systems, work flow, and organizational design. Organizational fusion is about the integration of departments, viewpoints, and the subtle forces into a self-organizing whole.

Personal fusion and organizational fusion can change concurrently. The interior and exterior selves are best integrated within a setting in which the individual and the collective are also brought together. This enables people to change as they buy into larger organizational changes in a genuine fusion of mutual interests.

In Chapter Two, we will lay the groundwork for awakening subtle forces.

Personal Remembering

- What makes you feel successful? Fulfilled? What do you value most about yourself?

- Describe a time when you felt truly alive and excited in your work. What was affirmed in you at that time?

- How do you express yourself in work, in relationships, in play? What potentials are not expressed?

- Do you have an inner voice that you sometimes respond to? Do you ever not respond? Why?

CHAPTER TWO

BREAKING WITH THE PAST

Before reading this chapter, try an experiment. Pick up a quarter in your hand. Hold your arm in front of you, palm down, and clutch the quarter tightly in your fist. Look at your fist. What do you see? Think of words that describe your fist in that position. What are your feelings about holding your hand in this position? Now relax your hand completely. What happens?

Pick up the quarter again, and hold your hand in front of you, only turn your hand so the palm faces upward. Relax your hand so that the quarter lies in the palm, fingers extended. Look at your hand carefully. What words describe what you see? What do you feel about holding your hand in this position? Squeeze your hand tight. Is anything gained? Relax your hand. Notice how the coin is still under your control. Think for a moment what you have learned from this experiment.[1]

In the clenched fist position, words like *control, tightness, stress, restraint, keep, possession,* or *fear* (of losing the quarter) may have occurred to you. When you relaxed your fist, the quarter tumbled to the ground.

With the palm held upward, a different set of images and feelings probably emerged. This position is characterized by words and phrases like *uplift, freedom, openness, joy, relaxation, independence, lack of restriction,* and *absence of control.* And even with freedom and openness, the quarter did not tumble to the ground. Clenching the upturned hand seems pointless. It isn't needed.

The palm-down clenched fist is symbolic of how strong-force management is practiced in many organizations. Managers grasp, control, and cling to budgets, people, and goals. They fear that relaxation of these strong forces will mean dropping the "quarter"—things will spin out of control. The open hand represents a paradigm shift—to uplift, to free people, to stop grasping and controlling, and still not drop the quarter. To manage in this way is to gain enormous power and influence, unlocking the subtle potentials of people working with you.

We believe the clenched fist represents the management style that evolved in the industrial age and that we have inherited, whereas the open palm represents the style managers need to embrace if their organizations are going to thrive in the century ahead. The question then arises: Is it possible for people and organizations to break with the past? We believe that most people in organizations can "remember" or learn to develop subtle forces, coach and facilitate others, give away authority, and create a sense of community, all the while achieving bottom-line results. We have frequently watched employee groups adopt a new mindset that involves personal responsibility, initiative, and accountability for their company's success. Individuals will give up some of their need for personal security and safety and become part of an adventure with others. Employees can learn to act from their dreams, ideas, and intentions rather than waiting for directives from bosses.

If these subtle forces are really available in organizations, why aren't they used? If creativity and ingenuity are within people, how were they forgotten? In this chapter, we look at the evolution of leadership in organizations to explain why the subtle forces have been forgotten and why remembering them can create a revolution in empowerment and participation.

THE STRONG FORCE HABIT

The strong forces are the habit of most organizations. The subtle forces have fallen into disuse from a combination of misleading experience and a desire for stability and certainty.

Misleading Experience

Winston Churchill said that we shape our buildings and thereafter they shape us.[2] The industrial age and the methods of assembly-line production gave rise to organizational structures that were based on division of labor, individual accountability, formal authority, control, and competition for limited resources. Modern organizational structures represent the twentieth-century application of Isaac Newton's seventeenth-century assumptions about machines. The Newtonian perspective assumes that humans can understand, predict, and control things through logic, reason, and data. The world is orderly, predictable, and controllable.

Designing this orderly world was not without cost, however. Human forces such as love, creativity, risk taking, vision, and integrity were relegated to the background. People were socialized to believe in hierarchy of authority, analysis, and efficiency. Subtle forces have atrophied in today's society and in hierarchy-based organizations.

Imagine wild animals raised in captivity and dependent on the zoo for survival. When a wild animal is raised in a zoo, the

instincts and potential to survive in the wild atrophy, so releasing the animal into the wild would result in its death. The
animal's innate potential has to be reawakened and remembered. An elephant in Thailand, pressed into service as a tourist
attraction, was chained to a stump beside a temple from the
time it was a small calf. After eighteen years, it was released and
had to be taught how to walk and do every simple thing for itself. This phenomenon is seen among humans, too. When prisoners are released after many years of passivity, dependence,
and regimented living, they often find the freedom threatening and need help developing new behavior and habits.

Citizens of Western societies have become conditioned to
control-based organizational structures and the limited roles
they offer. Most people do not know anything else. Every step
in socialization demands acceptance of formal structure. Schools
insist that students stay in their seats and learn information by
rote for multiple-choice tests. Families are based on the hierarchy of parent and child. The pressures for conformity at each
step are considerable, even in college and graduate school.
Newtonian thinking and strong authority structures have created generations of people who go along with the system.
Hence, the granting of empowerment is resisted both by those
who would have to give away responsibility and by those who
would receive it.

In our own M.B.A. classes, we encounter resistance when we
empower students to participate equally with us in class.
Trapped in their own psychic prison, students want structure.
They want to be told what to do so that they can know with
certainty what to expect, work for the desired grade, and get
on to the next class. They argue, "You aren't doing your job.
You're supposed to tell us what to do." But after a month or so
of coaching and facilitation, they begin to change. As they learn
to express their own vision for the course, find the courage to
embark on a new adventure, and learn to dialogue with each

other and create a fusion process, the classroom comes alive. Students become excited and enthusiastic, taking responsibility for their own destiny.

Time and again, we meet managers who face the same resistance. A plant manager, a finance vice president, a software company supervisor have all been told by subordinates that they are not doing their jobs when they attempt to empower employees. Equally, we meet people who have resisted their own empowerment simply because they didn't know what to do with it. They have been conditioned to small jobs and roles, and prefer certainty and predictability. When a retail firm fails to empower employees, or shop-floor workers resist a quality initiative, the motivation can usually be traced to a single syndrome: people are doing what they know, what they have been taught and trained to do. They have become dependent on the structures society has created.

False Beliefs

Along with being socialized into structure and control, people have learned to believe in the value of permanence and stability. It is almost as if managers want the world to be permanent and stable and try to make it so. They surround themselves with plans, strategies, budgets, retirement programs, resources, and formal authority in the vain belief that everything will work out as they want, that things really can be controlled. A Tibetan sage said that "planning for the future is like going fishing in a dry gulch; nothing ever works out as you wanted."[3] Traditional structures are maintained as if they provided safety. Many managers seem to want everything to continue as it is, the future to unfold according to their needs and plans. So organizations are designed and run as clenched fists, with constant fear that the quarter might be lost. Yet impermanence, turbulence, and change are the only sure things anyone can build on.

The new sciences, encompassing quantum physics, self-organizing systems, and the related sciences of complexity and chaos, say that an organization is not a machine, that information cannot be gathered to control the future.[4] Today's surprises inform us of the future. And everything in the organization is connected in some way. Thus reality and truth are in the relationships among elements, not in the elements themselves. Departments may seem like autonomous parts, but in reality they are interconnected, with important information and relationships flowing horizontally to produce the larger whole.

In an out-of-kilter world, it is hard to predict what you will be thinking or doing in a few hours. To know for sure, you must actually live through those hours and experience what happens at the time. To know exactly where your company will be one year from now, you have to live through the year and then experience what happens.

An executive at a major Italian communications company, STET, has said: "Our universe is changing every six months. First it is privatization, then deregulation, then technological revolutions, then mergers and strategic alliance. . . . We can no longer plan beyond six months or a year, and frequent discontinuities have become a way of life."[5] These influences are felt all around the world, and are enough to cause many managers to question whether old habits of thinking and controlling are still appropriate.

EVOLVING TO THE FUTURE

Our point is that the long-established habit of strong-force hierarchies has been reinforced by generations of people socialized into them. Yet as the example of the Ciba-Geigy chemical plant in Chapter One illustrated, real change is possible. Corporations are at the threshold of breaking with the past as they learn to free themselves from strong-force dominance and unlock personal subtle forces.

Transformational Versus Transactional Leaders

An important distinction among leaders has been whether they adopt a transactional or transformational approach.[6] When managers have detailed knowledge of work processes or the staff behaviors necessary to achieve a goal, they can micromanage the specific steps that will lead to execution of the task. For example, they can calculate the financial incentives that will induce employee compliance and work accomplishment. This approach is called *transactional leadership* because managers control each piece of the relationship with their staff. It is a logical, objective approach to leadership.

Transformational leaders do not analyze and control specific behaviors of their subordinates. They engage employees in the big picture that provides common ground, vision, and larger meaning. The transformational leader manages the context within which people work—for example, mission, shared values, and ideas that cannot be translated into specific, controllable actions. Such a leader shapes the setting that employees occupy, the mountain peaks to which they will aspire.

When a mountain climb is predictable, there are clearly marked trails to guide followers, and safety rails to prevent them from falling. A transactional manager can ensure that climbers stay on the trail; those who stray can be set straight. However, if no one has climbed the mountain before, there are no trails and no safety rails. In this potentially dangerous situation, what do managers control, and to what end? If you want staff to climb a mountain—pursue a vision—not attempted before, you don't want them limited by your own preconceptions, which may block their ability to learn how to overcome obstacles and surprises. High performance emerges from taking action without rules. The transformational leader empowers others and keeps them focused on reaching the mountain peak.

Four Eras of Leading

The progression of leadership styles through history is summarized in Exhibit 2.1, where account is taken of both the transactional/transformational distinction and the differences between stable and out-of-kilter environments. Each cell in this exhibit summarizes a way of thinking that was correct for its time.

Way One is *great man* leadership, the granddaddy of leadership styles. Great men, who tended to emerge in hospitable environments, were visionaries who understood how things fit into a whole. A single great man put it all together—the vision, along with the strategy, people, and resources to achieve the vision. Principles of administration and strong forces were important parts of new corporate hierarchies. Early corporate leaders like Vanderbilt and Carnegie are examples. Historical figures such as Napoleon and Julius Caesar, and great kings like Richard III and Henry V of England are also examples of great men leadership.

Way Two is that of the *rational* or *fission manager.* The rational manager was suited to a stable environment in which things could be taken apart and analyzed, and he learned to control every detail of the work performed under him. This approach was consistent with early scientific research in business schools. Newtonian thinking dominates here. This is the world of scientific management. Managers designed the organization so that people could be controlled and directed through hierarchy and division of labor. Strong forces were at their peak. Employees become dependent on tasks characteristic of the assembly line.

Way Three is that of today's *overwhelmed manager.* The world has turned chaotic, so managers pedal faster. They are not sure what to do. Because of downsizing and global competition, managers have more work than they can handle. Trying to cope with

Exhibit 2.1
Leadership Evolution

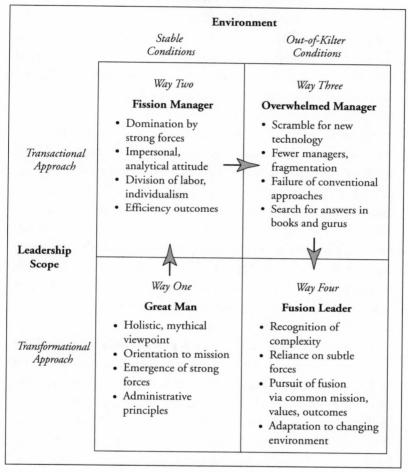

Environment

	Stable Conditions	Out-of-Kilter Conditions
	Way Two	*Way Three*
Transactional Approach	**Fission Manager** • Domination by strong forces • Impersonal, analytical attitude • Division of labor, individualism • Efficiency outcomes	**Overwhelmed Manager** • Scramble for new technology • Fewer managers, fragmentation • Failure of conventional approaches • Search for answers in books and gurus
	Way One	*Way Four*
Transformational Approach	**Great Man** • Holistic, mythical viewpoint • Orientation to mission • Emergence of strong forces • Administrative principles	**Fusion Leader** • Recognition of complexity • Reliance on subtle forces • Pursuit of fusion via common mission, values, outcomes • Adaptation to changing environment

Leadership Scope

out-of-kilter conditions, they buy "how to" books that they hope will resolve their dilemmas. Gurus are hired to lecture employees and teach correct fixes. The manager's job here is action-oriented. "Do something, try something" takes precedence over "Analyze the problem." Companies may merge to become bigger and less vulnerable to the environment. Managers may preach empowerment but not know how to give up control.

Technology plays a role in Way Three. Information technologies speed up activities and data. Companies reengineer, redesign structure, and use information technology to hold things together. But managers and employees often behave in the old way, their habits causing many corporate redesigns to fail. Way Three is where most companies are right now, facing destabilized environments but still operating with a heavy dose of traditional management.

The next stage, Way Four, is what we call *fusion leadership*. Fusion leaders are beginning to emerge in the out-of-kilter world of organizations. As changes descend on companies like killer bees, careful prediction and tight control seem pointless. Fusion leaders breathe life into dormant subtle forces. They facilitate the development of an overall vision that employees believe in. The fusion leader in Way Four successfully empowers others rather than reinforcing hierarchical control, and builds partnerships on shared values and information. Fusion leaders appreciate their interdependence with others who are also striving to adapt to the environment.

The struggle most leaders face is that of breaking with Ways Two and Three. Many well-meaning managers have been locked into a rationality box by organizations that use old-style structure and control. Most managers use just part of their leadership potential. Perhaps they are unaware that they have more, or if they are conscious of it, they may be uncomfortable letting it out. Fusion leadership means leading from subtle forces such as heart and vision. In Way Four, mindsets and structures are adopted that incorporate personal subtle forces along with organizational strong forces. In our experience, most people yearn for the opportunity to awaken their personal subtle forces.

USING SUBTLE FORCES

The challenge for the future is to empower the subtle forces of human potential in Way Four. Such forces may seem delicate and fragile, but recall how information brought down the Iron Curtain, and how invisible electronic signals have united the globe.

Often the unseen is more real and powerful than what we see. The things we do not see are fundamental. Look at the table or desk in your room. What do you see? A piece of furniture? Look deeper. That table is composed of wood, which you probably overlooked because your perception was dominated by the shape of the furniture. Look at something you are wearing. Do you see a shirt or blouse? Do you see fabric? Again, look beneath the surface. The fabric consists of woven thread, and the thread is made of cotton or some other fiber. Typically, we are unconscious of the underlying wood or fiber, even though it is the essential material of the furniture or clothing.

Think back to the experiment you performed at the beginning of this chapter. There was a powerful subtle force at work in the upturned palm. Did you notice what it was? Gravity. Gravity is invisible and often taken for granted. But when the quarter is lying on the upturned palm, this subtle force does all the work and your hand can be at rest. By contrast, when the palm is facing downward, energy must be exerted—in grasping—to resist gravity's pull. Can you or your organization learn to harness subtle forces so that they make financial success easier to achieve?

The new leaders at Hugh Russell, Inc., a three-thousand–employee distributor of steel and industrial products, learned about unlocking subtle forces by direct experience. We were fortunate to see Hugh Russell's transformation through the eyes of a friend, David Hurst, who wrote a book about the experience.[7]

Hugh Russell was the quintessential strong-force organization, with an established hierarchy, good performance, and vigorous top-down management oriented to growth and earnings. As much as 100 percent of managers' salaries could come from performance bonuses.

One day, Hugh Russell was put in play by a corporate raider and was subsequently acquired in a hostile takeover. A few weeks later, the price paid was clearly seen to have been too high. The transaction was vastly overleveraged, and the once agreeable bankers began to back out. Hugh Russell needed to refinance $300 million of debt at a time when interest rates were rising and the economy in decline. From one week to the next, a mature, successful company found itself desperately fighting for survival, with a new focus on downsizing, layoffs, closures, delayering, and asset sales. The two top managers left.

The remaining managers had to figure a way out of the mess. In the face of this crisis, people started talking to each other across traditional boundaries. The formal structure disappeared as ad hoc action teams emerged. Two people would start a conversation in the corridor, and others would gather around. Later, the new president and the executive vice president decided to share the same office so that each could hear what the other was doing in real time. Everywhere, employees were acting out of newly discovered subtle potentials.

In the head office chaos, individuals abandoned traditional tasks and began to do whatever they did best. The management team identified nineteen major issues, and members took on responsibility to deal with them. One person found his talent as a facilitator-networker. He developed team agendas and made presentations to bankers, suppliers, and shareholders. The president filled the role of entrepreneur-negotiator-inspirer.

Another change was in relationships with suppliers, bankers, unions, and governments. Rather than using formal systems to keep these parties at arm's length, managers made trips to see them, built personal relationships, and explained the trouble Hugh Russell was in. Thanks to these efforts, suppliers, bankers, and unions supported the company despite monthly reports of huge financial losses.

Nearly everyone broke out of his or her box. With the strong forces of formal structure reduced, attitudes and motivations changed. The traditional compensation system collapsed. Performance reviews were suspended. Salaries were frozen, and in some cases rolled back. Morale went straight up. The important thing seemed to be the shared sacrifice. Everyone suffered equally, but with the new personal freedom, work itself was becoming fun. People were engaged in an adventure, and everything a person did was potentially significant.

Hurst wrote that management had responded to the crisis by creating a new context for action. This new context had many of the characteristics of fusion. Management modeled egalitarian behavior, broke out of old boundaries, and let the formal structure weaken so that employees could coordinate and take action on their own. The shared mission infused everyone. Once the correct climate was created, the system organized itself. People were thrilled to leave individualistic self-interest behind. They did not have to be controlled, rewarded, or closely managed. As top management's trust increased, employees took personal initiative to solve problems.

Hugh Russell survived the crisis with a new culture, a new logo, a statement of shared mission, and various safeguards to prevent the organization from regressing to its earlier strong-force hierarchy. With a flatter structure, the company prospered, keeping the best of the old while adding the new. The balanced system of strong and subtle forces enabled Hugh Russell to survive, then thrive.

As shown in Exhibit 2.2, the magnets that have commanded attention, time, and resources in companies like Hugh Russell (as it used to be) are formal authority, goals, structure, the bottom line, and control. These forces are an outgrowth of the mass-production mindset. Unlocking the subtle forces of courage, mindfulness, heart, vision, integrity, and communication opens up an entirely new culture in which subtle and strong forces exert equal influence.

The strong forces impinging on you are easy to identify. Think about the organizational requirements that keep you so busy that you don't have time to think. In a brokerage firm, it may be maintaining the level of sales transactions. In a decentralized service firm, it may be meeting budget requirements

Exhibit 2.2
Balancing Strong and Subtle Forces

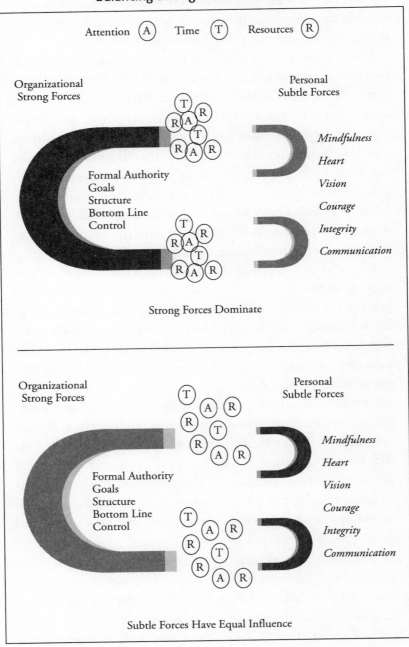

Attention (A)   Time (T)   Resources (R)

Organizational
Strong Forces

Personal
Subtle Forces

Formal Authority
Goals
Structure
Bottom Line
Control

Mindfulness

Heart

Vision

Courage

Integrity

Communication

Strong Forces Dominate

Organizational
Strong Forces

Personal
Subtle Forces

Formal Authority
Goals
Structure
Bottom Line
Control

Mindfulness

Heart

Vision

Courage

Integrity

Communication

Subtle Forces Have Equal Influence

because bonuses and promotion are tied to cost efficiency. In an entrepreneurial firm, it may be rapid growth at any cost. In a manufacturing firm, it may be achieving 10 percent growth within established budget guidelines.

But as the world changes, executives are beginning to look beyond the obvious. They are seeing beyond the clothing to the fiber, beneath the ground to the potential gusher, beyond the statistic to the whole employee, and they are redesigning the organization to become a self-adapting and learning organism. As you begin to see and trust the subtle forces, you will spend more time connecting with people rather than controlling them. You will be sharing ideas, information, and dreams. When work relationships include shared vision, values, and trust, control is easier, often taking care of itself through delegation and participation. The gusher of subtle forces is there for the taking. Are you ready to uncap it?

THE NEW REALITY

The new reality is fusion leadership in Way Four. The development of human subtle forces and ingenuity means treating people the way you would treat a flower in your garden. The potential is contained in the flower, which blossoms not because you direct it to, but because you release its potential by providing positive conditions of light, water, temperature, fertilizer, and soil.

If you have spent a lifetime grasping and controlling, changing your approach will be a challenge. Without reliance on the familiar organizational props of rules, regulations, measurement, and bottom line, you may feel uncomfortable. Without the security of structure and control, you will have to face yourself. Managing from within, using your own vision, mindfulness, heart, courage, and integrity, may be like confronting a stranger who has been present in your life but whom you have never met. You might as well be a primitive person looking in a mirror for the first time. You cannot put off this meeting any longer if you are to discover your own and others' subtle potentials. Keep in mind that your desire for control has grown from your experience in organizational hierarchies built on a false belief in permanence and stability. If you cannot give up the props of structure and control, then they control you. You need them because they support your sense of psychological safety and identity, not because they are best for you, your people, or your organization.

In Part Two, we probe more deeply into the subtle forces and the ways in which personal fusion unlocks them. This knowledge will provide a basic foundation for your transformation. However, if you are interested only in applying large-scale fusion technologies for organizational change, you may want to just skim Chapters Three through Nine. A casual survey of these chapters will illustrate the kinds of leadership potentials that can be released through the large-scale fusion technologies and events described in Part Three.

Personal Remembering ■

- What strong forces divert your time and attention from your personal creativity, dreams, and personal aspirations? What is their hold over you?

- How do you feel about attending a so-called "soft" or "touchy-feely" seminar on personal growth? Explore what your reaction means.

- What is your response to the idea that order is essentially free, that self-organization occurs naturally when traditional management methods are removed?

- In which of the four "ways" would you prefer to lead? How is this way of leading supported or resisted within your organization as it currently operates?

PART TWO

UNLOCKING SUBTLE FORCES THROUGH PERSONAL FUSION

CHAPTER THREE

THE CHALLENGE OF PERSONAL FUSION

A frog lived all his life in a large, deep stone well on a prosperous farm. One day a frog from the sea paid him a visit.

"Where do you come from?" asked the frog in the well.

"From the great ocean," he replied.

"How big is your ocean?"

"It's gigantic."

"You mean about a quarter of the size of my well here?"

"No, bigger."

"Bigger? You mean half as big?"

"No, even bigger."

"Is it . . . as big as this well?"

"There's no comparison."

"That's impossible! I've got to see this for myself."

They set off together. As they came over a rise and the frog from the well saw the limitless ocean, it was such a shock that his eyes glazed, his head was in great pain, and he fell unconscious.[1]

The stone well represents the frame of reference and comfort zone that define a person's view of the world. A big challenge for a leader is to understand that he or she resides in the well, not by the ocean. Managers often are trapped unknowingly in a strong force mindset. They don't see the ocean of subtle forces when their lives have been spent in a stone well of hierarchy and control. No wonder most organizational changes fail. A fundamental change in corporate mindset is essential to enable reengineering and restructuring programs to work. Leaders and employees alike need to see new possibilities.

The whole notion of leadership is changing rapidly. A few years ago, the concept of leadership seemed simple: employees had to be motivated to achieve the leader's goal. Leadership was about managing and controlling people for the sake of a goal. In recent years, leaders have been asked to develop new capacities within themselves—for self-inquiry, stewardship, egolessness, personal responsibility, relationships, passion, vision, empathic communication, empowerment, risk taking, partnership, nurturance, facilitation, and the welcoming of paradox and ambiguity.[2]

These capacities, which depend on subtle forces, are dizzyingly unfamiliar to managers living in the stone well of a traditional corporate hierarchy. However, thanks to increased competition and an out-of-kilter environment, more managers are ready to leave that well to visit the ocean of fusion leadership.

In this chapter, we explore personal fusion, which is about becoming whole, about integrating the subtle forces into one's approach to leadership. We will identify the source of these subtle potentials within the personality, describe the particular forces that will be explored later in the book, and provide a formula for guiding personal fusion—bringing together all parts of one's leadership potential.

THE SOURCE OF PERSONAL FUSION

Personal fusion is bringing the forgotten subtle forces into one's leadership style. Where are the subtle forces? Within you. Your long subjection to the influence of organizational strong forces has caused the subtle forces to atrophy. Fusion leadership requires that they be rediscovered and restored.

The point of fusion leadership is to become whole as an individual, to become one, to seek unity. Personal fusion brings together the rational qualities of traditional management and the subtle forces within you and others. It means understanding yourself, your humanness. Personal fusion unites the physical, mental, emotional, and spiritual qualities that together constitute a human being with the capacity to lead others.

Yet the images of fusion leadership suggest a separation in human nature. There are both strong and subtle forces in people. Each individual has an external person who operates in logical fashion and an internal person who can be awakened to express subtle forces such as vision and heart. A similar leadership duality is being and action. "Being" represents who we are, "action" is the use of our nature to change and improve an organization. But separations are artificial. Strong and subtle, external and internal, action and being—in each case, these are two sides of the same coin. They exist together. They need each other. Leaders are in some sense both monk and warrior. The monk is centered, grounded, and wise. The warrior is focused on a mission and is fiercely determined to reach it, regardless of obstacles. Both characters exist in the same person and are there to be used in union.

The source of subtle forces also can be understood in terms of an apparent duality, as illustrated in Exhibit 3.1. The figure illustrates the exterior and interior aspects of an individual. The part above the boundary in Exhibit 3.1 represents our conscious

Exhibit 3.1
Source of Subtle Forces Within Individuals

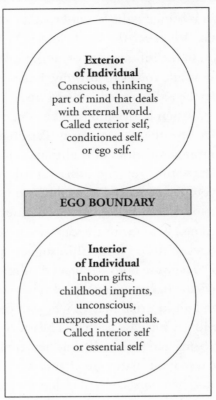

**Exterior
of Individual**
Conscious, thinking
part of mind that deals
with external world.
Called exterior self,
conditioned self,
or ego self.

EGO BOUNDARY

**Interior
of Individual**
Inborn gifts,
childhood imprints,
unconscious,
unexpressed potentials.
Called interior self
or essential self

mind or exterior self, the day-to-day cognitive processing that enables us to operate in the external world, and our rationally chosen behavior. This part of our psyche is also called the ego self or conditioned self.[3] The boundary is like the waterline for an iceberg or the groundline for a tree—the visible part above the surface is only part of the whole. Most managers improve themselves and others by shaping the conscious mind; they attend courses, read books, and hire experts to improve what they do, hardly realizing how limited all this work is. At a deeper level within them, a whole ocean of possibilities awaits discovery.

Beneath the boundary in Exhibit 3.1 is the store of unconscious and subjective potentials. An adult has accumulated thousands of experiences that have shaped and focused his or her personality. The conditioned self is formed by a wide range of experiences from childhood, family, school, movies, TV, and popular culture. The adult personality is the residue of early experiences such as touching a hot stove, playing with Daddy, being spanked for running into the street, receiving praise for catching a ball, and so on. Through such experiences, people learn what works for them, what to approach and what to avoid. Gradually, their experiences are narrowed down to a few that work effectively in childhood and become the dominant source of adult personality. The conditioned mind above the boundary in Exhibit 3.1 contains a small percentage of the potentials that were available to the person at birth. The challenge of personal fusion is to become aware of the subtle forces in the interior or essential self and to integrate them into one's leadership style.

It may be hard to believe in something you can't see or touch, such as subtle forces in the unconscious. But they do exist, and they shape your behavior even when they are unrecognized. This is illustrated by the following story.

A company that makes doors decided to advertise them by emphasizing their strength and safety. The advertisement showed a closed and locked door, virtually unassailable. Sales did not improve, and actually decreased slightly. A research study investigated the unconscious feelings associated with doors. Talking to people about their early life experiences, the investigators found that closed doors were associated with anxiety. People recalled Mommy closing the bedroom door at night and shutting off the light, or their coming home from school to find the front door locked, or the door to their parents' room being closed when they were scared and wanted attention. The advertisement with the closed doors created anxiety and avoidance in consumers that they were not consciously aware of. Check this out in yourself. What do you feel when someone says, "Come in and close the door"?

Open doors, by contrast, were associated with attractive and reassuring feelings in the unconscious. People recalled the open door to their parents' room on Sunday morning when they could run in and join their parents in bed. They recalled feeling safe when the door of their room was open at night because they could see the light in the hall and hear reassuring noises. The unconscious residue of these experiences attracts adults to open doors and makes them anxious about closed doors. When the company ran a new advertisement picturing open doors, the response was far more positive.[4]

The images of open and closed doors are also highly relevant to leadership styles. Does a leader represent an open door that invites others to enter or a closed door that creates fear and anxiety? Do leaders shape the conscious minds of employees or help them get in touch with their deeper potentials? Leaders who know how to appeal to the subtle forces and yearnings in others are able to circumvent the habits of the rational, conditioned self.

From Ego to Subtle Forces

Leaders cannot simply decree new thinking about the unconscious forces that underlie teamwork, cooperation, involvement, and personal fusion. *Leaders first have to change themselves.* They have to see the ocean of their own potential before they can see it in others. Rather than handing down edicts, fusion leaders first learn to connect with themselves at a deeper level, to find their own heart. But how does one find one's own heart and then speak to the hearts of others? If there are untapped potentials of leadership beneath the surface in every person, how are they found and released?

The struggle for most aspiring leaders is between the ego or exterior self and subtle potentials. Ego is the conditioned part of ourselves that operates rationally in the outer world to get what we need. It is concerned with "I" and "mine." Ego is initially developed, during childhood, to meet the individual's physical needs. Gradually it grows to include the acquisition of social goods such as money, status, and recognition. A healthy ego is functional, enabling the person to succeed in a society based on competition, self-orientation, and materialism.

The story at the beginning of this chapter about the frog in the well is about the conditioned ego. Because of life experiences, the ego holds limited and even false beliefs about the self and others. Life experiences create a frame of reference about who one is and what one can do. A manager may believe he does not have leadership skill, that the display of emotion is a bad thing, that he has no imaginative capacities, or that vision and caring are frivolous things for his organization. These beliefs derive from the rational ego and belie the awaiting subtle forces.

One manager we know views the world in terms of financial incentives. He believes financial rewards motivate behavior— for example, whether employees stay with the company or leave. Even when resources from which to draw such rewards are severely limited, he will not consider creating a congenial emotional climate as a way to keep or galvanize his engineers. If they say they need a vision or ask for more team relationships, he responds with dollars and cents. This narrow and false view of people is based on the experiences that formed his ego. But just as the frog learned the truth about the limits of its well, albeit painfully, leaders can learn the truth about themselves.

A sixteen-year-old anorexic girl weighing ninety-five pounds may look in the mirror and see someone who is overweight. This false belief is rooted in the conditioned self or ego. A woman who believes she is intrinsically unlovable because of rejection by her parents has created an ego belief that accommodates the experience of rejection. Similarly, an employee who is obsessed with perfection to the point of driving others crazy has learned to value accomplishments over his personal worth. In each of these cases, the false belief of ego can be corrected by allowing the inner truth to express itself.

The ego is to a manager what formal structure is to an organization. Watchdog managers enforce rules and standards, believing that the rules will keep everything under control and provide security and safety for the organization. What they fail to see is that the rules and regulations limit the creative potential of those within the organization. How often have you had to work around such rules to do your job well?

Ego behaves in exactly the same way. It is a vigilant watchdog that looks outward and controls inwardly. It wants to maintain stability and safety for the manger rather than free the greater creativity, vision, and courage that lie within. Learning the truth about how your ego limits your potential can relax it and allow the subtle forces to emerge. This is similar to what happens when top leaders of an organization realize they have limited the potential of employees and relax the rules to enable creativity to flourish. Your leadership potential can flourish also.

One task you can set for yourself as a leader is to work toward less ego. Even small steps can free great potential. Personal fusion means slowly dropping ego blind spots. Management is based on ego; leadership is based on the subtle potentials that become available when ego, like the rind of an orange, is peeled away.

Subtle forces have existed since the beginning of mankind. They show up again and again in art, literature, folklore, myths, dreams, and patterns of human behavior. The same deep images appear in every culture. Each person is born with these subtle potentials, but they are not fully developed in modern life. Robert Bly says that every individual is like a pie. Only one or two slices are eaten in life, while the other slices are put in a bag and carried over one's shoulder.[5] Ego is the slice most people eat. The subtle forces are the pieces in the bag, unconsumed in modern corporate life but with us nevertheless. When a leader remembers the other slices are there, she can bring them into fusion with the conscious and rational elements of her personality.

One type of subtle potential pertains to art. An artist friend of ours teaches people with no drawing or painting experience how to draw portraits. Managers in her classes are fearful and certain they cannot draw. They report experiences from childhood where they learned they could do only "rational" things; they could not paint a picture, least of all a portrait. This is a manifestation of the conditioned self—the belief that you can't do something because some early experience suggested you couldn't. People who learned as children that they were poor artists carry the belief into adulthood, certain that they have no potential at all. This belief is the frog in the stone well.

As our artist friend demonstrates in class after class of disbelieving managers, everyone has artistic potential. Even rational managers quickly see their artistic possibilities. Not everyone will become a famous artist, but all can do well, find pleasure and joy in the drawing or painting of portraits, and enjoy the artwork of others. The discovery of artistic potential is no different from the discovery of the subtle forces of leadership described in this book.

FUSION LEADERSHIP

There are three aspects of fusion leadership, as we use the term in this book. First, personal fusion means embracing and bringing together both rational ego and subtle potentials. It means becoming whole by nurturing and developing all of your potentials. Personal fusion means empowering yourself and acting from that power. *Fusion leadership can be defined as recognizing one's subtle leadership gifts, potentials, and passions and acting from them to lead organizational change and improvement.* Leaders like Jack Welch, Sam Walton, and Warren Buffett are all noted for acting from their inner compass or gyroscope. They act from deep knowing and strength to make the things that they believe in happen.

The greatest part of leadership is the impact we have on others. A leader has followers. In our experience, followers yearn to be inspired rather than controlled. Leaders develop others by showing the way to vision, courage, heart, communication, mindfulness, and integrity, and by enabling others to discover and act from their own subtle potentials. Thus, the second aspect is that *fusion leaders appreciate the potential subtle forces in other people and create fusion processes to help people develop and act on their gifts and potentials.* Leaders don't create anything new, they simply unlock the subtle yearnings and abilities that people already have. Fusion leaders help people remember what has been temporarily lost.

Personal fusion thus involves self-inquiry, finding one's own subtle potentials and acting from one's whole being—from a sense of the ocean rather than the well.

The third element of fusion leadership is *facilitating organization change by understanding and using the integration of organization needs and individual subtle forces through organizational fusion.* Research shows that most managers are hardworking, nice people. But they typically idealize logic, objectivity, order, efficiency, and control. They are impersonal, believing emotions should not be a part of the workplace.[6] Fusion leadership is the opposite. It looks deeply into self and others, seeking to release the vital inner being. As the Buddhist masters advise, it is time to turn to the "inner teacher."[7] The personal subtle forces are a treasure chest whose key is believed by managers to be lost. But they hold the key in their hands. They can unlock the chest whenever they choose. Then all that is required is to hear the message and trust its potential.

Mort Meyerson was away from EDS for five years before being asked to join Perot Systems as CEO. He saw from his experience as a consultant that old leadership techniques didn't apply during this revolutionary time in business. He looked deeply into himself, reinventing his personal concept of leadership. In the old days, he used strong forces to drive people to eighty-hour weeks and abandon family, community, and other obligations. Profit-and-loss excluded all other values. Each manager had to be tougher, smarter, and sharper than everyone else. People were in ruthless competition with each other, and also took a ruthless view of customers.

At Perot Systems, Meyerson created a new understanding of himself. He saw that he could no longer lead in the old way. He couldn't do everything himself, as he did when competition was stable. He was like a caterpillar entering a cocoon, not knowing whether he would ever come out as a butterfly. So he spent time probing into himself, into the durable principles and values he could embody as a leader. He became concerned with human relationships and how to facilitate others. He found that his top priority was not profit and loss, but building a great organization around values and people, building financial strength with a team of people who supported and nurtured each other.[8]

Achieving fusion between the subtle and the strong is the step many managers take as they move from management to leadership, from control to empowerment. Personal fusion can also happen in other fields.

Sam Powell teaches cowboys how to break horses. Early in his career, he dominated horses as a buck-proof, tough-as-nails cowboy. He believed in dominating horses through a rough 'n' tough style of spurring hard, pulling the horse's ears, and holding on for the ride. As a young man, he

*thought his father was a wimp because he could be riding
a horse within thirty or forty minutes without kicking up
any dust. How? By talking to the horse and developing
trust. As horses became more expensive and cowboys less
willing to break their bones, Powell remembered the subtle
approach. Now he reads the animal's body language to
understand its needs. He uses his own voice tone and body
language to build a relationship of trust. As soon as the
animal understands it won't be hurt, the saddle is quickly
in place and the riding begins. Now Powell teaches only
the subtle approach, and he is one of the most sought-after
teachers in the country.[9]*

PERSONAL FUSION

To achieve your leadership potential, let go of that part of yourself that needs order, predictability, and dominance. Let go of
control and grasping, let go of being the logical manager or the
overwhelmed manager. Awaken the deeper resources of yourself and your people for their and the organization's good.

The broad historical literature on leadership has emphasized
that leaders are whole human beings. Leadership, as opposed
to management, is about the subtle forces of mind, heart, and
spirit. Indeed, surveys about what people want in their leaders
also point to qualities that include mental, emotional, and spiritual dimensions.[10]

The following story (adapted from William Faulkner) suggests the sort of personal subtle forces that might be harnessed
within you:

*Imagine a small rural community in Mississippi in the
1880s. People live simply, off the land. Each family has a
plot of land for growing food, and all share the resources of
the larger wilderness. Each year, the men undertake an*

expedition into the wilderness to hunt, not just deer and game but their famous local enemy, a bear called Old Ben. Old Ben has taken on mythical proportions as the biggest, most ferocious grizzly bear imaginable, and as king of the wilderness. The hunt has been conducted annually as long as anyone can remember, and the men tell stories of past hunts as warriors speak of battle. They dream of the glory of killing Old Ben and talk of the sacrifices they will make for this personal accomplishment.

The story is told through the eyes of a teenage boy who will join the hunt for the first time. Hunting Old Ben is the motive for the hard work of learning a woodsman's skills. The boy is befriended by a half-breed who lives on the edge of the community and teaches the boy about the woods. The half-breed develops a close relationship with the boy, mentoring and coaching him about the subtle aspects of the wilderness, about loving and thriving in it. The boy masters the skills of using hunting dogs, tracking, riding, and shooting, and acquires self-confidence in his relationship with the wilderness.

The story builds momentum as the boy and the men prepare for the imminent hunt. Old Ben is the enemy, blamed for killing sheep and cattle, and his death is the mission of the group. He has been sighted on previous hunts, and once part of his ear was shot away, but he always survived. At last, everything is ready. Supplies are loaded and the group rides into the woods. Old Ben is the highest measure of each person's worthiness as a hunter.

In the course of events, the boy gets separated from the other hunters. He maintains presence of mind, and rather than searching randomly for the men or Old Ben, he sits quietly in a small clearing to be in touch with himself and the surroundings he cares about. Time passes. Suddenly, the boy hears a noise on the edge of the clearing and finds himself face to face with Old Ben. The bear does not attack, but watches as the boy stands and lifts his rifle. In that moment, the boy has an opportunity to kill Old Ben and become a hero. Studying the bear, the boy has a chance to do what all the men have dreamed of doing as long as he can remember. Yet, in that moment, he does not squeeze the trigger. Sensing safety, Old Ben leaves the clearing. The boy subsequently has another opportunity to shoot Old Ben, and again chooses not to kill him.[11]

Why didn't the boy shoot the bear? The wilderness and Old Ben represent surprise and threat that could destroy the livestock and livelihood of the community. The men saw themselves as separate from the environment and wanted to create a predictable, safe world by hunting Old Ben and destroying what was hostile to them. The boy, by contrast, did not see himself as separate from the wilderness, did not feel threatened by it, nor did he want to kill the bear. He seemed to have a broader understanding about adapting to a threatening world so that the community could grow and change in a positive way. The boy's actions in the woods, especially in his confrontation with Old Ben, reflect intuitive wisdom. He relied on subtle forces within himself, which led him to do the opposite of what might have been expected.

• The boy experienced *mindfulness* in his ability to see the big picture, be open to new experience, and be mentally present in each moment. The boy's greatest learning about the woods came from someone unlike himself—the half-breed—someone on the community's periphery. The boy understood the wilderness and saw that the process could be more valuable than the outcome, the hunt more important than the kill. He stayed present in each moment rather than chasing in several directions at once. By comparison, how many managers today welcome the potential of people and ideas radically different from those they are familiar with, or focus on the moment rather than being obsessed with multiple goals and outcomes in the future?

• The boy operated from his *heart* as well as his head. He loved nature. He loved animals. He loved the woods. He appreciated the magnificence of Old Ben's wildness. He was in his bliss, because he chose to do what he loved. Rather than keep himself apart, he let himself merge with nature and the woods. He had little sense of separateness between himself and the trees, animals, and surroundings. By contrast, how many managers today welcome emotions such as bliss and joy and encourage people to become one with the processes, people, and unfolding events of which they are a part?

• The boy had an intuitive sense of higher purpose and *vision*. He understood that killing the bear would destroy the community. The hunt united the community in a shared purpose, providing it with a common direction. The bear was the vision that transcended the men's fear of the wild and of their own deaths. With Old Ben dead, the community would fragment, would have no unifying dream, becoming a collection of isolated individuals without a larger purpose to serve. In today's organizations, how many managers build a shared vision that binds people together into community to achieve a shared purpose?

• The boy displayed the *courage* to deviate from norms and expectations. He was a nonconformist, subjecting himself to disapproval and ridicule in order to serve the higher purpose of the community and the wilderness he loved. He did not go along to get along. He had the courage to deviate, and in so doing protect the larger community. In today's organizations, how many managers risk ridicule and rejection by authority figures to serve a higher good?

• The boy experienced a deep sense of *communication,* both within himself and with the woods. He understood that practicing silence and meditation can be productive behavior even in a crisis. He heard his inner intuition. He did not feel the need to chase the men or the bear, thrashing around, trying to get what he wanted. How many managers today resort to listening and quiet rather than talking, noise, and busyness before moving ahead?

- The boy displayed the highest level of *integrity*, transcending his own selfishness. He took personal responsibility for the community. He seemed to traverse the passage into adulthood, acting from a mature perspective that embraced the woods, the bear, himself, and his community. He gave up personal glory. Rather than acting for himself, he gave to the larger group, becoming a servant to this higher cause. How many people in companies today take personal responsibility, giving up their personal rewards for the good of the whole?

The boy achieved fusion in his close relationship with the half-breed, in his oneness with the wilderness and his community. The half-breed, for example, became a friend, mentor, and coach. This close relationship enabled the boy to learn about the woods, and perhaps more important, to discover and awaken parts of himself that could be expressed in the wilderness.

Unlocking the full potential on one or more of these qualities will draw people to you as followers. People want to follow someone with courage, heart, and integrity. Fusion leaders transcend their formal position to speak directly to the yearnings and subtle potential in others.

Most of us hate to be controlled, so it is no wonder that many reengineering, restructuring, and downsizing initiatives fail to flourish. Employees are criticized for not embracing change, but the problem is the attitude of leaders. Managers tend to see employees as the barrier to change, which traps them in the mindset of wanting to fix others.[12] Through subtle forces and fusion leadership, leaders can unlock the natural energy and inherent capabilities of those whose courses they are piloting.

Although subtle potentials may not be fully awake within you, you can discover them. Individuals can achieve personal fusion to release their own subtle forces through knowledge, will, and action, as illustrated in Exhibit 3.2. By bringing together interior and exterior elements of self, subtle forces can be unlocked and used to lead others.

Achieving Personal Fusion

The formula we use to help people unlock their subtle forces is as follows:

$$\text{Personal Fusion} = \text{Knowledge}_{E, I} \times \text{Will} \times \text{Action}$$

Awakening a subtle force to make it a part of one's leadership approach requires knowledge, will, and action. Two types of *knowledge* are needed. The first kind, external knowledge, is knowledge about the subtle force obtained from the outside world. In the case of vision, this means reading everything you can lay your hands on about vision, and talking to or observing others. Similarly, you can use your rational mind to learn about courage or communication.

The second kind of knowledge is internal. In the case of vision, you would need to seek an understanding of your own higher purpose in life, your hopes, and your dreams. These not only determine your personal vision but enter into your vision for your department or organization. When exploring courage, you must identify your own fears and your own sources of courage. In seeking internal knowledge of mindfulness, you must come to understand your own frame of reference, your assumptions about life, the outline of the stone well in which you live. Internal knowledge is not available in books, nor can it be cultivated during a hectic work schedule. It is derived from reflection, contemplation, meditation, and feedback from close associates, through all of which you gain access to your essential self, your own inner feelings.

Exhibit 3.2
Achieving Personal Fusion

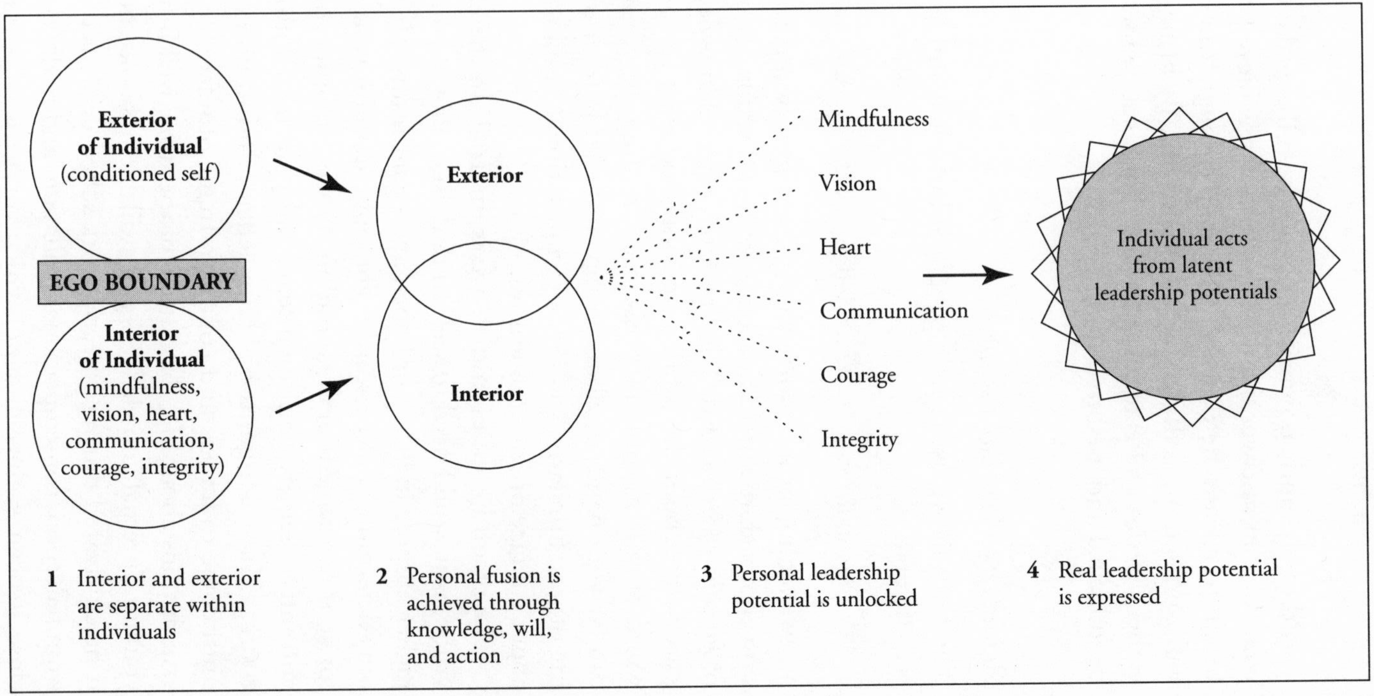

Individual acts from latent leadership potentials

Mindfulness

Vision

Heart

Communication

Courage

Integrity

Exterior

Interior

Exterior of Individual (conditioned self)

EGO BOUNDARY

Interior of Individual (mindfulness, vision, heart, communication, courage, integrity)

1 Interior and exterior are separate within individuals

2 Personal fusion is achieved through knowledge, will, and action

3 Personal leadership potential is unlocked

4 Real leadership potential is expressed

Will is the desire, intention, or willpower to change and grow as a leader. Willpower is necessary to acquire internal and external knowledge about the subtle forces. There is no personal change without intention. Knowledge is of no value—indeed, knowledge probably will not be acquired—without desire. The will to move forward often arises from dissatisfaction or from a crisis that tells you growth is necessary. Often the most difficult periods in life, including utter failures, turn out to be positive experiences because of the resulting motivation to grow and change. Will can also be harnessed by changing your focus. If no crisis is present, perhaps the desire for more money or promotion can be shifted toward desire for self-inquiry, personal competence, and change. Willpower is within each person as a motivating force: the challenge is to direct it toward leadership growth and away from mere objects and possessions. Willpower will enable you to seek your own vision, to surmount your fears of rejection, to serve the larger good of your team.

Action is embodiment of the subtle force, the practice that fuses it into your personality and leadership style. A new behavior performed ten times becomes your own. For example, a manager who develops a vision of high quality for his manufacturing department and uses the phrase "No defects" as his message becomes a visionary leader. If previous employee meetings have involved only the sharing of data and statistics, he now introduces a new emphasis. Ten times in scheduled meetings, he asserts, "No defects is our mission." Expressing the desired vision becomes a natural part of himself. Similarly, when the subtle force in question is courage, stepping beyond one's comfort zone to delegate additional responsibilities to subordinates becomes easy after it has been done several times. Practice any newly understood subtle force ten times and it becomes a quality of leadership.

Action is essential to personal fusion, for new behaviors enable the old behavior to die away. Action is the practice that enables the new behavior to become part of your new, integrated self. Consider the hands on a clock. The second hand moves rapidly. The minute hand creeps slowly, but movement can be observed. The hour hand cannot be observed to move at all, but a later look shows that movement has indeed occurred. Practice or action is like the fast second hand. Move quickly. Try a new behavior several times. The minute hand is your self-perception; after practice, you will soon think of yourself as having a new force of leadership. The hour hand is your conditioned self; you may not observe the change right away, but after a time you will see a difference. The subtle force slowly becomes a full part of you.

In the next few chapters, we describe each subtle force in detail, providing a base of knowledge for your growth toward personal fusion.

Personal Remembering

- How do you feel about the idea of changing yourself before you lead the transformation of others and the organization? How would you go about changing yourself to unlock your subtle forces?

- A philosopher said that one great fear is that of total insignificance. How afraid are you of insignificance? What does your answer say about your ego?

- What is the bear in your life? Have you wounded or killed it?

- When have you felt your involvement with your organization was most meaningful? What subtle forces were expressed at that time?

CHAPTER FOUR

MINDFULNESS

In the movie Star Trek II: The Wrath of Khan, *officer cadets are involved in a training exercise called the Kobayashi Maru. The exercise is a computer simulation of an attack by the Klingons. The cadets go through a realistic war scenario, trying many options, hopeful of victory against the Klingons. The cadet in charge isn't doing well. The Klingons blow up the* Enterprise. *Admiral Kirk walks into the war room, flips on the lights, and stops the game. The cadets lost. Kirk orders them to the briefing room.*

The cadet in charge complains to Admiral Kirk of her frustration at not being able to win, that winning seemed impossible. The simulation wasn't fair. Kirk is philosophical, replying it was real, that life sometimes confronts us with no-win situations. He assures her that life builds character and that she will learn and grow from it.

Later the cadet confronts Kirk again with her frustration. She has to know if there is a solution, if anyone ever passed. The Doctor, who is nearby, says she is looking at the only

*person who ever passed the Kobayashi Maru. It is the
Admiral!*

*The cadet immediately asks how he did it. Kirk replies
that he reprogrammed the computer software so he could
win. He even received an award for original thinking.*

Leaders like Kirk change the frame of reference. In an out-of-
kilter world—ambiguous, unpredictable, constantly changing—
the familiar way of doing business doesn't last. The lesson from
Admiral Kirk is that leaders question the premises, look for new
ideas, and know that rules must be changed in new situations.
There is no checklist, recipe, or rulebook that will tell people
how to act in each situation. Leaders need and encourage
unique solutions to novel problems. This releases the subtle
forces in them and others, helping all to remember the creativity they have forgotten.

Traditional corporate hierarchies provide cruise controls for
organizations. The ideal hierarchy is a series of linked robots—
people conditioned to their jobs—performing programmed
activity. This is the image of corporate efficiency in many manager's minds. Hence thinking human beings—leaders like
Admiral Kirk—are needed to recognize the programs and over-
ride them. Leadership is having someone awake at the wheel.
Leadership overrides the cruise control.

Recall Churchill's statement that we create our structures and
then they create us. In a more stable time, managers created cruise
control bureaucracies that let people sleep at the wheel. For companies today, it's not as if there is just one object on the road to
steer around. They might as well be driving in the Baja off-road
race, bouncing through hills, sand, and gullies at high speed. In
a world that is out of kilter, there is never a chance to use cruise
control. A leader—in fact, everyone—needs to think constantly.

Issues of mind are critical to fusion leadership. The world is
usually viewed through a limited and conditioned mind, but

fusion leaders can learn to "see" and appreciate the subtle forces
and unlock them as a resource for change. They can begin to
realize the narrowness of the ego's perspective and perhaps
recreate a blank slate for learning. *Mindfulness* is the ability to
appreciate new possibilities and new ways of thinking, to see
the subtle forces, to see the potential in people as being more
powerful than the safety of traditional structure and control.
Without the ability to see and understand things in a new way,
there is no chance of making fundamental change in yourself
or your organization.

A leader's open and questioning mind is the all-important
element that shapes his or her approach to the world and sets
the tone of the organization. Admiral Kirk illustrates how a fusion leader unlocks the force of mindfulness, which includes:

1. A beginner's mind that is open to a new world of ideas
   and people
2. Independent thought and the encouragement of such
   thought in others
3. The ability to see and appreciate subtle forces and
   relationships
4. The ever-deepening process of becoming more mindful

BEGINNER'S MIND

Mind potential is released when people open to new information and multiple perspectives. Mindfulness knocks down the
barriers of conditioned thinking and brings ideas and diverse
people together. Consider the following story.

> *A Zen master asked a student, "Would you like a cup of
> tea?" The student answered, "Yes," so the master poured the
> tea until it filled the cup and then spilled over the saucer*

*and tray. The student asked the master, "Why didn't you
stop pouring when the cup was filled?" The master sent him
to clean up the trash, and when he returned, the master
filled the cup properly and gave him his lesson: "You can't
put anything new into your cup until you take out what's
already there."* [1]

Education is learning how to forget. The full cup rejects new
tea. The full head, the "expert's mind," rejects new ideas. Managers conditioned to a programmed hierarchy have to learn to
forget, to jettison ideas and habits that are no longer needed.
It isn't just what leaders know that hurts them, but what they
know that isn't so. Managers have to forget some of their conditioned expertise so that they can remember things that truly
count—such as the subtle forces yearning for expression.

The challenge to leaders in chaotic times is to be open to
strange new assumptions about the world—new assumptions
that are at odds with basic beliefs. This openness—putting
aside opinions, beliefs, and preconceptions—is what a Zen
teacher called "beginner's mind." The beginner is open to new
ideas. The beginner has the openness and innocence of a child.
The expert has become closed, because he "knows the answer."

Welcome New People and Ideas Without Fear or Prejudice

The beginner accepts new tea like an empty cup. Leaders can
use the beginner's mind to approach new situations and complex problems. They can ask questions rather than provide answers. If they don't, they may miss the essence of opportunity
in an unfamiliar circumstance. One of Dick Daft's experiences
illustrates this:

*On a flight from Nashville to Los Angeles, I felt nervous
about the seminar to come, where I was expected to learn
more about my inner emotional life. Arriving at the*

*workshop early, I sat on the floor with a few other people
to await sign-in.*

*Strange-looking people straggled in, and one woman in
her late twenties was especially off-putting. She wore a
black leather jacket and skin-tight black pants. Her hair
was shaped into a long spike that rose several inches above
her head and was colored green. Her facial expression was
hard, even fierce, and the V of her blouse revealed a tattoo.
I knew I had made a mistake coming to this workshop.*

*The workshop finally started, and the leader asked each
of the almost 180 people to look around and pick out "your
scariest person." That was easy for me. Ms. Spike Hairdo
was sitting in the second row. The leader suggested that,
some time during the workshop, we get to know our scary
person. "No chance," I said to myself.*

*The next afternoon, we were asked to work in pairs in
an exercise to forgive others and to ask forgiveness for pain
caused others. As I walked around to select someone to
work with, Ms. Spike Hairdo appeared before me.*

*Our eyes met for a moment, asking the question of
whether we wanted to work together. I heard my voice ask
if she would do this exercise with me. She hesitated, looking
me over in a frightened way, and answered yes.*

*The exercise astonished me. Beneath the surface, this
person was struggling with the same emotional issues as I
was, and she had been treated far worse. She had been
emotionally rejected by her parents early in childhood and
had suffered multiple rejections since. She had constructed
a tough, rebellious exterior to protect her from those rejections. She borrowed money from friends to attend the workshop and was devoting herself to breaking through her deep
hurts to find loving feelings for others. I was astonished. I
learned so much from her experience and her forgiveness.
She no longer seemed so scary. She had seemed so threatening, yet beneath the surface she was a rich human being.*

When Dick saw Ms. Spike Hairdo, he was closed to the idea that she held value for him, that he could learn from her. His subsequent experience illustrates the importance of remaining open to new people and ideas, even when they seem threatening. Ideas that have the greatest impact on us are those we disagree with, those we don't like. Only by staying open to things dramatically different from what we have known before can we change, grow, and improve as mindful leaders.

The folklore archetype of a mindful person is the sage. The sage has knowledge and insight that is not apparent to others and seeks the truth wherever it lies. The sage's willingness to learn from multiple points of view, and to remain tentative, is stronger than his need to be proven right. Each person is born with sage-like wisdom waiting to be awakened.

Let Yourself See What Is Outside the Box

Human thinking can be thought of as operating inside a box. The walls may be solid, preventing us from thinking and accepting viewpoints "outside the box." A beginner's mind, being open to unusual ideas, allows us to escape the limiting box of our beliefs, enables the world of diverse ideas to enter from outside. The box is like the stone well that limited the frog's perspective in the Chapter Three story.

Plato used a cave allegory to explain how the unquestioning acceptance of prevailing truths makes each of us a prisoner in our box of beliefs.

> *Imagine a group of people who have been chained inside a cave all their lives where they cannot see the cave opening. Just beyond the opening is a roaring fire that casts shadows of the outside people on the cave wall in front of the prisoners. These shadows become the whole world to the chained viewers, who name them and even construct stories about*

*them. Blocked from direct view of the outside world, the
prisoners create their own reality, and the stories they weave
give them a sense of security and understanding of the
world outside.*

*Now imagine that one of the prisoners is allowed to
leave the cave. He would soon see the flaws in the stories he
had believed before. He would see that the shadows cast on
the cave wall were merely a reflection of a larger and more
complex social reality. On returning to the cave, he would
never again accept the old way of thinking. But when he
attempts to share his knowledge with the others, his ideas
are ridiculed and rejected. The familiar beliefs and stories
are more comforting to the prisoners than the big, threatening world described to them. In the end, in the face of the
new viewpoint, the cave dwellers cling to their old beliefs
more tightly than ever. The voice from the person who
ventured outside is not believed.*[2]

Plato saw the mercantile class of his day as people impris-
oned in a cave of simplistic and often mistaken beliefs. How
many executives today defend the comforting beliefs held by
their companies against the real world described by outsiders?
The beginner's mind assists us in seeing a broader reality. It is
only when we open ourselves to the possibilities of other truths
that we recognize the limits of our own beliefs and the validity
of others'.

Successful corporate leaders have a magician's open mind,
like Henry Kissinger's, not a closed mind, like Archie Bunker's.
Elliott Jaques, a psychoanalyst and management expert, developed the Stratified Systems Theory about leaders and organizations.[3] His research indicated that sage-like cognitive abilities
are essential to leadership today. He identified leadership potential by asking people questions like, "Should we legalize
marijuana?" High-potential leaders considered two or three

lines of reasoning simultaneously, such as the underlying moral issue, the symbolic implications of legalization, and historic parallels such as Prohibition. Such leaders also welcomed additional perspectives. Jaques found that people without leadership potential were closed-minded, considering only a single dogmatic viewpoint such as "Legalizing marijuana would be wrong."

Mix in New and Different Truths

The beauty of the beginner's mind is manifested at Spartan Motors, a manufacturer of chassis for fire trucks, motor homes, and other heavy-duty vehicles. Spartan revolutionized its industry by looking at its product in unexpected ways. Spartan experts know how to forget. Under the leadership of chairman George W. Sztykiel, mindfulness is manifested throughout the company.[4]

The Spartan secret is to mix old pro engineers with youngsters right out of high school or off the farm. The young workers come in with beginners' minds and practical knowledge acquired from tinkering with their cars and family tractors. They temper their new ideas with the older workers' feeling of the marketplace and practical knowledge acquired within the system. "The old engineers pass on the feeling to the new guys," Sztykiel says, which allows us to "produce ten times faster and cheaper than big companies, where they have lost the feeling. . ." Spartan employees are encouraged to go to trade shows, talk to customers, and get to know the market, as well as cross-train in more than one job within the company. Creating soft-sided mental "boxes" in this company expands the possibilities of a novel future without losing the value of past experience.

One team at Spartan Motors, Larry Karkau and Tim Williams, produced a dazzling result. Twenty-five years apart in age, the two men developed a low-cost chassis for high-end motor homes that the rest of the industry had given up on. Karkau, a thirty–year veteran in the industry, freely credits Williams with a lot of the ideas and tenacity that kept the project alive for a year and a half. One-year sales of their chassis totaled $30 million. A year later, that number doubled. Williams's résumé, which showed a little drafting in high school and experience driving a semi as his only prior employment, would not have qualified him for an engineering position at an orthodox company, and the door would have remained closed to a $100+ million butterfly that looked at the time like a bothersome moth.

INDEPENDENT THINKING

Mindfulness comes from within. It is remembering how we were before we accepted an organization's structure as our reality. As defined by Harvard psychologist Ellen Langer, mindfulness is the creation of new labels and categories with which to interpret the world.[5] Mindful people question assumptions and interpret data and events according to their own thinking. It is the opposite of mindlessness, which means using the labels and categories given to us by others. People may become mindless because they find it too hard to stay mentally alert or because they do not trust themselves to interpret data from their own perspective.

Our society encourages mindlessness. At any moment, much of the population seems mesmerized into mental passivity. Schools encourage students to memorize facts and pass multiple-choice tests rather than to think independently and wrestle with ambiguous problems. Youngsters and adults alike spend long hours in front of video and television screens where the thinking has been done for them. They are not required to create their own experiences or thoughts.

A consequential example of mindlessness occurred in 1985, when an Air Florida jet crashed into the icy Potomac River shortly after take-off from Washington, D.C. The pilot and copilot, unaccustomed to snowy conditions, mindlessly followed their standard preflight operations without questioning their assumptions. Although the ground crew applied de-icing fluid to the wings, the flight crew, in their habitual mindset, did not turn on the airplane's electric de-icers in the long wait for take-off.[6]

In the chaotic world of organizations, a leader's weather and flight conditions change daily, so mental categories and habits that worked in one situation may not work in the next. Mindful leaders question patterns, labels, categories, and habits. In our opening example, Admiral Kirk realized that old categories would not let him beat the Klingons. He demonstrated mindfulness by challenging the assumption that the Klingons were his opponents in the war simulation. He saw the computer as his real adversary, so he attacked its software to win.

Mindfulness Is Determined by Rudder, Not Radar

Leader mindfulness means being willing to stand apart, to say what you believe, to have opinions, to determine your course by your inner rudder rather than by external radar. Managers often steer their course by determining what is acceptable to bosses and the peer culture. They use a technique like radar, learning what other people think before deciding their own path. Their watchword is "Tell me what to do and I'll do it." Mindful leaders determine their path by what they believe from within. They trust the subtle inner voice of creativity and independent thought.

Mindfulness is hard work. It means constantly questioning things as they are. It means challenging assumptions, challenging the mental and organizational structures usually taken for granted. Bernard Bass studied charismatic leadership and found that subordinates admired leaders who questioned assumptions and stimulated them intellectually.[7] "Why do we do this job this way?" Such questions energized people. Mindfulness also means finding the inner confidence to act on creative impulses. Mindfulness means reading between the lines of a report, and seeing beyond the explicit argument of a written proposal. Mindfulness means constantly asking, "Why?"

Everyone finds it easy to relax into temporary mindlessness, accept black and white categories, pick the right answer from habit, and rely on the old pattern. Many of us like having the correct answers and categories given to us, because it spares us the exertion of figuring them out for ourselves.

James Gleick, of chaos theory fame, wrote a book about the Nobel physicist Richard Feynman.[8] Feynman maintained a childlike curiosity, which was the heart of his genius. He was always in doubt. He was always starting over. He resisted any authority that prevented him from doing his own thinking, finding his own answers. Certainty and authority work well in a mechanical world, but doubt and questioning are the basis for understanding relationships in a destabilized world. When things are always changing, mental laziness and acceptance of the answers and rules favored by others are dangerous. The trick is to stay mindfully alert, welcome a sense of uncertainty and doubt, and keep asking questions.

The struggle toward mindful leadership requires you to turn within. It depends on your finding the subtle part of yourself that Richard Feynman found. Everyone has a mindful inner voice, but often people don't listen to it, or fear acting on it.

When You Know Something, Look at It in a Different Way

Another approach to independent thinking is to act like John Keating, the teacher in the movie *Dead Poets Society,* who urged his private-school students to break out of their categorized

thinking patterns. He told them to tear a worthless introduction from a book of poetry. He climbed on to his desk and
declared: "I stand on my desk to remind myself we must constantly look at things a different way. The world looks different
from here." He not only sought mindful thinking in himself but
also led others on the same path. By looking at things a different
way, his students found wellsprings of poetic creativity.

A simple change in perspective can completely alter how we
see the world and act in it. The following story tells of such a
turning point in Bob Lengel's life:

*My approach to classroom instruction changed after
watching an episode of the* Paperchase *TV series. The
critical program was entitled, "The Day Kingsfield Missed
Class." Kingsfield was a stodgy, old-fashioned law school
professor. The day before a major examination, when he
was scheduled to lecture on breach of contract, he failed to
appear in class. His absence was completely out of character
and deeply troubling to his students. As they left class to
prepare for the exam, the class broke into two camps. One
group believed they did not have to study the breach of
contract material because it was not covered in class. The
other group believed that his absence did not relieve them
of their obligation to prepare on their own. As the second
group grew increasingly frustrated with the complexity of
the breach of contract material, they suddenly realized that
Kingsfield had breached his contract with them to lecture
on the material before the exam. As they thought through
this breach issue, they began to understand the subtleties
that had previously confused them.*

*On exam day, Kingsfield was asked by the first student
group if the "breach" material would be included. He
answered authoritatively, "Yes, of course." The students*

responded with the charge that he had breached his
contract with them. In a brief dialogue, the class quickly
concluded that Kingsfield was not in breach of contract
because his contract was to teach, not lecture. Lecturing is
just one method of teaching. His absence provided an
object lesson in breach of contract law. I never again
approached teaching as mere lecturing. This example
expanded my capabilities as both teacher and learner.

Only Ideas Outside Your Paradigm Can Save You

How many corporate managers are trapped in a Plato's cave of appearances and mistaken beliefs because it feels "right" or is accepted within the company? In times of fast change, our current beliefs are based on circumstances that no longer exist, yet these beliefs control our view of the world. During the 1970s and 1980s, American auto manufacturers lost 38 percent of the U.S. market to German and Japanese car companies by not recognizing that public preferences had shifted from style and status to quality and economy. Management expert Ian Mitroff found that General Motors operated on a set of assumptions that had been their "magic formula for success" for many years.[9] These assumptions were regarded as fixed truths rather than as thinking to be challenged and overturned by leaders. Only after enormous business losses did General Motors executives question whether their assumptions fit the reality of the new marketplace.

The beginner's mind is more open to a paradigm shift than the expert's mind. Joel Arthur Barker, in *Future Edge*, described the notion of *company paradigm*—the company's fundamental shared way of thinking and perceiving and understanding the world.[10] The paradigm is the box within which "expert" managers think and believe.

Most managers accept their paradigm as truth, discounting other people's beliefs as mistaken good intentions. Belief in a paradigm prompts managers to say, "Doing it that way won't work," "You can't change the rules like that," and "When you've been here longer, you'll understand why." Even when people see a new paradigm outside the box, they stick to the old way of doing things because it succeeded in the past and feels comfortable.

One great paradigm resister was the German scientist who synthesized Novocain, which he intended for major surgical procedures.[11] Surgeons preferred general anesthesia for major surgery, but Novocain found a ready appeal among dentists. The inventor spent his life traveling to dental schools making speeches that forbade dentists to misuse his noble invention. The German scientist is part of each person, and he must be ignored in favor of greater openness to the outside world.

No matter how much you resist, your paradigm won't last. General Motors, IBM, and Sears certainly learned this. Variety stores held on to their belief in a 45 percent markup until their paradigm was obliterated by Wal-Mart and other discounters. Barker pointed out that, in 1968, Swiss companies had 65 percent of wristwatch sales and more than 80 percent of world profits. Everyone predicted continuing Swiss domination of the market. However, a paradigm shift occurred from mechanical to quartz watch mechanisms. Despite these changed conditions, the Swiss stuck with their old way of doing business. By 1980, Swiss world market share had collapsed to less than 10 percent, profits to less than 20 percent.[12]

Only ideas you disagree with have the potential to change you. When Dick rejected Ms. Spike Hairdo, he nearly missed the opportunity to learn from her. Who is your Ms. Spike Hairdo? Welcome scary people and ideas like long-lost relatives who bring news of your forgotten past.

SUBTLE FORCES AND DUALITIES

Organizations are composed on the surface of concrete objects—computers, buildings, offices, new products, the accounting department, the parking lot—and the strong forces of structure and control described in Chapter Two. If you see only the objects and strong forces and attempt to structure and organize them in some meaningful way, the essential flow and process of subtle forces are lost. Engaging the fusion potential of an organization means dealing with subtle forces and intangible relationships.

Look Beyond the Obvious to See Flows, Relationships, and Processes

The important processes in learning organizations occur between the objects. In the physical sciences, invisible force fields like those of magnetism, gravity, and radiation are known to exist in the space between objects. In the social world of organizations, subtle force fields between people contain love, caring, information, culture, values, and a sense of belonging. These subtle forces connect people to one another and to the whole.

In the old stable world, a manager gained power and influence through formal position and the number of people and tangible resources controlled. In the out-of-kilter world, influence is based on building relationships with other people and by seeing and managing relationships among key elements in the organization.

Insight often arises when a leader understands more deeply his relationships with other people. One manager we worked with was courteous and helpful toward women but left them feeling demeaned, hence they avoided working with him. He

came to see that he felt like a big brother and protector in relation to women, thinking of each as "little sister." His approach made it impossible for women to feel that he was
dealing with them as equal, independent adults. When he recognized this pattern, he was able to change his behavior and
create a new set of positive relationships at work.

In another case, a domineering manager expressed his frustration at subordinates who were too passive and dependent. As
he discussed this with others, he gradually saw that his domineering style was creating the dependence. He was creating the
very behavior he disliked. Once he saw that people's behavior
was not something they brought to the workplace but was a result of his manner of relating to them, he was able to change his
behavior and help subordinates act with greater independence.

An effective manager we know plays the subtle processes of
change like a musical instrument. Understanding the subtle
forces, he is alert to the possibility that pockets of failure, dissatisfaction, or crisis may provide the beginning point for
change. He helps people face the reality of their negative conditions, then coaches and mentors them into greater success
and celebrates the result. As each project completes itself, he
seeks subtle opportunities to start over again, touching the right
strings to bring the organization to higher and higher levels of
performance.

Yet, unlike this change manager, many people fail to see the
subtle forces. The following myth from Europe illustrates the
point:

> *An old count believed his son was stupid and couldn't learn
> anything. So he turned the son over to a famous master.
> The son studied for a year, and when he returned, the
> father was disgusted to find that all he had learned was
> "what the dogs bark." Sent out to study with a different
> master for a year, the son returned to say that he had*

*learned "what the birds speak." Furious again that his son
had wasted his time, the father sent him to a third master,
with a warning that this was his last chance. The son
returned after a year to explain that he had learned "what
the frogs croak." In a rage, the father cast his son out.*

*The son began his wanderings and came to a land where
the people were in trouble because the furious barking of
wild dogs permitted no one to rest. Since the son understood
the dogs' language, the dogs talked to him and explained
why they were so ferocious. He then explained to the people
what to do to pacify the wild dogs, and they soon left the
country in peace.*

*After some years, the son traveled to Rome. On his way,
croaking frogs revealed his future to him. Arriving in Rome,
he learned that the pope had died, and the cardinals could
not agree on a new pope. The cardinals wanted to see a
dramatic symbol that would identify the future pope, and
two snow-white doves settled on the son's shoulders. Asked to
be pope, the son did not know if he was worthy, but the doves
counseled him to accept. He was consecrated, as the frogs had
prophesied. When the son had to sing mass, the doves, which
sat on his shoulders, told him the words in his ears.*[13]

In this story, the practical-minded, hardheaded father could
not see value in the subtle relationships the boy had built with nature, the very relationships that carried the boy to the highest position in the church. The father was unable to share his success.
The needs and learnings of the son were not understood by the
father, just as the subtle yearnings and relationships of employees
may not be understood by the manager. The son manifested his
subtle potentials, yet the father could not see their value.

To a manager trapped in the hard-sided box of rational management, talk of sensitivity, sharing, and encouragement—the
building blocks of relationships—may sound appallingly soft.

But it is through these subtle aspects of organization that the leader's real work is accomplished. For this reason, Jack Welch of General Electric, hardly considered soft by associates, mandated that he, along with the rest of his senior people, become softer, more human, more collegial.[14]

In a world far from equilibrium, where everything depends on everything else, mindful leaders do not perceive themselves as autonomous or as acting alone. Skills such as caring for the work group and building relationships are what make a company successful. The fusion leader sees the fluid, organic flows and processes within organizations, and traditional boundaries and concrete objects are no longer dominant. An unfortunate holdover of Newtonian thinking is that important organizational problems, such as low morale or poor quality, are seen as reducible to simplistic, tangible solutions that fail to capture systemic processes. Mindfulness encourages us to move toward an understanding of relationships rather than things, toward holism rather than concern for discrete parts. As Wheatley describes in *Leadership and the New Science,* mindful leaders look for patterns of movement over time, and focus on the qualities of rhythm, flow, direction, and shape, on networks of relationships and the energy flows required to accomplish the work of their units. The intellectual capital that mindful leaders bring to a company is not technical knowledge of finance or marketing but a vision of subtle energy and work flows that used to look like empty space.

Balance Organizational Dualities

Leaders moving toward mindfulness appreciate the subtle dualities inherent in organizations: hard versus soft, masculine versus feminine, old versus new, the big picture versus the part, stability versus change, logical versus emotional, tangible versus intangible, union versus management. As the fusion leader

becomes aware of the soft side of the organization, these dualities become more apparent. Black-white, good-bad, right-
wrong thinking, and attachment to one side of duality, can lead
to disaster, not only because rigid assumptions are quickly ob-
solete, but because they limit an organization's options for dealing with the ever-changing environment.

Consider the popular value of rugged individualism. When
applied in a corporate setting, it encourages people to be independent, to stand on their own two feet, to develop themselves
to the fullest. Yet when carried to the extreme, individualism
denies things equally important to a successful company. Too
much individualism means that people will not admit their
weaknesses, will not participate in co-creation to strengthen the
team, will not be interdependent with others, will not build relationships. Rugged individualism rejects interdependence.
Likewise, the opposite extreme that rejects individualism removes an important source of personal motivation and creativity. A leader can't have everything done in a team. The
mindful leader sees the paradox and embraces both sides.

Joseph Campbell wrote about the "wall of opposites," a
theme that runs through myths from diverse cultures throughout history. In Greek mythology, two islands in the Euxine Sea
were known to crash together in high winds, wrecking ships as
they tried to pass between them. In a mythical sense, these islands represent the opposites within ourselves and within our
organizations: individual and group, liberal and conservative,
masculine and feminine. What allows a ship's captain to pass
safely between the opposing island forces is finding a point of
balance that brings together aspects of both. After Jason, in his
search for the Golden Fleece, sailed the *Argo* between the islands, they remained forever apart.[15] In the same way, a mindful leader who can disengage from one side of the organization's
"wall of opposites" expands the possibilities for safe passage
through the treacherous straits of a chaotic world.

Open-minded balance, not rigid belief, triggers the creative flow of ideas and energy. As we saw in the experience of Spartan Motors (page 74), integrating opposites can achieve astonishing results in the midst of a changing environment.

Another subtle relationship is between the whole and the part. The collective vision must sometimes be achieved at the expense of the part. Mindful leaders accept personal or departmental sacrifices necessary to achieve the larger gains. And sometimes it works in reverse, with the interest of the part given primacy to accomplish the need of the whole. The mindful leader must measure his or her own needs for additional budget, personnel, and efficient operations against the yardstick of the corporate purpose. It is by simultaneously living the visions of the whole *and* the part that fusion leaders inspire success.

We interviewed a fusion-oriented air force general in the Systems Acquisition Command. His wing was responsible for contracting with suppliers for some of the air force's inventory of smart weapons that were later used during Operation Desert Storm. His organization used a dual-authority matrix structure in which conflict was rampant.

The general encouraged people, regardless of rank, to meet face-to-face to resolve their conflicts. When we asked him what single quality most accounted for the success of his conflict resolution, he responded instantly: "Corporate mindset." He meant that individuals had to see the whole as well as their part. When people were immersed only in their personal interests, championing them and defending them against those of everyone else, the system started to break down. By contrast, when individuals could negotiate and make decisions to honor the whole as well as their part, this awesomely complex organization worked just fine.

It is easy to get lost in organizational parts. Traditional managers have been trained to break things down into pieces, and the success of each piece is believed to add up to the success of the whole. Mindful leaders learn that the subtle *relationships* among the parts, and between the whole and the part, are what counts.

BECOMING MINDFUL

The aspects of mindfulness presented in this chapter are summarized and contrasted in Exhibit 4.1. Beginner's mind, open-mindedness, seeing the whole, being aware of subtle forces and relationships—all mean breaking free of the limitations of your mental box. This releases subtle forces of mind in everyone. What better way to stimulate ideas for change? For strong-minded conventional managers, seeing and embracing the subtle view may be the most difficult thing described in this book. It means abandoning a deeply ingrained way of living and thinking, and stepping outside one's mental comfort zone.

Exhibit 4.1. Mindfulness

Conventional Strong-Force View	Fusion Leader Subtle View
• See strong forces	• See subtle forces
• Take position as expert	• Take position as beginner
• Maintain fixed mind	• Maintain open mind
• Project certainty	• Be tentative
• Hold firm opinions	• Set aside opinions
• Know answers	• Ask questions
• Accept labels and categories	• Create labels and categories
• Accept assumptions	• Challenge assumptions
• Reject opposites	• Welcome opposites
• See objects and things	• See subtle flows and relationships
• See own part	• See whole and part
• Believe in one best way	• Encourage multiple approaches

There is no easy path to fusion leadership, but one place to start is the practice of being fully present in each moment. Instead of mentally racing around and worrying about the future, or chasing in ten directions at once, simply become present to the reality of the moment. You will find that everything around and within you is uncommonly vivid. An example of presence is a mother picking up her crying baby. The baby is in distress but can't talk. The mother's complete mental and emotional concentration is on him. In that moment, she's not worried about tonight's dinner party or returning a phone call. She looks at the infant deeply, seeking to understand his need. Her focus and complete presence can be felt by the baby, and he may calm down. Becoming mindful means eliminating noisy mind chatter and fragmentation so that you can hear your subtle inner voice. The daily practice of contemplation or meditation may help unlock your subtle forces of creativity and independent thinking, generate assumption-challenging questions, and connect you with fresh insights and deeper truths.

Another approach is to honestly recognize and accept your limited view of the world. When a person is wearing tinted glasses, the whole world seems tinted. Only by becoming conscious of the glasses themselves does he recognize that they affect his perception. The ultimate challenge of mindfulness is to see the limitations in your own perceptions of the world. These perceptions are limited by the past experiences that have formed your mindset and ego structure. By recognizing the tint in your glasses, you enable subtle forces to liberate you from fallacious thinking. Mindful leaders struggle to think independently, to expand their perspective, to eschew expertise, to remain open to new ideas, and to encourage flexibility and change in others. Mindful leaders buy new glasses for themselves and their associates.

Yet another way to promote fusion is to welcome opposites into your life and your organization. This keeps the doors and windows of the box open. One leader we admire has a personal board of directors. These are people whose judgment he trusts and who often express views opposite to his own. He consults them on a regular basis, thereby maintaining a mindset expanded beyond his normal thinking. He has found that consultation with others is the quickest way to broaden his perspective.

Employees, too, can be exposed to diverse points of view. One means of doing this is to make sure every employee has "line of sight" to the customer—that is, he or she has direct contact with the people being served. Employees can visit customers, suppliers, developers of new technology, and so on, to create a keener sense of the urgency and outcome of what they do. Rather than hiring people who already share your corporation's mindset, try recruiting those with opposing views.

Almost any exposure to a different paradigm can help you see more deeply into your own subtle assumptions and those underlying your organization. Most people who have lived in a foreign country for a period of time no longer see their country of origin as they used to. They return appreciative of its good qualities, but much more aware of its negative aspects. They have a more balanced and realistic view, and have insight into the values of foreign cultures. Experience in other companies or countries provides this broader frame of reference. Bob Lengel has two illustrations of this principle:

> *I had a bright Japanese student in a graduate management class. One night during class, I asked her what she had learned about the United States. She replied that she had come to the United States to learn about its culture, but she found that she had learned more about her own. By getting out of her culture, the assumptions and beliefs that defined it became visible to her for the first time.*
>
> *I started my own career as an aerospace engineer, but as the aerospace industry hit hard times in the early 1970s, I decided to branch out into the study of business. Exposure*

to two unrelated disciplines brought the limited mindset of each discipline into focus. Once the power of assumptions became visible in one area, I became more sensitive to their effects in other areas.

All in all, the move toward mindfulness and the subtle view, as represented in Exhibit 4.1, requires continuous effort on the part of the leader. People are born open to the world and then learn to protect their feelings by becoming prejudiced, judgmental, and narrow. That is why Dick Daft initially rejected Ms. Spike Hairdo at the California workshop. To tear down the walls of your mental box, to operate with less ego and step out of the safety of your current opinions, is to face the fear that your world is not as you want it to be. This is the biggest challenge on the path to fusion leadership, but to duck it is to turn your back on immense opportunity.

Personal Remembering ■

- In a discussion with divergent viewpoints, do you feel the need to defend your ideas, to convince others that you are right? Why? What does this tell you about the Plato's cave you are in?

- What do you need to empty yourself of to be a better leader?

- Do you steer your course by rudder or by radar? Why?

- When assigning tasks to others, how much time do you spend on the larger *why* of the task as opposed to the *what, how,* and *when?* What does this tell you about yourself?

CHAPTER FIVE

VISION

A blind man was brought to the hospital. He was both depressed and seriously ill. He shared a room with another man, and one day asked, "What is going on outside?" The man in the other bed explained in some detail about the sunshine, the gusty winds, and the people walking along the sidewalk. The next day, the blind man again asked, "Please tell me what's going on outside today." The roommate responded with a story about the activities in a park across the way, the ducks on the pond, and the people feeding them. The third day and each day thereafter for two weeks, the blind man asked about the world outside, and the other man answered, describing a different scene. The blind man enjoyed these talks, and grew happier learning about the world seen through the window.

Then the blind man's roommate was discharged from the hospital. A new roommate was wheeled in—a tough-minded businessman who felt terrible but wanted to get work done. The next morning, the blind man said, "Will you please tell me about what is going on outside?" The businessman didn't feel good, and he didn't want to be bothered to tell stories to a blind man. So he responded assertively: "What do you mean? I can't see outside. There is no window here. It's only a wall."

The blind man again became depressed, and a few days later took a turn for the worse and was moved to intensive care.[1]

This story illustrates how dependent we all are on those who can connect us with a larger reality than our limited faculties can apprehend on their own. Leaders who provide a vision meet this need: they open a window to a larger, meaningful world that people may not see for themselves. Without such a leader, the yearning spirit of the employee will wither.

A vision is a potent subtle force in organizations. Recall the bear story from Chapter Three. Old Ben provided a focus for the community's energy in the face of awesome forces that existed in the wilderness. By not killing Old Ben, the boy preserved the sense of shared purpose and community. Today's world is one of change, unpredictability, and unlimited possibilities. In this world, the workplace can be isolating, abstract, and frustrating, with little connection between people and something larger. A vision enriches a mundane, dispiriting reality. A vision can create a future so compelling that it lifts people from their preoccupation with minor difficulties and refocuses them on the path ahead. Pettiness, small inconveniences, and other distractions have little impact when people see through the window to the larger world outside. An out-of-kilter environment can pull an organization apart; a vision provides the counterforce that draws it together. A vision helps people remember their unconscious dreams, their purpose, their common future.

A *vision* is an alluring, ideal future that is credible yet not immediately attainable. It is a propellant for change. Typically, a vision describes both the desired future and the values needed for its attainment. This chapter is about using the subtle force of vision to achieve fusion energy in organizations.

THE HIGHER PURPOSE OF VISION

A vision is powerful because it speaks directly to the heart—to unconscious yearnings to be great, to serve, to make a difference, to be involved in something meaningful, to pursue a dream, to achieve a higher purpose. A vision bypasses the rational ego to connect with deeper subtle potentials.

People love to have a larger meaning in their work. Consider three stonecutters talking about their job. The first stonecutter says, "I'm cutting stone." The second says, "I'm carving a cornerstone." And the third says, "I'm building a cathedral." The third stonecutter sees the larger vision, which infuses pride into his work. A leader can provide that vision and stir that pride.

Fusion leaders help stonecutters become cathedral builders. With a shared vision, employees will build the organization. Just as the acorn will grow into an oak tree because it contains a "picture" of the oak tree, people who are imprinted with a larger picture will transform the organization. No paintbrush ever created a masterpiece, no piano ever wrote a sonata, no spreadsheet or balance sheet ever created a great company. Inspired individuals do those things.

People want to achieve great goals, but they first have to be released from the psychic prison of rules and regulations. Without a vision, they go through life mechanically mimicking sounds or painting by the numbers. Leaders help them play great music or create masterpieces by providing a higher vision and the opportunity to grow into it. An organization really takes off when everyone starts to play the music. It is the ideas or music or poetry of a business that are attractive to employees, not its formal structures of authority.

Once articulated and assimilated into a company's culture, vision becomes a subtle force that pulls people together, aligning mindsets in a common direction. The vision is like a magnetic force that pulls individuals toward their desired future.

The Best Vision Is Widely Shared

In an earlier, stable world, where people believed in "great man" or "single actor" leadership, one person could have a vision, assemble the necessary people and resources, and design a structure to carry out the mission. In a destabilized world, everyone needs a shared mental picture of what is being aspired to.

Some visions are brief, compelling, and slogan-like. Visions like these can be communicated widely and understood by everyone in the organization. For example, what employee would not be motivated by the following:

"A Coke within arm's reach of everyone on the planet" (Coca-Cola)

"Encircle caterpillar" (Komatsu)

"Become the premier company in the world" (Motorola)[2]

The ideal vision is identified with the organization, not with the individual running the organization. When everyone understands and embraces the hunt for "the bear," the organization becomes self-renewing and adaptive, because each individual is acting independently but moving in the same direction. In the new sciences, this is called the principle of self-reference. *Self-reference* means that each element in a system will serve the direction of the whole system when the elements are imprinted with an understanding of that whole. In addition, as Peter Senge states in *The Fifth Discipline,* a shared vision changes people's relationship with the company. It creates a common identity and allows each employee to think in terms of "our company" rather than "their company." The vision becomes the common thread connecting people and involves them personally and emotionally in the organization.[3]

The Vision Is a First Step Toward the Future

To a conventional manager, the idea of creating an ideal future may seem strange or frivolous. Trained to discover and analyze things, conventional managers believe the world is objective and can be understood and predicted if data are available.

> *Consider the movie director who, tired of the hassles of temperamental actors and film crews, had the idea of making a movie with nothing more than a computer. He programmed the computer to generate thousands of random combinations of colored pixels and transfer them to film. He intended to select the best and sequence them for a ninety-minute movie. The miracle of computer data generation would create the future.*
>
> *He soon discovered that finding even one frame that made sense would take more than a lifetime. Coming up with a new* Gone with the Wind *would take longer.*
>
> *A huge stock of brightly colored frames did not solve the director's creative problem, just as infinite data won't solve a leader's problem. It is impossible to make a movie or to successfully lead an organization without first developing a strong mental picture of the desired outcome. There is no substitute for vision.*[4]

A part of that movie director is in each person. We often want to answer a difficult question by recourse to a standard formula or to computer data. But the subtle force of a challenging dream for the future is where the real fusion potential lies.

The organization that is far from equilibrium creates its own future. According to John Sculley, Steve Jobs's planning at Apple Computer considered questions such as what the world would be like in the distant future, and what kind of future the organization wanted to create for itself to succeed in that world.[5] A business, a department, a project all move forward as an image in people's minds. The vision changes and grows over time. It is never finished, but it is the essential first step. As Kouzes and Posner write, "There is no freeway to the future, no paved highway from here to tomorrow. There is only wilderness, only uncertain terrain."[6] The leader and the organization use the vision not as a road map but as a compass. Visionaries can't predict the future. They draw a conceptual map of an imagined future and guide the company in that direction.

What does this first step look like? Two examples of visions are offered below. If you were an employee of Disney or Giro, would the stated vision give you the kind of guidance you need? Walt Disney said of Disneyland:

> *The idea of Disneyland is a simple one. It will be a place for people to find happiness and knowledge. It will be a place for parents and children to spend pleasant times in one another's company: a place for teachers and pupils to discover greater ways of understanding and education. Here the older generation can recapture the nostalgia of days gone by, and the younger generation can savor the challenge of the future. Here will be the wonders of Nature and Man for all to see and understand. Disneyland will be based upon and dedicated to the ideals, the dreams and hard facts that have created America. And it will be uniquely equipped to dramatize these dreams and facts and send them forth as a source of courage and inspiration to all the world.*

Disneyland will be something of a fair, an exhibition, a playground, a community center, a museum of living facts, and a showplace of beauty and magic. It will be filled with the accomplishments, the joys and hopes of the world we live in. And it will remind us and show us how to make these wonders part of our lives.[7]

And here is Jim Gentes's vision of Giro's future:

The best riders in the world will be using our products in world-class competition. Winners of the Tour de France, the World Championships, and the Olympic Gold Medal will win while wearing Giro helmets. We will receive unsolicited phone calls and letters from customers who say, "Thank you for being in business, one of your helmets saved my life." Our employees will feel that this is the best place they've ever worked. When you ask people to name the top company in the cycling business, the vast majority will say Giro.[8]

These pictures are very clear. They translate hopes and dreams into words and free employees to take first steps. But a vision need not be detailed or elegant. A simple vision created Sweden's Ikea, a retail furniture giant. The vision "to provide affordable furniture for people with limited budgets" drives the entire operation, including new stores, furniture design, and manufacturing. An even simpler idea was Nike's "Crush Reebok."

Today's Picture Pulls People into the Future

A big frustration during organizational change is the tendency to cling to the past. George Land and Beth Jarman, in *Breakpoint and Beyond,* explain that *future pull* helps people break free of the heavy anchor of habit and history that prevents movement.[9] All elements of biological life—cells, trees, caterpillars, human beings—are pulled toward the future by DNA. We are programmed to dream and to seek the dream. The vision is a subtle force that evokes a memory of the dream and propels a person toward its realization. Unless the subtle force is killed by the strong forces of bottom-line thinking, rules, and performance appraisals, the dream will crystallize in the mind.

A clear mental picture has astonishing impact on progress toward a goal. One picture may be better than another, but *a picture is so much better than no picture at all.* Without the picture, one person's work in the moment may be disconnected from the work of others and from the future goal. A vision is the picture in the leader's and followers' minds that gives meaning and value to activity today.

Vince Lombardi, renowned coach of the Green Bay Packers, put the matter in a nutshell:

> *The best coaches know what the end result looks like. . . .*
> *If you don't know what the end result is supposed to look*
> *like, you can't get there. All the teams basically do the same*
> *things. . . . But the bad coaches don't know what the hell*
> *they want. The good coaches do.*[10]

Companies that harness future pull do the same thing. The founder of Weight Watchers had a vision of "teaching people how to eat for the rest of their lives." Merck's vision is "victory against disease and help to human kind."[11] Everyone yearns for a picture of a successful future. When imprinted in the leader and employees, the mental picture becomes the genetic code, the shaping force of the organization.

Self-reference leads to an emergent sense of identity for individuals. Each element of the system, when imprinted with the vision, will independently orient itself toward the desired future without traditional controls. In humans, the yearning to pursue a dream is imprinted in the unconscious. It is a subtle yet powerful force that leaders help others reconnect with.

A Working Vision Can Embrace the Part and the Whole

Many people think of vision as being for the company as a whole, but visions for departments and subunits are powerful too. As John Kotter writes in *The Leadership Factor,* CEOs of effective companies develop a vision of "what should be" for the organization, taking into account the interests of everyone involved.[12] At the same time, a project team leader seven levels beneath the CEO would develop a vision with team members for the new product they are working on.

Kouzes and Posner discuss a facility manager in a large corporation whose department received requests to fix toilets and air conditioners. The vision he adopted was "Use physical space to make people feel good." Employees in his department started planting flowers outside office windows and created an internal environment that lifted people's spirits. The Ritz-Carlton hotel chain asks each department in each hotel to write its own vision statement. Workers in the parking garage, in housekeeping, and at the front desk all wrestle with their purpose and develop a vision for their future.[13]

In *Real Change Leaders,* Katzenbach and others described visions that enabled employees in the various departments of an organization to clearly understand the changes their organization was pursuing and why change was necessary. These working visions gave meaning to the changes expected of employees, provided positive mental images of where everyone was headed, created pride and a sense of accomplishment along the way, and linked people's individual activities to performance results. Examples of working visions included:

"Eliminate what annoys our bankers and our customers"
(Texas Commerce Bank)

"The one others copy" (Mobil)

"No graffiti" (New York City Transit)

"Be our customer's best sales relationship" (AT&T
Business and Commercial Services)[14]

These visions had impact because they are memorable, motivating, and relevant to each person touched by them.

Each employee at a company like Motorola or Mobil is like a small piece of a large puzzle. Removed from the whole picture, each puzzle piece has limited meaning. The vision reveals the whole and enables each individual to appreciate his or her place within it. Without visions of the organization and its subunits, critical mass for fusion will not occur.

THE PERSONAL IMPACT OF VISION

People need visions to evoke their deeper potentials and inspire them about the future. A vision is a force that touches a person's "higher" self and subtle inner motivation. We all want to be proud of what we do, to be a part of something special, to take on challenging tasks, to collaborate with others, to take risks, to belong to something large and awe-inspiring. We want to build cathedrals, but often we aren't conscious of our need or don't know how to meet it. Like wild animals raised in captivity, we haven't been given the opportunity to develop our latent potentials.

As the world becomes increasingly chaotic, any sense of order and purpose must be based on shared vision and common ground. The old order of the past that pigeonholed people in rigid hierarchies and roles is no longer viable. The new order gives meaning and direction to fragmented working lives.

A vision taps into each person's unconscious need for spirituality, connection, and myth. It becomes a living, growing entity within the employee, expressing itself in active efforts to reach it. The combined energy of everyone it touches will ultimately bring about its achievement.

The employees of Bread Loaf Construction Co. created organizational fusion by jointly developing a vision to fit their potentials. The vision stated: "We are a family, empowered by the strength of our people; we seek challenges, we focus upon employee wellness and community responsibility."[15] The mission statement of Ben & Jerry's Homemade, Inc., likewise touches and motivates each employee by identifying three distinct goals: (1) making the finest-quality all-natural ice cream and related products; (2) achieving profitable growth and providing financial rewards to employees; (3) improving the quality of life of the broad community.

Visions transcend weekly production schedules and monthly sales figures. Employees are not motivated by the "vision" of providing an extra few dollars for shareholders. The wonderfully simple yet compelling purpose at Hard Rock Café is "Love all, serve all." The goal at Patagonia, a maker of outdoor clothing, is to serve as both a role model and a tool for social change. Steve Jobs once expressed the following vision for Apple Computer: "To make a contribution to the world by making tools for the mind that advance humankind."[16]

The Vision Is the Focus Button

You know how frustrating it is to watch a movie when the projector is out of focus, or a presentation when the visual aids aren't clear. Our out-of-kilter world, with its rapid change and complexity, often seems out of focus.[17] The vision is the focus button for the future. And if the leader—the person running the projector—does not fix the focus, the viewers-employees become frustrated and angry. They want and need clarity.

A Vision Beckons Toward Greatness

A vision presents a challenge to go where one has not gone before, to struggle and to risk failure in seeking success. It appeals to the adventurer within. A vision encourages nonconformity, asks for change, and leaves the old way behind. It is an invitation to achieve something great. Dick Daft witnessed the inspirational effect of vision when working on an earlier book.

For the first edition of my management text, the publisher assembled the production and editorial teams to explain the function each person would perform. After each person presented, I spontaneously took a few minutes to explain my dream for the text. I wanted it to be the first in a new generation of management textbooks that would use photo essays to bring management into the lives of students. The book would be so "interesting" that students would want to turn pages and professors would be proud to teach from it. This book would be the Rolls-Royce of the industry. A year later, when the book was in production, I heard about production staff and editors working nights and weekends to keep it on schedule. I asked the production editor why they were working such strange hours, and she said, "The vision speech." She explained that everyone was motivated by the talk I gave because, although they produce a lot of books, they seldom have an opportunity to work on something special. Her people loved to be part of something larger than themselves. "Many authors come in and say, 'Tell me what to do and I will do it.'" Spontaneously sharing my dream motivated them for a year and a half, and they produced a book far better than I had envisioned. It became the best seller in its field. And for each edition since, the editorial and production teams have asked me to give another vision speech.

At NCR Dundee (Scotland) in 1982, the vision was to achieve world leadership in automated teller machines (ATMs). Doing so would bring growth, profitability, job security, and pay raises. As John Kotter explains, leaders decided that their strategic path to market dominance would focus on fast-track development programs and personal visits to clients. Managers and employees, knowing that a mighty effort would be required to overtake the IBM colossus, were energized by the challenge and, within a few years, brought the vision to realization.[18]

A Vision Releases Subtle Forces and the Desire to Serve

A vision often appeals to people's desire to become fully who they are, to express the best of themselves rather than just use their hands or rational minds. A vision shows that the organization operates from excellent values, promotes the growth of its employees, and enables them to serve others. People grow into wholeness as a result of being part of the organization.

A vision provides the "why" of work and of change, giving meaning to employees and bosses alike. A shared vision can change people. Vision brings meaning even to the most mundane job, transforming stonecutting into cathedral building. Those mired in a bureaucracy will free themselves and change things when a vision connects them to a larger purpose. Bob Lengel found this demonstrated in an academic environment:

> *A few years ago, I spent a spring break writing a formal proposal to create a Center for Professional Excellence at the University of Texas at San Antonio. This center would live the principles of self-organization and foster the fusion potential we have been discussing. I had experienced success facilitating fusion in outside companies, but my efforts to communicate my vision of the center to university administrators and community leaders drew little response. How*

*could the spirit of the center be communicated so that its
ideals would be clearly differentiated from those of traditional continuing education programs designed for cognitive
learning? How could I change these people's minds and
enlist them in the cause of the center?*

One night I was rereading Ray Bradbury's Fahrenheit
451 *(1953). In a prophetic paragraph, Bradbury warned
of an ominous future in which people could be turned into
controllable, mindless robots by giving them huge quantities
of information that would take all their time to process,
and by taking away front porches so that they had no place
to relax and reflect together about their mindless plight.
That was it—"the front porch." The center was a front
porch for the university. It was a place to escape the crowded
information highway and to explore the deep and meaningful questions that define our common ground. Every center
activity would grow from dialogue that created a fusion of
interest.*

*The center and its resources have grown exponentially
as a result of the crystallization of the "front porch" vision.
People who heard the vision moved to support the center.
Now many individuals and groups around the university
are involved in creating this learning community.*

We yearn for fundamental values in our leaders and organizations. But even if such values are in place, they may not be
articulated. Often, a vision is required to crystallize them and
make them communicable.

*Bernard Marcus and Arthur Blank were let go from
the Handy Dan Home Center chain. Their distasteful
experience became the source of the values underlying
Home Depot, which they founded. Those values include
humility, the constant questioning of success, a daily*

*commitment to improved performance, and a willingness
to fix the inevitable mistakes without coverup. Hovering
over all is the larger vision of the company: "Customer
satisfaction through constant change and improvement."*[19]

CREATING THE VISION

Initiating a vision is a leader's responsibility. Leaders encourage
a dream for their department, team, or company. But the vision must be widely owned, so that it can grow through the
participation of many hearts and minds.

A Vision Is Based on Hope for the Future and Personal Experience

A vision will not survive in a purely rational environment. In
such an environment, people are not satisfied with the beauty
of a butterfly skittering through the woods on a spring day.
They must capture it, kill it, and pin it to a board. Then they
can dissect and analyze it. But the butterfly is dead, the fullness
of its beauty gone. To accept a vision is to enjoy the butterfly
without overanalyzing it.

Overly rational types also have difficulty letting go and
thinking big. A dream with scope and size can really have an
impact. At Sewell Village Cadillac in Dallas, antique lamps are
used instead of fluorescent lights. The expensive fixtures don't
make economic sense, but the setting captures people's imagination because it's special. And it succeeds. On TV's *Life Styles
of the Rich and Famous,* a man was interviewed who built huge,
majestic hotels around the world. He said he built each one
bigger than necessary because it attracted people and led to
long-term economic success. He never worried about making
money. People would come.

Vision should not be linear or logical or easily achievable. If it is, it will connect with the rational ego rather than with deeper yearnings for something great. To managers who have built careers dealing with tangible objects rather than concepts, with things rather than feelings, with hard data rather than dreams, creating an inspiring vision may seem impossible if not a waste of time.

If you are not a natural visionary, where does a vision come from? The answer is (1) from a foundation of personal experience—yours and others people's—and (2) from your own and others' hopes and dreams for the future. With these ingredients, you can go beyond numerical sales or production goals and develop a hopeful, inspired future for the organization. This image of the future is more a dream than a concrete goal, although tangible outcomes are often included in it.

A leader has to have a base of personal experience to envision a plausible future. Otherwise the vision will come from the head rather than the heart and will not inspire others. Most leaders develop a vision based on their ascent in their industry or company. An assortment of jobs has afforded them a range of experiences. They don't have to guess what employees or customers need or feel—they have been there. The deep intuition from which the vision emerges is seeded and grows from their personal and professional history. The relationships and events of their early years facilitate the development of a vision later on.

The other source of vision is your hopes and dreams for the future. To fully access these, you must quiet your conditioned rational mind so that inner images can emerge. Mental imagery is increasingly understood to have great power. In sports, for example, athletes repeatedly visualize successful performance, and the resulting improvement is often better than with actual practice.[20]

Let the vision emerge from your inner dreams for your company or unit and for yourself. Sometimes during periods of quiet reflection or meditation, such as on a plane trip, an inner voice will speak with clarity about your hopes for the future. Your hopes describe the ideal work environment, the ideal enterprise. This voice has the ring of truth. It cannot be heard during the noise and frantic pace associated with a leader's life. Simply taking quiet time to be in touch with your hopes and dreams will provide the mental images to begin developing the vision. The hopes and dreams gathered from others, too, are raw material for the vision of your group's future.

The Vision Defines Both the Destination and the Journey

Restful meditations and visioning may seem a far cry from rational management approaches taught in business school. And so is the realization that a leader's ultimate responsibility is to facilitate a shared vision for people in the organization. Leaders may not welcome the responsibility of shaping how others think. However, identity and culture will be influenced by somebody or something in your organization; it's a question of who or what exerts that influence. A shared vision of where the organization is headed and the common ground that must be created before it can get there creates the fusion that lets organizations succeed in chaotic conditions. The envisioned future can include specific outcomes. In a private business school, for example, these might include a top twenty ranking, the placing of 90 percent of students in summer internships, and job offers for 80 percent of graduating students by June of their final year. Less precise outcomes might be the preparation of students for lifelong learning, and increased knowledge of business, values, teamwork, and leadership. The business school vision may also espouse underlying values such as boundarylessness—no separation between fields of study or between professors and students—heartfelt concern for students' welfare, commitment to the expansion of knowledge in the field of business, and avoidance of prima donna faculty candidates who could create discord and damage the school's culture. An explicit vision is a powerful influence, and it includes both desired outcomes and the underlying values that will achieve them.

Several of the ideas described in this chapter are summarized in Exhibit 5.1. Fusion leaders understand that their primary responsibility is to get in touch with the dreams and values that drive the organization. They think big, create the future, verbalize higher values, shape corporate culture, and energize people in their work. In this way, they facilitate development of a vision and larger meaning for employees, while freeing them to create and solve problems in pursuit of the dream.

The subtle forces of yearning and dreams can shape minds more effectively than the strong forces of budgets and hierarchical control. An overarching vision creates a sense of purpose

Exhibit 5.1. Vision

Conventional Strong-Force View	Fusion Leader Subtle View
• Discover future	• Create future
• Analyze hard data	• Facilitate hopes and dreams
• Pursue goals and objectives	• Pursue higher purpose that touches the heart
• Direct people	• Inspire people
• Focus on measures, money	• Focus on values, yearnings
• Consider dreams fuzzy, unrealistic	• Consider dreams concrete, reliable
• Stick with the logical, doable	• Think big, do the impossible
• Scorn vision	• Cherish vision as motivating, energizing
• Live by tomorrow's deadlines	• Live by hope and personal experience

and community among employees; it is the mountaintop toward which employees climb together, and it empowers them for that climb.

Just as each acorn contains the imprint of the oak tree, so does the mind of each employee bear the imprint of the leader's vision, which is communicated by speeches, personal actions, awards, celebrations, and stories. Visionary leaders shape their subordinates' perceptions of the organization and their place in it. A shared dream and shared values, not formal authority, pull people toward the future, enabling them to advance in the same direction while they each take care of their own tasks. Failing to harness the power of vision is to fail as a fusion leader in an out-of-kilter environment.

Personal Remembering

- What is your calling or highest purpose in life?

- Do you open a window to a meaningful world for people with whom you work? How do you feel about this idea?

- Have you had positive or negative experiences in attempting to create a vision in your organization? What did these experiences mean to you?

- Often it is difficult for rational people to let go and dream big. Is it difficult for you? Why?

CHAPTER SIX

HEART

Imagine a time several hundred years ago, a broad grassy plain, and a wide river slowly meandering across the landscape. Settled on a bend in the river is a small tribe that lives in scattered mud, wood, and leather structures and teepees along the bank. The tribe has been settled here for a generation, and the men provide the tribe's sustenance by going into the river to fish. Previously hunters, they learned to create simple dams, nets, and tide pools from which fish and turtles could be caught, and this work was redone each day. Over the years, a friendly competition developed among the men, and a few became strong and expert, acknowledged by the others as the best swimmers and fishermen.

One evening at dusk, the last fisherman to leave the water paused on the shore. He sat down for a few moments on the sand, resting his forearms on his knees. Recognized as one of the most skilled fishermen in the tribe, he now studied the water and contemplated his last twenty years of daily work in the river.

Suddenly a realization hit him: there was no trace of his existence in the river. Everything he built each day over all those years had washed downstream, leaving no trace of himself. As that realization soaked in, he stood up and turned to face the village. The sun was setting behind the village, silhouetting its shape, and he could hear dogs barking, children at play, and adult voices.

Absorbed in the village, a second powerful realization struck him: the enduring things in his life were on the bank and not in the river. On the bank were the things that provided deep satisfaction and meaningfulness in his life—children, grandchildren, friends, relationships, art, music, and spiritual values. In that instant, he decided that the rest of his life would be devoted to relationship building and the nurturing of his community.

What happened to this warrior? He reappraised his values. The river represents the strong forces of ambition, drive, discipline, rationality, achievement, and action that made a contribution to the tribe. But these qualities only took him so far. He was becoming aware of the subtle forces represented by the bank—caring, listening, creative expression, and relationship building. The warrior's transformation symbolizes the change that can occur among leaders.

Companies traditionally reward the strong qualities of drive, ambition, and competitiveness, the sources of success and achievement in North America. Although these qualities are essential, it is the balance of strong and subtle forces that enables companies to adapt to ever-changing conditions. Strong forces alone carry us only part of the way. As we described in earlier chapters, organizations experience continuous change. Stability is impossible. The future cannot be predicted, much less controlled, and employees create solutions as they go along. The traditional hierarchy gets in the way. But without reliance on organization charts, rules, and authority, how do leaders hold people together?

In self-adapting organizations, employees can be fused together through relationships. Heart represents human emotions such as love, bliss, compassion, enthusiasm, and the desire to connect with others. It is emotion that generates attraction to shared vision and mission, shared values, shared culture, and shared information. In an out-of-kilter world, leaders must focus on relationships, not things. Influence comes from relationships, which are based on the heart qualities of caring and compassion.

Developing heart in leadership may go against the grain of the rational attitudes, training, and impersonal relationships that succeeded in a stable corporate America. Yet finding and releasing emotions in oneself and the organization provide many rewards. In this chapter, we will discuss aspects of fusion leadership that lead to those rewards.

LOVING WORK AND WORKERS

To those managers who have spent their careers dealing with rational things, what does emotion look like? In folklore, emotional energy comes from the lover within each person. The archetypal lover has access to his or her primal needs for food, reproduction, and well-being. The energy that moves people forward with enthusiasm is not intellectual or rational, but comes from feelings. Emotion is the life force. Having full access to emotions enables a leader to feel alive, connected, energized, and in love with life and work.[1]

Do you lead with heart? Live with heart? The leader who has access to emotions is able to bond with people, work, friends, children, and a mission or cause. Bonding enables a web of attachments to develop, and through these relationships the leader influences others. It is emotional attachments that lead people to care about one another and jointly pursue their shared vision with creativity and enthusiasm.

Emotions add sensitivity to life and relationships. A leader with heart is likely to enjoy sensory experiences such as the sun shining through an unusual cloud formation, the colors of the Arizona desert, a quiet morning, and the feeling of passion in work and play. Emotional aliveness means feeling pain and poignancy as well as joy. With awakened emotion comes compassion, acceptance, forgiveness, and a reduced propensity to judge others. The leader with heart helps people find work they love, work in which they can express their gifts and experience personal growth.

Influence Emotions and White Space, Not Objects and Things

Rather than managing objects and things, fusion leaders learn to manage the subtle "white space" between people. White space contains the emotional energy that binds people together and keeps the organization flowing along with changes in the environment. In the physical world, white space is filled with radiation, gravity, and radio waves. In organizations, white space contains the relationships, emotions, and spiritual values represented by the riverbank in our opening story.

In Western countries, high value has been placed on the mind and the rational approach to things. But a life of the mind misleads us about the larger life of emotions. The mind is just a small part of who we are. The rational mind is like a small boat in a stormy sea of emotion. The great sea of emotion is our source of life energy. Although a rational person often is not aware of emotions, forward motivation comes from the heart, not from the head. Emotion is a bottomless reservoir of leadership energy when leaders learn to use it.

Zen Lessons provides a similar image:

> *Ancient sages likened the human being to a boat, heart being*
> *the water—the water can carry the boat, and it can also*
> *overturn the boat. When the water goes with it, the boat*
> *floats, and when the water goes against it, the boat sinks.*
> *Therefore, when a leader wins people's hearts, there*
> *is flourishing, and the leader that loses people's hearts is*
> *abandoned.*[2]

The water, not the boat or its oars, is the deep source of motivation available to leaders and organizations. The challenge for leaders is to accept the lover archetype within themselves and to release the emotional energy within others.

Leadership Grows from Emotions

The emotion within us is harnessed by openly connecting with it. Yet the path between the head and the heart is little traveled. Managers with the fewest people skills, with least access to their softer, feeling side, often deny the emotional element in themselves and others. They may be detached, defensive, overly mental, or domineering, and waste energy covering up their emotions. Yet when integrated into personality and behavior, emotions become a positive force rather than a negative one.

Our society—family, school, church, organization—is effective at conditioning people to satisfy the external world rather than internal yearnings. We are taught to obey our parents, teachers, and bosses rather than follow internal guidance. Yet people need to honor their emotions too. The best-selling books *Women Who Run with the Wolves,* by Clarissa Pinkola Estes, and *Iron John,* by Robert Bly, carried to thousands of readers the same message: learning to act from within—from the authentic self, from your native emotions—is a source of satisfaction to yourself and to people around you.

Another aspect of inner emotion is "bliss," which Joseph Campbell described as rapture, ecstasy, activities that brim with good feelings. Campbell said that following your bliss is the left-hand path through life that is chosen by the heart, with no guarantee of material success because the journey itself is the reward. The right-hand path is the practical, logical alternative. This path is selected by the conscious mind in collaboration with the expectations of others, and often overrides the wishes of the heart.

Every year we have students in our offices describing their plans for graduate school, law school, or a career in finance based on ambitions and expectations that go back as long as they can remember. Expectations are powerful. A student's face may light up when talking about her love of filmmaking, but she decides to go to law school because it seems the right thing to do. It doesn't even occur to her that there is a path other than the "logical" career choice.

Bliss has been referred to as a precious thing that we love. This precious thing is not another person—it is within us. Only our emotions can tell us what it is. When people identify this object of their desire, it awakens them, excites them, brings them alive. Warren Bennis calls this the "inner voice" that leaders follow.[3] Leaders break away from the beaten path, just as Norman Lear did in the 1970s by filling television drama with average Americans rather than larger-than-life or glamorous characters. Fusion leaders are directed from within. They operate on instinct because they are in touch with it.

You have found a moment of bliss when you are so absorbed in something that you lose track of time. This is emotional motivation being released. If you believe you haven't experienced bliss, it can sometimes be remembered by recalling the activities you loved as a child, or fantasizing what you would do if you won a $100 million lottery prize or had only six months to live. The nature of bliss is richly expressed in this verse by Susanna Clark:

> *You've got to sing like you don't need the money.*
> *You've got to love like you'll never get hurt.*
> *You've got to dance like there's nobody watching.*
> *You've got to come from the heart if you want it to work.*[4]

For many people, the absence of bliss is easier to recognize— for example, when they are doing a dreary task just because they are "supposed" to. Procrastination over such tasks arises from an inner battle between the willing head and the resistant heart. If you cannot find at least a small amount of bliss in your job or in your leadership tasks, then quit. To work without some love is to work only out of fear.

Over the years, Bob Lengel has found, lost, and gratefully rediscovered bliss:

> *I first felt a passion for learning and creating when I was eleven years old. This passion attracted me to the physical sciences and led to two degrees in engineering. As an engineer, I loved to apply knowledge but felt disconnected from people. I left engineering to become a stockbroker. During this four-year experience, my yearning for creativity and learning was buried beneath the short-term lure of big money. But I gradually discovered that my heart was not related to my bank account, and that suppressing it induced a slow death. Headaches, stomach acid, back pain, and anxiety were the surface symptoms of abandoning my passion. I'm thankful that I had this lesson early in life. My career decisions since have followed my heart's desire to do something meaningful rather than become somebody with social or financial position. Work became a joy again, not a difficult chore.*

Leadership Charisma Is Being in Love

Charismatic leaders attract people to them by personality rather than position. They are charismatic because they are pursuing an idea, vision, project, or activity they truly love. Charisma is simply releasing your inner emotional power, engaging your bliss in daily life. A person becomes charismatic by being true to his or her essential self.

Charismatic leadership is not a personality trait that only a few possess. People who pursue what they love are attractive. Other people want to follow them and be part of their dream. Leaders who are enthusiastic about their work are brimming with ideas and energy. *Charisma* originally referred to a gift of the Spirit. A charismatic person touches his inner, spiritual self.

When we talk to students about their best teachers, about teachers with charisma, they say things like "That teacher really *cared* about her subject," "He *loved* teaching," "He really *cared* about me." This caring and loving is from the heart. It is the source of charisma and is available to each of us.

Kouzes and Posner, in *The Leadership Challenge*, report the response of Major General John H. Stanford, U.S. Army, to a question about developing leaders. He said:

> *When anyone asks me that question I tell them I have the secret to success in life. The secret to success is stay in love. Staying in love gives you the fire to really ignite other people, to see inside other people, to have a greater desire to get things done than other people. A person who is not in love doesn't really find the kind of excitement that helps them to get ahead and lead others and to achieve. I don't know any other fire, any other thing in life that is more exhilarating and is more positive a feeling than love is.*[5]

Leaders in love have a magical quality. And love in its broadest sense is the source of leader wisdom, the subtle inner voice that connects people to realities the rational mind may not perceive. Love is hard to fake. Finding exhilaration from what one loves is a basic premise of leadership. To do it any other way is to lack charisma, to lack authenticity.

BUILDING RELATIONSHIPS

In out-of-kilter conditions, things are unpredictable and constantly changing. The organization chart is flat, with cross-functional teams, horizontal structures, and interorganizational alliances. Conventional vertical structures of hierarchy and authority have diminishing value. In a destabilized world, the subtle forces in the white space between people are the source of leader influence. This space can be filled with relationships based on shared values, a strong culture, information, and caring.

Influence Derives from Relationships

A heartfelt, loving connection with another person is a source of leader influence. Children who feel loved and nurtured by parents are less likely to rebel. A strong bond between parent and child creates an attitude on both sides of going along with the needs of the other.

In companies, a leader with a clear sense of self-worth and a heartfelt respect for others is open to the advantages of shared responsibility, or what Judy B. Rosener, professor at the University of California at Irvine, calls "interactive leadership." Leaders who use this approach "encourage participation, share power and information, enhance other people's self-worth, and get others excited about their work."[6] They eschew the use of hierarchy, formal authority, competition among subordinates, and overbearing logic as means of exerting influence. Because this interactive style of leadership draws heavily on "feminine" qualities, women seem to adopt it more easily.

Grace Pastiak, director of manufacturing for one operating division of Tellabs, Inc., a maker of sophisticated telephone equipment in Lisle, Illinois, is a classic example of an interactive leader. Her leadership style builds relationships. She is in constant and direct communication with people on the plant floor, works for consensus in decision making, and develops self-reliance in her teams by delegating major responsibilities to line workers.

As she explains, "I have the bias that people do better when they are happy. The old style of beating people to get things done does not work." The proof of the production line's self-reliance is their ability to fill 98 percent of orders on time.[7]

A dispute arose between the North Wind and the Sun, each claiming that he was stronger than the other. They agreed to try their powers upon a traveler, to see which could soonest strip him of his cloak. The North Wind had the first try; and gathering all his force for the attack, he came whirling furiously down upon the man, and caught up his cloak as though he would wrest it from him by a single effort. But the harder he blew, the more closely the man wrapped it around himself. Then came the turn of the Sun. At first he beamed gently upon the traveler, who soon unclasped his cloak and walked on with it hanging loosely about his shoulders. Then the Sun shone forth in his full strength, and the man, before he had gone many steps, was glad to throw his cloak right off and complete his journey more lightly clad.

Persuasion is better than force.[8]

The persuasive warmth of a relationship builder is like the sun in Aesop's fable. Why is the gentle quality of caring relationships more powerful than brute force for enhancing productivity? For one thing, it encourages cooperation. People help each other succeed. Perhaps the more important reason is that friendship taps into heart emotions of both the leader and the led, allowing them to experience intimacy with work, to be a part of things, to be emotionally invested in the proceedings. Is it any wonder that a Forum report on leadership found that subtle relationship skills are what distinguished high-performing leaders from average ones?[9]

Leadership based on emotional connections is not "natural" in U.S. organizations. From childhood, we learn the ideals of individual rights and initiative. Our political and justice systems, and our capitalist economic system, encourage competitiveness. The masculine energy that these values represent is a major contributor to our national success, but organizations that emphasize the masculine at the expense of the feminine lose an important resource. Recall the games you played in childhood, such as "king of the mountain" and "musical chairs."

> *One of the earliest games you played was probably musical chairs. As new music is played for each round, one chair is removed, and another loser in the competitive battle is left out when the music stops. At the end of the game, one person sits in one chair as the winner, and everyone else is a loser.*
>
> *How different might organizations be if our culture were based on games like "musical pillows"? In this game, large pillows would be placed on the floor, and each time the music stopped, everyone would pile on the remaining pillows. At the end of the game, only one pillow would remain, and on it would be a giggling pile of children feeling joy from their togetherness.[10]*

As a leader, do you want your people to play musical chairs or musical pillows? Under which set of relationships will they and the organization thrive?

Hearing Builds Relationships

Relationships are not built with strong forces. Subtle forces, touching the heart within, are the basis of connections between people. Leaders act from heart potential and touch this potential in others.

Hearing another is one simple yet powerful way to connect with another, to touch the heart of another. Listening honors and affirms the other person, whether a family member, friend, associate, or subordinate. Taking time to do this is a symbolic expression of caring and respect.

> *There is an [Asian] Indian folktale of a poor widow who lived with her two sons and two daughters-in-law. She was constantly ill-treated by the four, but she kept her woes to herself, as she felt she had no one to hear her. Holding in all of this misery, she grew fatter and fatter, which became a source of more ridicule from her children. One day she wandered away from home, and came to a deserted house where she went inside. Unable to carry the burden of her troubles any longer, she spoke to each of the four walls in turn, expressing the pain from each of her four tormentors, until each wall came crashing down under the weight of her transferred grievances. Standing in the ruins, she felt lighter in mood and body, and looking down, saw that she had lost all the weight she had gained in her wretchedness.* [11]

How many businesses have come crashing down under the weight of their employees' repressed miseries? An effective leader hears and diverts the force of negative emotions before they interfere with performance and bring down the walls of the organization.

Leaders who value relationships show their concern for employee miseries, thereby winning respect, gaining wisdom from a different perspective, and opening up possibilities for the correction of legitimate grievances. Leaders must hear bad news as well as good to create meaningful relationships. When the leader is responsive to the pain and anger of an employee, a bond is created.

When Westinghouse was preparing to put its synthetic fuels division up for sale, management decided that the unit would be more attractive to prospective buyers if all jobs not considered essential were eliminated. The task of announcing these layoffs fell to William Peace, general manager of the division, who opted to deliver the news in person.

In his face-to-face meeting with the fifteen workers to be laid off, he allowed them to vent their grief and their anger at him and the unfair situation. He took their painful blows without attempting to defend himself. His action sent a message to all remaining workers that management valued each of them as individuals, that the layoffs were a last resort, and that the management team was doing everything possible to keep the business alive and as many jobs as possible in place.

The remaining employees rededicated themselves to saving the division. A buyer was found, and management was able to rehire half of those laid off. The loving way they had been treated in difficult circumstances overcame their negative feelings about the layoff.[12]

UNLOCKING HEART POTENTIAL

The subtle potentials of the leader, not the external resources of the position, are the basis of fusion leadership. What counts is having intimacy with yourself, knowing yourself down deep so that you are fully aware of your strengths and weaknesses.

In coming to terms with their emotions, fusion leaders connect with a profound source of relationship power that helps them steer the organization through chaotic times. Emotionally balanced leaders are able to welcome other people and their ideas without defensiveness, to share information and resources without a fear of loss, to accept their own limitations and use the superior ability of others for the good of the organization, and to achieve a sense of joy and fulfillment in their work, as well as fostering it in others. Relationships are built by sharing yourself, listening, having significant moments together, and being vulnerable—experiences that are threatening to many managers. The quest for emotional openness requires rational people to overcome their deepest fears, to go beyond the belief that emotions represent inferiority or weakness. The interior world of your personality is where the power of fusion resides. The masculine approach to leadership is blind to the potency of relationships, the emotional energy that connects people. This energy is provided by feminine qualities that fill up the white space between one person and another.

Awaken Sleeping Beauty

The quest for the heart deep within is an underlying theme in many of the world's mythologies. In our own culture, "Sleeping Beauty" is a perfect metaphor for the awakening of the heart potential and the union of the active and receptive principles within us.

> *The prince, the embodiment of active masculine energy, overcomes numerous obstacles and temptations to arrive at the bed of the sleeping princess, who represents his ideal of beauty, love, and desire. In the original folk tale, he not only kisses Sleeping Beauty but has sexual union with her, which signifies complete union of the masculine and feminine. She awakens from her slumber, bringing the prince lifelong bliss in their marriage, as well as abundance in the kingdom they rule.*

This life-enriching union is not available to those who remain emotionally asleep. The lovers' myth is a metaphor for the difficulty of each person's inner union, of awakening the feminine when the masculine is well developed. Overly rational, masculine managers resist these heart qualities. Managers who have not found the subtle forces within themselves reject these qualities in others. Fear of emotion leads to obsession with the masculine.

One woman described her experience at an accounting firm, where certain partners claimed that all women were "emotional, irrational, and illogical." Even when women established professional credibility, they were not invited to play golf with the partners or attend other recreational activities. The men's discomfort with feminine qualities was obvious. Only when women acted like men were they welcome in this organization.

A close friend of ours who was smart, financially successful, and not very emotional, told us about what he discovered as he began to connect with his emotions.

> *I've had a massive blind spot all these years about things emotional, because I never experienced many feelings. I didn't have intimacy with my own feelings and couldn't feel sensitivity to other people's feelings. As a child my family was cold, and I decided touching and hugging and loving that other kids received was for weaklings and babies. I believed it was foolish to be anything other than strong, independent, and unemotional. I couldn't see the value of taking an extra moment for someone's birthday or anniversary, or buying flowers, or celebrating a job well done, or just listening to someone as a way of connecting with them. It didn't seem important. Frankly, I didn't know how to do those things. I wasn't aware of the emotional side of my personal and work life. I lived my life "doing" so I wouldn't have to "feel."*

Our friend was uncomfortable with other people's subtle heart qualities until he found those feelings within himself. His blind spot and denial of emotion for a long time prevented him and his organization from achieving a balance between strong forces and subtle forces, because he couldn't connect with people or awaken their passion for work.

The Strong Are Gentle, the Gentle Are Strong

If leaders were strong, they would have no need to defend themselves against women. Defensiveness comes out of emotional weakness and fear, not strength. Heart leaders understand that welcoming the feminine side adds both to their own strength and to that of their organization. A fusion leader strives to be both monk and warrior, to be like the mother lion who can be either gentle or fierce as circumstances demand.

The martial arts offer a useful perspective on the kind of transformation that a fusion leader would be seeking.

> It is not self-defense but self-mastery that the adepts have learned. To maintain and assert the illusory sense of a separate, contending self, to encourage and nourish a preoccupation with adversity and defensiveness—this is precisely what martial arts is not. Self-mastery involves developing the concept of self quite different from the contemporary meaning implied when using the English words "self" and "defense." Self-mastery involves overcoming the illusion of the isolated self.[13]

The alternative to a separate self is the collective. A sense of the collective self eliminates the we-they mindset that insulates men from women, bosses from subordinates. Defending your company against females or any other group sustains a divisiveness that will prevent the organization from excelling in a chaotic world.

Many managers achieve high positions with the energy of strong drives they don't fully understand. They are extroverted, driven to the point of obsession, highly persuasive with potential investors, and unrelenting in their assault on obstacles. These external qualities leave little room for introspection and emotional connection to others. But at some point, such managers may be prompted to look inside themselves and start on the path that will take them beyond management to true leadership.

Keith Dunn allowed this transformation to occur within him and saw the results in the increased success of McGuffey's restaurants. He and two partners in Asheville, North Carolina, started McGuffey's with the ideal of treating employees well. But pursuit of that goal was sidetracked by the overwhelming pressures of running a growing business. Employee alienation increased turnover, reduced service quality, and slowly eroded profits. As Dunn told an unhappy manager, "We're a big company, and we've got to do big-company things."

When one of his partners hit a car head-on while riding his motorcycle and, around the same time, an employee survey slammed his own management style, the combination of personal and business trauma caused Dunn to reevaluate his relationships with employees. In recalling this period, he told a reporter, "All you do is sit and wonder, 'What could I have done to make them hate me so much?'" The virtues of drive and ambition that had helped him become president did not serve him in connecting with people and ultimately hurt him and the company.

After trying to impose his ideas for morale building and incentives on employees, Dunn changed the thing that counted: he opened his heart. He began *listening* to employees, and found that the dialogue not only gave him a wealth of new ideas, it improved morale and transformed the workplace. Dunn began demonstrating his caring and respect for workers. He opened himself to their concerns and found that the power of their emotional response enriched his organization and brought greater success. He awakened the emotional energy— Sleeping Beauty—first in himself and then in his company.[14]

Leaders Can Develop the Capacity for Love

Remember, "what is softest in the world drives what is hardest in the world."[15] Each of us differs in our capacity for love-based leadership. The fully developed leader is able to love country, family, work, children, and a significant other, all with passion and playfulness. Some people are natural "lovers." Lee Iacocca, for example, though driven to work hard, found time to call his daughters every day. Ronald Reagan cared deeply for his wife and was seen by millions on television displaying tender feelings for World War II veterans revisiting the Normandy beach and for bereaved relatives of the astronauts lost on the *Challenger.*

For many managers, emotion does not come as naturally, and direct intervention helps. Danaan Parry wrote in *Warriors of the Heart* how emotionally repressed he was as a project manager with the Atomic Energy Commission. He used a tough style of leadership, motivated by his own insecurity. Things came to a head when Sam, one of his engineers, slumped into his office in a desperate emotional state. Sam's wife and two children had left him. He had been unable to find them. He felt hopeless. He cried. Parry's stomach was tied in a knot in the face of this emotion, and he responded in the only way he knew: "Sam, we don't pay you to bring your domestic problems to the office."

As Sam left the office, Parry knew he needed help more than Sam. He was unable to deal with emotion. He could not put his arm around his employee, console him, care for him, provide emotional support.

Parry's solution was to join an "organizational dynamics" course at UCLA, also known as a T-group or encounter group.

Ten middle-management types were locked in a suite of rooms
for seven days. The group started out pleasantly enough, as
members got to know one another, but by the end of the second day, they had run out of polite conversation.

> *On the third morning, someone told the group how fed-up*
> *he was with the rest of us, how shallow he thought we were.*
> *We ate him alive. Like a team of piranha, we systematically*
> *tore him apart emotionally and picked his bones clean.*
> *When he was a pile of quivering rubble, we turned on the*
> *next-weakest member and did the same. Finally, here was a*
> *vent for our resentments and fears, and we used all the skill*
> *we had accumulated on our paths to becoming managers to*
> *viciously attack each other. By the fourth day, we had*
> *attacked everyone.*

Then they attacked Abe, their facilitator. But he was different. Abe had done his emotional work.

> *Then we remembered Abe. And we attacked him. We were*
> *good at it, screaming incompetence, hurling charges of*
> *mediocrity and stupidity at him. . . . How dare he call*
> *himself a professional. We were surely going to advise our*
> *superiors to demand our tuition back and sue this charla-*
> *tan for malpractice.*
> *But it wasn't working. . . . He wasn't defending his*
> *position. He was just there. It was like he could take in the*
> *whole world and love it and feel it and not be crumbled by*
> *it. Damn him!*
> *I told him he was a fake and he asked me how I felt*
> *when I said that. I told him he didn't give a shit about me*
> *or how I felt, so stop pretending. He asked me if my father*
> *had ever given a shit about how I felt and I started to cry.*
> *Oh, God, not now, not in front of all these men, please—*
> *I'll do anything not to cry. Please.*

*And he's got his arms around me and he's holding me.
And he's telling me about his father who died in a Nazi
concentration camp and he's crying and I'm telling him
about my father who never touched me, never told me he
loved me and I'm crying. . . . Oh, God, if my father had
pressed his body against mine like this, if he had cried with
me, not just when he was stinking drunk. But this is now
and I'm healing; I am feeling. I can feel and it's so, so good.*

*In the final three days, we somehow were able to reach
past the years of deadness and confront and comfort and
heal one another. Not everyone, but most of us, learned to
cry and to touch and to feel, together.*[16]

In this striking transformation, Parry and the others melted
the conditioned ego's defenses that had kept their emotions suppressed. Parry received support from Abe that reinforced his
newly discovered emotions, and he thereby began his transformation from a tough manager to a heart leader. Truly the softest
things in the world overcome the hardest things in the world.

Balance the Strong and Subtle Forces

Don't mistake the point of this chapter. Masculine traits are ter-
rific in organizations. And as organizations become more chaotic,
such traits will continue to be important. Our point is that masculine ways by themselves aren't enough in an out-of-kilter
world. Merging the subtle feminine with the masculine gives
managers new tools of leadership that humanize and strengthen
an organization. The ideal is to find a point of balance between
the two poles—to affirm individuality while creating a team
spirit, to encourage drive and assertiveness while listening and
caring, to build a company while building relationships.

A lean, muscular company can use the soft stuff to grow and
improve, while the soft stuff gets diffused in a flabby organization. It is almost too easy to focus on masculine hardness. In

that most masculine of occupations, military service, successful generals from Patton to Schwarzkopf know the secret that many people in the corporate and academic worlds forget: heroic action is not undertaken by people who are out for themselves, who think of themselves in competition with each other. The heroic achievements of war occur because soldiers love one another, and in the workaday world of peace, the same principle prevails.

The columns in Exhibit 6.1 summarize the ideas discussed in this chapter. The conventional strong-force view reveres rationality and expectations over underlying emotions. Leaders who understand fusion know that people create organizational fusion through relationships that touch the heart. These leaders use the strength of strong forces and the strength of subtle forces to compete and adapt in a turbulent world. Seeking bliss, seeing hidden potential, affirming others, and trusting emotions are sources of motivation and creativity that are not available when people are kept in the cage of rational expectations.

Exhibit 6.1. Heart

Conventional Strong-Force View	Fusion Leader Subtle View
• Stay emotionally distant from people and work	• Stay emotionally connected with people and work
• Base choices on career expectations	• Base choices on finding bliss
• Look at track record	• Look for hidden potentials
• Look down on people who are emotional	• Seek out people who express emotions
• Hold that emotions block truth	• Hold that emotions are truth
• Be individualistic, adverserial	• Be collaborative, interdependent
• Pay attention to rational ideas and people	• Pay attention to ideas and people with emotional power

The story at the beginning of this chapter described the awakening of the inner spirit, which leads to life satisfaction and impact. Those who invest in the emotional aspects of life and community find their impact and satisfaction more enduring. There is no substitute for the heart. Leaders in a far-from-equilibrium world welcome Sleeping Beauty along with the prince into their workplace. United, they inspire zealous cooperation and achievement.

Personal Remembering

■ How do you react to the idea of developing a balance of masculine and feminine qualities in yourself or your organization? Do you know why you feel this way?

■ "People must both give and hear bad news to create emotional relationships." Do you agree?

■ Are you more comfortable with words like *individualism* and *competition* than with words like *partnership* and *cooperation?* Why?

■ How does being cared about make you feel? How do you show that you care about someone? (Answer each of these questions with a list.)

CHAPTER SEVEN

COMMUNICATION

Back in the third century AD, *the King Ts'ao sent his son, Prince T'ai, to the temple to study under the great master Pan Ku. Because Prince T'ai was to succeed his father as king, Pan Ku was to teach the boy the basics of being a good ruler. When the prince arrived at the temple, the master sent him alone to the Ming-Li Forest. After one year, the prince was to return to the temple to describe the sound of the forest.*

When Prince T'ai returned, Pan Ku asked the boy to describe all that he could hear. "Master," replied the prince, "I could hear the cuckoos sing, the leaves rustle, the hummingbirds hum, the crickets chirp, the grass blow, the bees buzz, and the wind whisper and holler." When the prince had finished, the master told him to go back to the forest to listen to what more he could hear. The prince was puzzled by the master's request. Had he not discerned every sound already?

For days and nights on end, the young prince sat alone in the forest listening. But he heard no sounds other than those he had already heard. Then one morning, as the prince sat silently beneath the trees, he started to discern faint sounds unlike those he had ever heard before. The more acutely he listened, the clearer the sounds became. The feeling of enlightenment enveloped the boy. "These must be the sounds the master wished me to discern," he reflected.

When Prince T'ai returned to the temple, the master asked him what more he had heard. "Master," responded the prince reverently, "when I listened most closely, I could hear the unheard—the sound of flowers opening, the sound of the sun warming the earth, and the sound of the grass drinking the morning dew." The master nodded approvingly. "To hear the unheard," remarked Pan Ku, "is a necessary discipline to be a good ruler. For only when a ruler has learned to listen closely to the people's hearts, hearing their feelings uncommunicated, pains unexpressed, and complaints not spoken of, can he hope to inspire confidence in his people, understand when something is wrong, and meet the true needs of his citizens. The demise of states comes when leaders listen only to superficial words and do not penetrate deeply into the souls of the people to hear their true opinions, feelings, and desires."[1]

In a world where managers are trained to make a good impression, to take action, to think quickly and solve problems, the deep listening of Prince T'ai seems strangely out of place. Many people think of communication as persuading others to accept their ideas, as talking another company into buying your product or service. Yet fully half of communication is listening— really listening, in order to understand people and affirm them.

A consultant friend of ours does an amazing listening exercise with managers. The exercise begins in a large room with, say, sixty people who are paired off with one another. The partners are blindfolded and are instructed to find each other by sound alone. By the final round, the partners find each other without any explicit sound whatsoever. They must feel like Prince T'ai, because blindfolded, they listen in a new and profound way. They use all of their senses to detect breathing, energy, warmth, smell. And they succeed. The managers find a capacity to listen that exceeds all their expectations.

Another feature of leader communication is that it seldom conveys data, answers, or instructions. A leader's role is far bigger. Leaders communicate to manage mindsets, imprinting people with the big picture and the basic ideas that will stimulate high performance. Leaders create images in people's minds. They provide meaning, purpose, and a sense of community by articulating the vision and where employees fit into it. With the use of stories, symbols, and rich language, they direct people's attention to what is important.

LEADER DISCERNMENT

Everyone wants to be heard and understood for who they are. Each person wants to be appreciated and valued. Leaders give this gift to others.

First Understand, Then Be Understood

When a leader can really listen, magic happens. Robert Greenleaf argued that a natural leader responds to a problem by listening first. Listening enables the leader to understand a situation fully and to be a servant by expressing concern and caring for the other. Listening builds trust, letting the other person know that he or she is fully seen and heard. It strengthens others by affirming their humanity. It enables you to know another person so that they can lower their defenses and know you. Trust and respect are engendered by listening even when the parties to the conversation disagree. Stephen Covey suggests that leaders rediscover others each time they meet. Without expecting to know the answer in advance, leaders ask questions and listen. Listening can transform a relationship.

> *A friend of Covey's was heartbroken over the deterioration of his relationship with his teenage son. Covey advised him to stop lecturing the boy and to work on the assumption that he didn't understand his son. The father eventually came around to accepting this assumption, and one evening approached his son. "Son, I'm not happy with our relationship, and I'd like to see what we can do to improve it. Perhaps I haven't taken the time to really understand you." The son exploded, "Boy, I'll say you haven't! You've never understood me!"*
>
> *The father burned, but he did not respond with anger. "Well, son, perhaps I haven't, but I'd like to. Can you help me? For instance, take that argument we had last week over the car. Can you tell me how you saw it?"*
>
> *Slowly, the son's defenses started to drop. He began to soften. He was being heard. The father showed genuine interest, and the son began to reveal some of his real problems and feelings. The father also opened up and shared his feelings and concerns rather than justifying his past actions. They talked until midnight.*
>
> *When the father relayed this experience to Covey a few days later, he tearfully said, "I feel like I've found my son again, and he's found his dad."*[2]

Listening allows a leader to be seen as a servant, not as a parent, judge, or critic. Listening builds others.

Being a Good Listener

What is good listening? A good listener is present in the moment and is not thinking of his own desires, attachments, or agenda. A true listener sets aside his own needs and is totally merged with the other. Listening is reaching out to understand the inner world of another person. Hearing is different from seeing. Hearing is extreme empathy. Hearing is feeling oneness with another. Hearing is giving. Hearing what needs to be done is different from seeing what needs to be done. Hearing can know the inner person, seeing observes the outer person. Hearing is focused on the person, seeing is focused on the problem. Our own agenda shapes what we see. When we rely on seeing, we move into problems, solve them, and defend our solution. Seeing often misses the basic humanity of others.

Dick had the following experience that demonstrated the power of listening.

> *The power of listening was brought home to me by a manager friend. The manager showed me the vision he had developed for his department. We discussed it over lunch. I asked a number of questions to understand what he was trying to do. Then I offered my own judgments about the quality of his vision and explained my ideas about how to write a vision statement. When I talked to him later, he thanked me for the conversation and said his revised vision statement was much improved. I graciously accepted his thanks, with a comment about the power of the ideas I had discussed with him. He said it wasn't the ideas that had helped him, but my listening and asking questions. That had helped him clarify his purpose and what he wanted to say. He didn't remember the suggestions I had made.*

Listening demands effort. Deep listening is pure concentration. It may seem passive, but is just the opposite. Listening is the action of giving. Doing it well requires that we focus on and develop sensitivity to others. When we listen, we don't argue. We are completely present in each moment.

Successful relationships are created with active listening. This is as true of top salesmen as of leaders. Good salesmen do not pressure others. They sell by discerning the underlying needs and problems of others. They draw people out. For example, superbroker Richard F. Greene of Merrill Lynch prides himself on customer satisfaction. With a new client, he establishes a relationship.

> And how does he establish this relationship? He listens. "I don't go to the meeting with something to sell," Greene says. "I want information about his risk profile so I can do the job right for him."
>
> Greene is an instinctive expert on human psychology. "If you talk, you'll like me," he explains. "If I talk, I'll like you—but if I do the talking, my business will not be served. Now, this fellow is the same as everyone else. His kids don't listen to him. His wife doesn't listen to him—and he doesn't listen to her. When he goes to parties the person he's talking to is looking over his shoulder to see what else is going on in the room. Then all of a sudden he goes to breakfast with me. He starts to answer a question. And he doesn't get interrupted."
>
> Before the eggs have cooled, Greene has won another client.[3]

Rather than chasing transactions, Greene builds long-term relationships, and he does it by listening. It seems natural. And it's powerful.

Yet real listening seems so hard. Why? The transition from talker to listener is a paradigm shift. The shift from being understood to understanding another is a shift from wanting our way to giving another person her way. Listening is hard because we have to step from the role of parent, judge, critic, and authority figure into the role of partner, helper, facilitator, empowerer, and witness.

Listening has the potential to change you. If you listen carefully, you may learn you are wrong. The father in the Covey example learned he was wrong in the way he dealt with his son. If we truly understand another point of view, we understand the person's struggle, difficulty, and suffering. We may change our minds. We may change how we view that person. If you have to always be correct, real listening is impossible. To really hear is to change both listener and speaker, and that is what organizational fusion is about.

Discern the Larger World

Perhaps the most difficult and profound listening is that of Prince T'ai in the story at the beginning of this chapter. He listened beyond mere sound. He listened beneath the surface to detect deeper patterns and relationships. As Joseph Jaworsky writes in *Synchronicity*, "Leadership, ultimately, is about collectively 'listening' to what is wanting to emerge in the world, and then having the courage to do what is required."[4] This kind of listening hears complaints not spoken of, discerns what will delight and surprise customers, knows when something is wrong, and enables the leader to discuss the true needs of associates and clients.

Tom Peters and Nancy Austin use the term *naive listening* to describe what takes place in "management by wandering around"—the process of keeping in touch, asking innocent questions, and paying attention to what goes on with employees, customers, and suppliers.[5] Wandering around lets people know you are interested and are listening to them.

Leader roaming and listening facilitate organizational change. Leaders pick up the first hint, the first subtle vibration, of something new in the air. A geologist who gets out of the office and feels the sand of a delta between his toes is a better geologist than one doing analyses at his desk. The software designer who meets customers in a computer store can build in more user friendliness. The executive who fields calls on the toll-free 800 number has substantive raw complaints from which to form impressions. A top executive who brings in a dozen tough customers to talk with company managers helps everyone obtain much valuable information. Leaders know that many good ideas for innovations originate outside themselves. If you are not listening to employees and customers, you are missing great suggestions.

Another way to listen is to bring employees together for conversation. Customers can be invited too. Beer blasts and other social gatherings help to dissolve boundaries, which is vitally important for a learning organization in a chaotic environment. Managers can institute "360 degree feedback," in which each manager hears opinions about his or her performance from people on all sides. These are the beginnings of organizational fusion. Listening produces change and growth.

MANAGING MEANING AND MINDSET

Being a leader involves a special kind of outward communication. Managers traditionally learn to sell themselves, win arguments, communicate correct answers, solve problems, pass data and decisions to people who need them. Leaders, by contrast, define the psychological container within which other people work. They shape the big picture, tell people how they fit into it, and direct attention to what counts.

Defining Reality and Vision

People who join a company know that they are taking on the rights, values, obligations, and purpose of the organization, and they therefore want a frame of reference that tells them where the company is headed and what is expected of them. Leaders provide this frame.[6]

Jack Welch of GE found that employees' reality could be shaped by providing lots of information from the top and by encouraging them to share information with each other—important steps toward fusion. Information sharing across boundaries helped people understand one another, changed many minds, and created a consensus about GE and where it was headed. Conversations also provided peer support for decisions. But as leader, Welch himself took responsibility for winning the large mass of employees over to the new way of thinking.

> *It's not that I changed. We just expanded the reach of our communication. We refined it, got better at it, and it began to snowball. If you have a simple, consistent message, and you keep on repeating it, eventually that's what happens. Simplicity, consistency and repetition—that's how you get through. It's a steady continuum that finally reaches a critical mass.*
>
> *You've got to be out in front of crowds, repeating yourself over and over again, never changing your message no matter how much it bores you.*
>
> *You need an overarching message, something big but simple and understandable. Whatever it is—we're going to be No. 1 or No. 2, or fix/close/sell or boundarylessness— every idea you present must be something you could get across easily at a cocktail party with strangers. If only aficionados of your industry can understand what you're saying, you've blown it.[7]*

Leaders communicate more like evangelists than accountants. They articulate values, paint the big picture, and make jobs meaningful for subordinates. Leaders take communication seriously. They seize every moment to stand in front of people and repeat the message. At the foundation of all leader communication is a vision that is repeated and shared until imprinted within everyone. Convey meaning, not data. A person could memorize every word in the dictionary and every definition, but that doesn't mean he would understand novels or poetry. The words and definitions are just facts, pieces of data. To be human, facts have to be part of a larger landscape, story, picture, or emotion that gives them meaning. It's the bigger idea or story that counts.

To create fusion, leaders give data away. Most information can be handled better at lower levels. But it's just noise to people unless they have the big picture within which to use it. Leaders provide a mental picture and then free people to act within that picture. Employees welcome images that say what the organization is about and where it is headed. Such images enable them to find a path through the forest of company data and determine what serves them and the organization.

Leaders who forget to communicate the big idea make a mistake. Facts don't change or shape mindsets. Only a higher purpose and vision can do that. Statistics are good for solving problems, but not for shifting attitudes and values—the essence of survival in an out-of-kilter world. Data are cold. Stories and images have warmth and emotion.

Leader communication exemplifies the difference between show and tell. As we all learned in kindergarten, telling alone doesn't communicate; it's no fun, and people don't understand. But showing makes an impact. The role of the leader is to show—with stories, with symbols, with mental pictures. Organizations would do well to go back to kindergarten.

Success as a leader depends partly on the ability to teach. Leaders don't teach technical skills, they teach vision and values.

They talk about what they believe, often engaging constituents in a dialogue and then articulating the shared perspective that emerges. This is the day-to-day hard work of the leader.

Leaders keep the vision in mind, and it is always there when they make decisions and talk to others. As Jack Welch candidly admitted, "Without question, communicating the vision, and the atmosphere around the vision, has been, and is continuing to be, by far the toughest job we face."[8]

And when it doesn't work, the results are painful. Consider Roger Smith, former CEO of General Motors.

> *I sure wish I'd done a better job of communicating with GM people. I'd do that differently a second time around and make sure they understood and shared my vision for the company. Then they would have known why I was tearing the place up, taking out whole divisions, changing our whole production structure. If people understand the why they'll work at it.*
>
> *I've had a vision for this company for a long time. It goes back to 1972 . . . but I've also known for a long time that if I was the only one who had that vision, it was no good.*[9]

STORIES, SYMBOLS, AND RICH CONVERSATION

Leaders engage stories, symbols, and language as powerful stimulants of desired behavior.[10] They use subtle communication to reach and change people's minds. Shaping mindsets is the primary source of leader influence in a changing organization.

People Hunger for Stories

David Armstrong, president of Armstrong International, was inspired to write *Management by Storying Around* by observing how people listened to his minister's stories each Sunday. Even when congregants had heard a story many times before, their attention always perked up at that point in the service. Armstrong realized that people loved to hear stories.[11]

Just as myths help human beings understand the larger universe and how they fit within it, stories help employees understand the larger organization and the place they occupy in it. Stories are the means by which people make sense of life. The story of Adam and Eve helps us understand the meaning of life and death. The story of George Washington chopping down the cherry tree illustrates a fundamental truth about how to live life successfully.

Stories have power beyond facts. Stories guide us. They touch the subtle self within and make us part of something larger. Facts are outside, separate from us. Facts appeal only to the rational mind. Stories bind us together. Stories are told and retold. They connect the landscape of the mind to the landscape of the outer world. Stories provide continuity with organizational experience and history.

Evidence for the power of stories was obtained in a study at Stanford Business School. The point was to convince M.B.A. students that a company practiced a policy of avoiding layoffs. For some students, only a story was used. For others, statistical data were presented that showed little staff turnover in comparison with competitors. For a third group, the statistics and the story were combined. A fourth group was simply given the company's policy statement. Of all these approaches, the story alone engendered the greatest conviction that the policy was practiced.[12]

A personal experience of Bob Lengel's confirmed how compelling a personal testimony, a special kind of story, can be in relation to objective facts.

I was shopping for a laptop computer. Trained as a researcher, I gathered objective data from computer magazines and assembled a matrix detailing all attributes of competing laptop computers. I computed a numerical score for each computer model, and decided on XYZ computer because it scored highest.

That evening, I attended a business dinner. In a casual conversation, the subject of laptop computers came up. The person said, "I don't think you can go too far wrong these days, but stay away from XYZ computers. I bought one two months ago and it has been back for service more time than I have had it for work." I did not buy XYZ computer. Even with all my research training and objective data, that one story carried far more weight.

It has been said that all societies need drummers and warriors and storytellers. Drummers unite people behind a cause. Warriors fight for the cause. Storytellers interpret the cause and create history.[13] The Ute Indians of Utah made the best storytellers their tribal leaders. The storytellers interpreted experience. They provided the context and meaning for the tribe. They espoused values and dreams.

For many Americans, President Reagan's gifts as a storyteller made him a particularly persuasive leader. The same is true of Abraham Lincoln and Martin Luther King, Jr., who used stories to define their visions of civil war, emancipation, and the nonviolent struggle for fundamental rights.

David Armstrong of Armstrong International replaced rules and regulations with stories. He told a story about an individual traveling for the company who spent money just the way he did at home. This story replaced the company's travel and entertainment expense manual. Stories eventually replaced the entire policy manual at Armstrong International.

One of the most compelling stories used by Armstrong was about the decision not to expand the plant in the direction of a neighbor's property. As Armstrong International expanded, the building committee recommended a new building right next to the old one. The layout would be efficient. All that was needed was to buy the home of Fred Kemp, then in his mid-seventies, a retired Armstrong employee.

> *The president vetoed the plan.*
> *"Fred has lived in the house forever," he said. "His children grew up there, and it really is the only place he's ever called home. I know he loves that place. We bought it from him years ago, when it looked like we'd have to expand onto his property someday. But when we bought it, I promised he could stay there as long as he liked. Making him move now might upset him to the point where it shortens his life. We'll build a new plant on the other side of the property."*[14]

This story vividly illustrates to everyone who hears it that human values outweigh planned efficiency at Armstrong International.

Some stories grab employees. One story told how Ray Kroc, founder and chairman of McDonald's, would throw every burnt-out bulb against the wall in each store he visited. Supposedly, he once fired a store manager for a burnt-out light bulb. This story kept managers on their toes with respect to details of customer service.

A symbol is typically a visible, concrete object that stands for abstract values and concepts. The flag is a symbol of our nation. The Liberty Bell, the Declaration of Independence, and the Constitution all have symbolic value. Religious symbols include the cross, the Star of David, and the figure of the Buddha.

Symbols have astonishing ability to tell people what counts. A physical symbol can create a bond, connecting individuals together through the shared meaning and values they find embodied in it. Leaders use physical artifacts, as well as rituals and celebrations, to symbolize important values.

Leaders at Sequent Computer Systems rely on symbols to help the company thrive. A bicycle came to have symbolic meaning, so when a project was passed from one department to another, it was done through a joint meeting and the actual handing over of a bicycle. The red light on the manufacturing floor symbolized a quality problem, and it burned until the problem was solved. If a major problem arose, most employees would wear green "How can I help?" buttons, while those on the critical path to a solution would wear red "Priority" buttons. The "greens" would remove obstacles for the "reds."[15]

Leaders, who are themselves symbols, convey important messages through the choices they make. Sam Walton's distaste for frills, for example, was symbolized by the sparsely decorated Wal-Mart headquarters, which has the designer appeal of a truck terminal. Walton flew coach class, and executives often slept two to a room.

Rituals and ceremonies are important symbols. One CEO of a computer company uses a quarterly ceremony to recognize superior performance. She invites top performers to spend five days with senior executives in a vacation setting to talk about new technologies and to learn about each other.

When Bill Arnold was president of Centennial Medical Center in Nashville, he tore his office door from the hinges and suspended it from the lobby ceiling to emphasize his commitment to an open-door policy. New ideas from employees were referred to as "jumper cable" ideas, symbolized by a pair of jumper cables displayed on his desk. They encouraged employees to think of "shocking" new ways of working.[16]

You Are Watched

Even if leaders are not supplying stories, symbols, rituals, and celebrations to impart meaning, employees will see meaning in their actions. Every behavior of a leader is watched and interpreted by associates. Leaders make use of this tendency to shape mindsets and shared understandings.

When Ignacio Lopez took over General Motors' worldwide purchasing operation, he immediately communicated symbolically. He called his purchasing staff "warriors" and distributed a copy of his "Warrior's Diet." His subordinates thought he was joking, but soon learned that he expected everyone in the purchasing operation to act as warriors. He called staff meetings as early as 6:00 A.M., and allowed no "poisonous" substances, such as coffee or sugar, to be served. He took the highly symbolic action of transferring his watch to his right arm, with the explanation that he would return it to his left arm when his task was accomplished. Other executives at GM switched their watches to their right arm as a sign of changing times.[17]

When Ren McPherson took over Dana Corporation, he symbolized the shift in corporate values by getting rid of the policy manual and substituting a one-page statement of corporate philosophy. He also cut four hundred monthly reports to none, thereby creating a face-to-face culture for Dana.

Roy Ash used a symbolic approach when he assumed control of A-M Corporation. He visited widely scattered spots rather than summoning managers to headquarters as his predecessor had. He made his own calls. He removed several copy machines to symbolize the decreasing bureaucracy. He flew to visit a dissatisfied customer, symbolizing the importance of service.[18]

The president of a retail chain, along with other corporate staff, worked in stores on the holidays, symbolizing their concern for employees.[19] At another company, a human resource executive learned that employees could predict a layoff announcement because he always wore the same tie (his favorite) on announcement days.

CEOs, division and plant managers, and heads of major departments and functions are watched. Employees want to make sense of the organization, to be given a sense of direction and purpose. Savvy leaders network, persuade, cajole, describe the vision, tell stories, create symbols and rich images to shape values and the corporate culture. As one CEO said while reflecting on his impact in communicating values, "The influence of the top person in the organization is quite frightening, really."[20]

Face-to-Face Conversation

Leaders thrive face-to-face. Personal meetings are the richest communication medium because they provide the opportunity to experience others directly, build social relationships, have eye contact, and observe body language. They offer instant feedback. Rich cues are needed in a chaotic world where things change constantly. One study found that managers who hid behind memos and electronic mail were less effective.[21] Successful leaders communicated face-to-face when conflicts arose, during times of change, when issues were ambiguous or emotionally charged, when personal relationships were important, and when it was necessary to build agreement.

One firm learned how face-to-face conversation contributed to the success of a major acquisition:

> *The company had sent senior management to every major installation of the acquired firm. In all, 75 percent of the required firm's employees had an opportunity to meet the CEO and other top officials. "We stood there for hours, until every question was answered," one participant recalled. What that gave employees, recalled another, "was the chance to take a measure of you, look you in the eye, ask some questions, and see how you responded. . . . You get to be seen as a person who understands what's happening, who is cognizant of feelings, who doesn't have all the answers but is willing to listen and learn, and who has a vision so that others will say, I'll work for that guy for a few months and see how it goes."[22]*

The relationship power of conversation was understood by senior leaders at ATI Medical, Inc. The 305 ATI employees were subject to a "no memo" policy that was laid down by Paul Stevenson, president and CEO. He found that employees loved the policy, except for those from large organizations who felt memo writing was sacred. People loved to build personal relationships. Everyone knew everyone in the company. Shared meaning was easy at ATI.[23]

Jack Welch described the importance of face-to-face conversation for shaping GE:

> *We've learned a bit about what communication is not. It's not a speech like this, or videotape. It's not a plant newspaper. Real communications is an attitude, an environment. It's the most interactive of all processes. It requires countless hours of eyeball-to-eyeball back and forth. It involves more listening than talking. It is a constant interaction process aimed at [creating] consensus.*[24]

Rich Language and Metaphors

Language itself is symbolic. Rich language, especially metaphors, spark pictures in people's minds that endure and create the future. During a budget message, Reagan described a trillion dollars by comparing it to a pile of dollar bills beside the Empire State Building. He created that image to persuade others to support his vision. Another time, Reagan was talking about a budget bill that was thousands of pages long. Remember what he did? He had it all brought into the room, pointed to it, and said, "Forty pounds of paper." He knew how to encapsulate data in an emotional nugget that people could relate to.

Rich, vivid language is a tool to unite people in a shared vision. Sue Tabor, general manager of Nordstrom's department store in San Francisco, used the following metaphor to bring home to store personnel the nature of retail competition as she saw it:

> *Every morning in Africa, a gazelle wakes up. It knows it must outrun the fastest lion or it will be killed. Every morning in Africa, a lion wakes up. It knows it must run faster than the slowest gazelle or it will starve. It doesn't matter whether you're a lion or a gazelle—when the sun comes up, you'd better be running.*[25]

Consider the image in your mind when a leader is described as a coach, facilitator, partner, teacher, or empowerer. Compare this with the picture evoked when a leader is characterized as a dictator, cop, autocrat, or rule maker. Now try two more leader images: the giraffe and the hyena. The giraffe with its long neck is farsighted, it moves fast on its long legs, and has a huge heart. The hyena is known for its slashing teeth, its attacks on others, and its fearsome laugh. Which image do you prefer?

The mixed feelings he experienced when about to let go of a bad acquisition were summed up by one CEO in the phrase "holding the dead baby to the breast." "Stretch objectives" dominated the attention of managers in a large finance company, almost as if they could see taffy candy in their minds. A leader in Australia's largest company used the slogan "Big is out, good is in" to shift mindsets from size to quality. One woman executive described her organization as a "wounded elephant—large, suffering, and enraged." This image was the catalyst for change toward a different culture. Another executive described his organization as a "1950s Edsel," evoking the image of an outdated failure.[26]

Leadership communication is "high touch" rather than high tech. It consists not of data, rules, or instructions but of rich conversation, stories, symbols, and celebrations designed to engage stakeholders—employees, customers, suppliers—in a shared mindset. Leaders also listen, demonstrating caring, respect, trust, and affirmation of others.

A summary of the key themes in this chapter can be found in Exhibit 7.1.

Exhibit 7.1. Communication

Conventional Strong-Force View	Fusion Leader Subtle View
• Talk	• Listen
• Persuade others to act	• Discern other's needs
• Focus on work issues	• Focus on big picture, frame of reference, meanings
• Transmit data	• Transmit symbolic images, stories
• Cultivate impersonality	• Cultivate face-to-face contact
• Assign next task	• Celebrate completed task
• Direct message to "head"	• Direct message to "heart"
• Answer questions	• Ask questions
• Controlled access	• Flood information across boundaries

Personal Remembering

∎ How might you advocate your point of view in a meeting without dominating or excluding other points of view?

∎ The next time someone wants to talk to you, look directly in his or her eyes, relax, hold your gaze, nodding and affirming the person but withholding your own thoughts and opinions. Note what happens.

∎ What was the most meaningful conversation in your life? Why was it meaningful?

∎ If you were to communicate with your team strictly to build trust with them, what would you say?

CHAPTER EIGHT

COURAGE

A farmer one spring enjoyed watching two eagles flying near a distant bluff. After failing to see the eagles for a couple of days, he went to investigate. He found an abandoned nest that held an egg, which he took back to the farm. With the faint hope that it might hatch, and a baby eagle grow up and fly, he placed the egg in a nest in the henhouse.

Two weeks later, the egg hatched, and the strange-looking baby eagle joined the chicks in the yard of the henhouse. As the first days passed, the eaglet learned the habits of the chickens, feeding on the corn provided by the farmer. Noticing birds flying overhead one beautiful morning, the eaglet remarked, "Wouldn't it be wonderful to fly like that! I wish I could fly." But you know how chickens are. They quickly admonished this foolish thinking. "You are a chicken," they said. "You are not meant to fly." The fearful mother hen said, "If you try to fly, you will surely get caught in the chicken wire and break your neck." The strutting rooster father added logically, "Even if you flew over the fence, it would be hard to find food and you would prob-

*ably starve." All the chickens agreed the baby eagle should
not try to fly.*

*"It sure would be wonderful to fly and soar like that,"
the eaglet repeated to himself. "I wish I could do it." But he
did not try. He believed the chickens. As the days and weeks
passed, the eaglet said little about flying. He spent more
time alone, often in the henhouse.*

*Then one day, the farmer noticed that the eaglet was no
longer in the chicken yard. He hoped the eaglet had grown
big enough to fly away, but went to investigate. The henhouse was dark, and when he turned on the light, he noticed
a clump of dark feathers in the corner. He picked it up,
saw that it was the young eagle. The eaglet was dead.*[1]

This story is sad because the eaglet saw his inner dream in
the birds flying overhead, and if only he had tried, he too could
have flown. Instead, he listened to the chickens and died without ever fulfilling his true identity.

The eaglet story is applicable to people, especially managers,
who have identified their dream but have not acted on it.
Dreams are not achieved automatically. You have to make
dreams happen in the face of resistance from the "chickens."

Companies that rely exclusively on strong forces appeal not
to courage but to fear. Fear appeals to the conditioned ego, not
to the deeper, essential self. When fear prevails, the deeper
sources of courage within managers and employees go untapped, and remain so until people begin to wonder why risk
taking and courage are so rare. Courage, like mindfulness and
vision, can be remembered and unlocked.

A dream comes from the heart. Acting on the dream takes
courage. Courage enables you to fly. Courage carries you through
deprivation, ridicule, rejection, and potential failure to achieve
something you love. Corporate America was misled by years of
stability, abundance, and the assumption that courage wasn't

needed. Managers learned: "Keep your nose clean. Don't fail. Let somebody else go first. Don't have a mark on your record. Be careful. If you are cautious and gather enough data, you won't make a mistake."

This approach is so safe, and so ridiculous. Life in an out-of-kilter world is as safe as a roll of the dice. Things constantly change, one thing depends on everything else, and nothing significant can be controlled. Leaders thrive by solving problems through trial and error, which means many errors. In a turbulent world, caution is no match for reality. Action is demanded. Acting precedes planning, not vice versa. Leaders create the future by moving forward in the face of uncertainty, by taking chances, by behaving with courage. Yet many aspiring leaders seem blocked from risk taking and initiating real change. Their fears overwhelm them. In this chapter, we will help leaders understand and break through such fears.

WHAT IS LEADERSHIP COURAGE?

In images from folklore, courage is seen as doing battle with intrusive elements from the external world.[2] It is the virtue of the archetypal warrior who takes the offensive, loves action, and abhors inaction. Similarly, the inner warrior has a strong spirit, engages life, seizes opportunities, and enjoys an outpouring of life energy toward a valued goal, a higher mission or cause. A courageous leader is an adventurer, an explorer. Courage is the stuff that underlies a leader's choice to put in long hours, endure pain, and overcome obstacles, lack of sleep, and repeated rejection.

In *Iron John*, Robert Bly asks the reader to consider whether he is made of copper or iron.[3] Copper is a conductor. A manager made of copper lives as an unhealthy bridge for others. The demands of the organization, the expectations of others, the boss's whims, all run through a copper person without resistance. The copper manager suppresses his real opinions and beliefs, carries out orders, tries to gain acceptance by being a nice person, and may become an apologist for actions that violate his own true values. Managers made of copper accept change initiated by others so that they will obtain corporate approval.

Iron represents strength, armor, and protection. Iron means healthy resistance. Arrows bounce from an iron shield. The leader made of iron sets limits, knows when to say "Enough," and will sacrifice charm, niceness, and the approval of others in the risky cause of the dream. Leaders made of iron have opinions. They disagree with the boss. They express subtle forces, and protect others' right to do so. They promote new ideas in the pursuit of a higher purpose. The leader made of iron has an internal shield to protect himself and his boundaries.

Courage and risk taking seem nonexistent in some of today's large, bureaucratic organizations. We visited a large agency of the federal government and were amazed at the obsessive avoidance of risk taking in that corporate culture. The slightest mistake created a whirlwind of blaming, finger pointing, and extra effort to avoid responsibility. Culpability was passed down the chain of command: one lower-level employee suffered the penalty for a superior's error because he had no power to avoid it. The absence of courage froze the agency. People were almost afraid to do normal tasks. Innovation was impossible.

Yet there are also examples of great courage in organizations. A study sponsored by Korn-Ferry International found many leaders unafraid to take risks. "They spoke out, they changed jobs, they argued with bosses, they tackled assignments with uncertain prospects for success. They consistently voiced a strong point of view, and pushed for what they believed."[4] Courage is the CEO who was proud to admit, "We make mistakes on an hourly basis." That attitude was the basis of his company's success. Courage is Hewlett-Packard's medal of defiance given to people who disobey the system and succeed anyway.[5] Courage is the executive who gave the highest performance evaluations to people who made mistakes while stretching beyond their traditional responsibilities.

Courage Is Nonconformity

Not too many years ago, large companies would hire business graduates by the truckload. The students who went to work in staff jobs at IBM would soon start to look and think alike in important ways. The same is true of those hired to work at the headquarters of General Motors or Ford. And the Ford people would be different from the IBM people. An important reason for homogenization is that the business graduates want to succeed. They want approval. The organization has enormous power over those who will do whatever it takes to succeed. Business graduates use their talent to tune into politics and protocol and give the company what it wants, hoping someday to "succeed" with a big salary and high position. But this success-oriented behavior is conformity, not leadership.

Leadership in a destabilized world means nonconformity. It means breaking tradition, boundaries, and norms. One obvious trait that distinguishes a leader from a manager is a willingness to take risks, to deviate from the system, to change the system. Leaders do not play it safe, and they encourage others to take chances. Managers are fine for stability, leaders are needed to initiate change. It takes courage to jump into a new way of doing things when you don't know for sure whether there is water in the pool. Leaders extend themselves, they try new things. Rather than avoid surprises, courageous leaders welcome surprises because this is where progress is made.

At its easiest, courageous leadership means championing change in the form of a new idea, product, procedure, or improvement. At its hardest, courageous leadership means being a maverick, pursuing guerrilla warfare, dismantling the system, perhaps creating a new culture or a new paradigm. The courageous leader does whatever is needed to help the organization and its people grow, improve, and adapt.

Understood in this way, leadership is difficult. Leadership is a struggle. Leaders who pursue a dream to improve the organization will find cooperation, but they will also meet resistance. Just as the Red Sea parted for Moses, the organization may yield to a leader's dream and passion, but leakages will slosh back on the leader. Well-intended people will resist, disagree, or drag their feet. When nudging subordinates into new territory, you will encounter opposition, uncertainty, and doubt. You will make mistakes, be outvoted, and fail. Other managers will challenge you, and you will feel hurt and rejected. Leadership is a struggle, both within yourself and within the organization. That's why warrior courage is so critical. *If what you are doing comes easily, it is probably not leadership.*

It is important to note that nonconformity must be verbal if it is to influence others. Consider the Texas farm family and guests who decided to drive forty miles to town for dinner on a hot day when their car's air conditioner wasn't working. They were miserable. Talking about it afterward, each person admitted that he or she hadn't wanted to go, but went along to please the others. The father said he had suggested going to town only as a way to make conversation and find out what the others wanted to do. No one in the family wanted to go to town on that hot day, yet no one honored their mindful inner voice and said no.

Jerry Harvey calls this The Abilene Paradox.[6] He found that people often don't voice their independent thoughts because they want to please others. The need to please blocks the truth. Often, in company teams, no one says how he really feels or what she really thinks. The reason is partly our cultural predisposition to conform. People want approval and hence fail to listen to or act spontaneously on the subtle voice within.

Courage Is Naming the Truth

The old Newtonian wisdom for a stable world was to fake it, to maintain an appearance of strength, to keep your nose clean, to go along with the company crowd. Steering a course through the chaos of the modern workplace requires that the hard problems that at first glance seem insurmountable must be faced honestly. Giant bureaucracies like IBM, GM, or Sears Roebuck were impossible to streamline as long as leaders failed to acknowledge the reality of their own and the companies' weaknesses.

Like the medicine man in a tribal culture, the courageous leader today recognizes and names the "undiscussable" demons that plague his organization. To face the faults within himself, his coworkers, and his organization is to acquire the demon's power.

> *Consider Pat Riley's naming of the demon in the New York Knicks after he took over as coach. The players couldn't see how their cliques and dislike for each other fed negative attitudes and a losing mindset. He had the players report to a room one hour before practice. They all sat together while Riley named the members of each clique and described their characteristics. Then he had each clique sit together in separate corners. The chair-shifting exercise made visible a new reality for the team. Riley held up a mirror to their separateness and hostility. The players fumed, but they got the message, along with an hourlong discussion about tolerance, openness, and team spirit. Riley's mindful naming of the demon started the team on a cooperative path that led to the playoffs. He helped the players remember the truth of why they were there.[7]*

A fusion leader seeks truth as the ultimate foundation for effective communication and trust. Denying the truth strains everyone as people tiptoe around obvious issues.

Expressing vulnerability takes courage, and leaders are admired when they acknowledge their responsibility for a blunder. President Kennedy earned great political capital from publicly admitting his responsibility for the Bay of Pigs fiasco. His honesty attracted people to him. Some think that Richard Nixon's refusal to admit mistakes about Watergate caused the threat of impeachment and his ultimate resignation. It is fear that prevents people from admitting failure.

A delightful example of vulnerability was Captain Asoh, a pilot for Japan Air Lines, who landed his DC–8 two miles short of the San Francisco runway—in the bay. When asked how he did what he did, Captain Asoh replied, "As you Americans say, Asoh f--- up." Asoh knew that admitting the mistake was the best strategy for himself and J.A.L. He continued to fly for Japan Air Lines until his retirement, and having made the big mistake, he was a better pilot than ever.[8]

As illustrated in the Greek myth of Orestes, even the gods admire people who openly take responsibility for their mistakes:

> *Orestes' grandfather was punished by the gods, who put a curse on his descendants. The curse upon Orestes was realized when his mother murdered his father. A son was obliged under the Greek code of honor to slay his father's murderer, yet the greatest sin a Greek could commit was to kill his mother. After agonizing over the decision, Orestes decided to kill his mother. The gods punished him by assigning three Furies to torment him day and night.*
>
> *After many years of trying to atone for his crime and be relieved of the Furies, Orestes asked the gods to reconsider. A trial was held. Apollo spoke in Orestes' defense, claiming that he arranged the situation in which Orestes chose to kill his mother. Orestes jumped up and contradicted Apollo. "It was I, not Apollo, who murdered my mother!" He took personal responsibility. The gods were surprised because*

people always blamed the gods for what went wrong. Never
before had the gods seen someone take total responsibility
for his behavior. They decided the trial in Orestes' favor.
They removed the Furies and assigned instead loving spirits
to ensure Orestes' good fortune.[9]

The moral of this story is clear: taking responsibility for your
actions and mistakes brings acceptance and respect from others, and even good fortune. Denial of your mistakes and responsibilities brings pain and punishment.

Courage Is Fighting for What You Believe

In today's corporate world, where people seem so focused on
their own careers, the idea gets lost that warriors use courage
in the pursuit of the larger purpose, dream, or social outcome.
Warriors venture beyond traditional boundaries, and risks are
taken for an important purpose. The warrior fights for what he
or she really believes in. A true warrior is not just out for number one, but fights for valued outcomes that benefit the community. Commitment to higher values is the foundation for
risk taking.

Leadership courage does not mean using warrior energy to
violate or hurt others. Courage is not conquest. Warriors do
not venture beyond boundaries to triumph over the weak and
powerless or to destroy things valued by others. True strength
is gentle. The desire for conquest or destruction arises from fear,
not courage. When the courageous leader becomes a destroyer,
it is to destroy senseless procedures, thoughtless actions, cor-
ruption, pettiness, abuse, stifling bureaucracy, or unfair corporate demands. The warrior battles against obstacles that stand
in the way of employee growth, the overall vision, and higher
values.

Courage Is Setting Boundaries

Although warriors venture beyond traditional boundaries, courage also protects boundaries. Risks are taken and battles fought to protect the warrior's family, community, department, or organization. The warrior battles evil and injustice that threaten his or her community. The highest use of courage is to protect others, to be assertive for human values. Marshal Matt Dillon in *Gunsmoke* stood for justice by drawing a line in the dust against a mob that wanted to lynch a prisoner. The "Magnificent Seven" used their courage to defend a helpless Mexican community against ransacking bandits. Courageous leaders protect associates who take worthwhile risks and fail.

Courage also means protecting one's personal boundaries. Courage is the ability to say no. A strong individual will not give his or her entire life to the company, working endless hours in the hope of gaining approval. Saying no to unreasonable demands from bosses or subordinates protects your personal boundaries. The courage to say no in the interests of self-protection is as important as saying no to protect your family, department, or community.

Managers with courage are able to claim their rightful power as human beings, as leaders, as employees. Such managers ask for what they want, for what their department or project needs. They pursue the department's vision, they facilitate change, they improve things, they say no.

FEAR AND FAILURE STRENGTHEN COURAGE

Courage is the ability to step forward through fear. Courage is the will to overcome fear. Courage means acting when you are afraid to act, whether giving a speech when you feel desperately shy or approving a multimillion-dollar contract that could sink your career.

People experience all kinds of fears, including fear of death, mistakes, failure, change, loss of control, loneliness, intimacy, pain, uncertainty, engulfment, abuse, embarrassment, rejection, success, and public speaking. Fear may reveal itself as a tightening in the stomach or as avoidance and procrastination. Recognizing the symptoms of fear is the first step in overcoming it. Avoidance is unproductive. Many fears can be conquered when you can admit to them.

Fears have a physical or psychological base. Physical fear has its roots in mortality. In our work with managers, fully 95 percent of the fears that influence their leadership behaviors are psychological. Psychological fear has roots in childhood, when we depend on acceptance and approval. The fear that the love of a parent might be lost persists into adulthood as an unconscious fear of any rejection or failure.

Everyone is vulnerable to fear when going beyond his or her comfort zone. In social or risk-taking situations, we may walk into an invisible wall—we would like to move forward, but can't. Single people may feel this wall of fear when asking someone for a date. Or it may loom up when a person is about to confront the boss, break off a relationship, launch an expensive new project, double the size of a building, or change careers. The wall is within us. It is our own fear projected onto the situation.

Fear Imagines Terrible Consequences

What we've learned time and again is that fear of failure is worse than the failure itself. The imagined loss of reputation, dollars, love, respect, or whatever, is typically far worse than the real loss that occurs when a risk does not pay off. We can handle failure. We dust ourselves off and move on. Actual failure is not so bad. It's fear that stops us.

At a critical point in his life, Bob Lengel found himself confronting the irrational fear of consequences:

*My disenchantment with Wall Street became a watershed
for courage in my life. The pull of financial success versus
fulfillment kept me from peaceful sleep. As my discomfort
mounted, my wife and I decided to join friends on a trip to
Bermuda. I love the sea and looked forward to some time
for serious thought. On the second morning, as the group
walked through the lobby of the Southampton Princess, I
spotted a ticker-tape machine on the wall. Four men sat in
front of it staring at the stream of symbols and numbers
that passed before them. I told my friends I would join
them at the beach after I learned how the market was
doing. As I focused on the stream of stock quotes, I felt sorry
for those men spending this beautiful morning worrying
about their money and ignoring the beauty and spiritual
joys only steps away. Then I realized I was one of them.
During the downhill stroll to the beach, my mind was
on fire. My impulse was to call in my resignation, but
anxiety stopped me. What would I do to make a living?
Would others think I quit because I couldn't cut it in the
world of investments? The stream of terrible consequences
that would surely occur if I acted from my heart blinded
me. I walked along the water's edge by myself, absorbed in
the sights, sounds, and smells that brought back memories
of my childhood summers on the beaches of New Jersey.
I remembered what it felt like to be fully engaged in a
moment. Every sand crab, every seagull, lives at the edge
of life and death. The lives of people like myself were
insulated from living and dying by artificial walls of
certainty and security. Maybe to be alive is to be at risk.
A source of courage began to flow from within me.
Within minutes, there was no doubt—there was a choice*

between preparing to live and continuing to die. As I
rejoined my friends, the song I Want to Live, *by John*
Denver, was playing on the radio, and the lyrics about
growing and giving and being will forever mean courage
to me. Within two months, I was back in school studying
to become a teacher.

Bob faced the invisible wall of fear that in the moment
seemed to be made of concrete. He was scared and asked,
"How can I do it?" But when he stepped forward, the wall disappeared. Suddenly the question changed to "Why did I wait
so long?" Looking back, the decision was obviously correct, no
matter how it turned out. He had to try. By stepping through
fear, new opportunities sprang up.

Risk takers discover parts of themselves waiting to blossom.
They grow strong. And they often experience unimagined success. The majority of risks work out. Either the risk succeeds as
planned or the so-called failure produces growth that exceeds
the originally desired outcomes.

Whenever leaders defer to fear, they lose their voice, the opportunity to express themselves. This is powerlessness, and it is
self-imposed. It comes from not asking for what you want, not
stepping into your fears, and not speaking your truth. People
never really know themselves until they step through the wall
of fear and gain the enormous benefits of either "success" or
"failure."

Failure Is the First Step Toward Success

An ice skating instructor who had trained several "star" pupils
was asked if she could tell which students would become champions. She answered that future champions were the ones willing to make fools of themselves. Nonconformity involves risk
and the possibility of failure. And the failures are more impor-

tant than the successes. Without failure, we don't learn. Many people mistakenly believe that failure leads to failure and must be avoided at all costs. This is absolutely untrue. Over time, success breeds failure, and failure breeds success. Everyone can recall an embarrassing failure that was the trigger for growth and learning and new success. Success and failure are phases in the normal cycle of leadership growth.

Sam Walton understood that his role was to take risks and change things. As David Glass, Wal-Mart's CEO said:

> *Two things about Sam Walton distinguish him from almost everyone else I know. First, he gets up every day bound and determined to improve something. Second, he is less afraid of being wrong than anyone I've ever known. And once he sees he's wrong, he just shakes it off and heads in another direction.*[10]

If you don't have failures to look back on, something is wrong. You aren't acting like a leader. You've been playing it safe. One of our friends was proud of having skied all day without falling, and she said so. Another friend replied, "If you're not falling, you're not skiing." His point was that when a skier stretches to improve, she will naturally fall. In a short time, this woman became an outstanding skier.

A Zen teacher said, "Having many difficulties perfects the will; having no difficulties ruins the being."[11] Thus gain is the edge of loss, loss is the heart of gain.

The poet Kahlil Gibran wrote that we must know fear and failure to enjoy success: "Your pain is the breaking of the shell that encloses your understanding. Even as the stone of the fruit must break, that its heart may stand in the sun, so must you know pain."[12]

The strength gained from risk taking grows from a transformation similar to rebirth. The image of death followed by new life is symbolic of courageous leadership. The writings of Joseph Campbell emphasize that failure and destruction are the beginning of new life. Death, decay, and pain are the creative forces producing new possibilities. Leaders affirm the life-giving opportunities in failure. The old life, the familiar organizational routine, has been outgrown. Leaders see that the time has arrived for the organization to cross a threshold into the new.

The leader may symbolically go inward, to be born again. Jonah went into the whale and survived. The Greek hero Herakles threw himself into the throat of a sea monster, then cut his way out through the belly, killing the beast.[13] Each move forward is associated with loss, with the pain of giving up something. No leader or company can transform itself without ceasing to exist in some sense, leaving the old behind, leaping into the maw of the monster. The courageous hero, intent on protecting others, risks his or her own death in the effort to slay the monster. But having passed through fear, the hero comes away from the act a new person, stronger than ever.

This process of death and rebirth was experienced at Video Star, a company that provided temporary satellite networks to corporate clients. Executives took no chances in bidding for an all-important order from Digital Equipment, a prized special-event customer. All sixty employees geared up to win the order, which they expected to receive.

The order went to a competitor. Stunned and bewildered, Video Star undertook an agonizing postmortem. Its harsh self-analysis revealed much about how the company positioned itself in relation to prospective clients, and these findings led Video Star to redefine what it was and what it wanted to be. The company underwent a transformation that produced astonishing dividends in future bidding competitions.[14] Without the failure, the rebirth and subsequent growth would not have happened.

SOURCES OF LEADER COURAGE

To be a fusion leader in a destabilized world is to frequently live outside your comfort zone. What can you do to push through your fear? How can you be forcefully assertive in the face of risk, let your warrior energy flow outward, and serenely accept losses and failures? Perhaps the best way to find courage is to connect risk taking to other subtle forces—emotions, a higher vision, and an attitude that welcomes failure.

Emotion Is a Source of Courage

Emotion is the foundation of courage, the source of forward energy. Anger and love are two powerful emotions. Harnessing anger occasionally allows people to blast through fear. When someone has to be fired, it is often put off until an incident makes you angry enough to carry it out. In moderate amounts, anger is a healthy emotion that provides forward energy.

Perhaps less obvious, but even more important, is love. Positive emotions such as love, passion, and bliss pull us toward the objects that inspire them. When we are engaged with our hearts, our head is less likely to overanalyze possible shortcomings (a symptom of fear), and we have greater confidence to push ahead. It's like being in love with an opportunity, however risky. As Barker described in *Future Edge,* rational judgment does not empower us to move into a paradigm shift.[15] The courage to move forward is a leap of faith based on attraction, belief, and trust, rather than logic. When rational evidence is the only basis for risk taking, the path chosen is likely to be the safe one.

Emotion also means being connected to other people, which increases courage. Clarissa Pinkola Estes tells a story that describes the way of old African kings:

*An old man is dying, and calls his people to his side. He
gives a short, sturdy stick to each of his many offspring,
wives, and relatives. "Break the stick," he instructs them.
With some effort, they all snap their sticks in half.*

*"This is how it is when a soul is alone without anyone.
They can be easily broken."*

*The old man next gives each of his kin another stick,
and says, "This is how I would like you to live after I pass.
Put your sticks together in bundles of twos and threes. Now,
break these bundles in half."*

*No one can break the sticks when there are two or more
in a bundle. The old man smiles. "We are strong when we
stand with another soul. When we are with another, we
cannot be broken."*[16]

Having support from others is a potent source of courage in
an out-of-kilter world. Although rugged individualists in corporate America prefer to stand alone, being part of a team that
is supportive and caring, or having a loving family at home, reduces the fear of failure. When a person is all alone, the consequences of failure seem enormous.

In *Band of Brothers,* Stephen Ambrose describes the astonishing fusion among members of E Company, 101st Airborne,
in Europe during World War II. Having bonded together
under seemingly impossible conditions during eighteen months
of training and six months of fighting, these men cared about
each other more deeply than brothers, more deeply even than
lovers. In the harsh cold of a German winter, they gave up
blankets to one another. When surrounded at Bastogne in Bel-
gium, running low on supplies, they gave up food to one another and accepted scouting assignments to protect one
another. If wounded, a soldier would use every device to get
back to the front and rejoin the company. E Company was assigned the most difficult engagements, suffering 150 percent

casualties (some soldiers were wounded multiple times). On learning that they were surrounded by Germans at Bastogne, one of the soldiers was heard to say, "They've got us surrounded, the poor bastards." A short time later, the company broke out and overran the German positions. Loving one another was their source of extreme courage.[17]

Courage Responds to a Higher Purpose

The archetypal warrior has courage because he fights for what he believes. He is committed to something larger than himself, whether a community, a people, a task, a nation, a cause, or a god. Higher values and service to a larger vision are the great enablers of our inner warriors. Courage is easy when we fight for something that really matters.

Gandhi endured many deprivations in pursuit of the higher goal of expelling the British from India. Martin Luther King, Jr., received death threats against himself and his family almost every day during the civil rights movement.[18] The moral rightness of his cause enabled King to move forward. What is the higher cause, the larger meaning, in your work and in the work of your division or department? Finding a meaning as simple as serving others can release the courage to innovate and even shift the paradigm. Immature leaders often pursue goals just for themselves. To them, failure means the loss of everything, rather than a minor setback on the road to a larger vision.

Bob Lengel witnessed a striking demonstration of the motivating power of higher purpose in a class he taught:

> In a policy course, I had a student group that produced a creative paper about the downsizing of middle management. The group made the unusual argument that a company has a responsibility, beyond producing goods and services, to create jobs for people. I talked to a couple of the students in

*the group after their paper was graded, and they explained
that they saw the paper as a big risk, but they took the risk
so that Betty could receive an A. Betty was the first in her
family to go to college, and now she wanted to go to medical
school. The group decided to pull out all the stops for an A,
which would increase the chances of her realizing that dream.
These students had a higher mission, and they cared about
each other. Their passionate priorities gave them the courage
to make a daring leap. And they did earn their A.*

Courage can increase simply as a result of your clarifying
what you want to achieve. Risk taking then is only a matter of
trying to reach your goal. Trial and error produces plenty of errors, but it also creates ultimate success.

Welcome Failure as a Natural Part of Things

Joseph Campbell, in the study of myths and dreams, pondered
why images of failure seem fewer in the twentieth century. He
commented on an early saying by Heraclitus: "The upward way
and the downward way are one and the same."[19] The point is
that our life journey can be seen as a harmonious relationship
between upward and downward movement. It is a life-death-
life cycle. Success and failure form a unity; these opposites are
two sides of a coin. But modern man wants to have success
without failure, believing that everything should be good and
perfect, and that success arrives without difficulty.

Acceptance of failure fosters courage. Japanese samurai warriors learned to face the biggest possible failure—death. *The
Book of Five Rings,* written centuries ago, prescribes the samurai practice of visualizing death in battle before the actual encounter.[20] In a meditative state, a warrior could vividly see his
own death and accept it. This allayed his fear, and he could go

on and fight with abandon. Accepting failure and the worst possible outcome makes it easier to move the mission forward.

Leaders know that failure ultimately leads to success, that pain of learning strengthens the person and the organization. A courageous leader understands that the biggest risk of all is not taking risks, not experimenting, not taking action. Both the leader and the organization become healthier, trimmer, and more capable through trial and error. They know that danger comes from change that is too slow. A frog that jumps into a pan of boiling water will immediately jump out again. A frog that sits in a pan of cold water that gradually comes to a boil will perish.

Authentic courage is a human attractor. People want to follow someone with courage, especially the courage to be a nonconformist, pursue a higher purpose, serve others, admit failure, and be willing to act on faith and trust.

These ideas about courage are summarized in Exhibit 8.1.

Exhibit 8.1. Courage

Conventional Strong-Force View	Fusion Leader Subtle View
• Assert conformity	• Assert nonconformity
• Follow self-interest	• Follow higher purpose
• Seek to conquer	• Seek to serve
• Act as copper	• Act as iron
• Deny fear and failure	• Feel fear, admit failure
• Support success, avoid failure	• Support failure as way to grow and learn
• Avoid demons	• Name demons, speak truth
• Go along	• Disagree, say no
• Seek rational evidence	• Act on faith and trust
• Be self-sufficient	• Accept support from others

Courageous risk taking is the price of fusion leadership. The eagle cannot soar if it listens to the chickens and remains afraid to fly. Courage is the foundation for personal action and achievement. Courage mentors others by its example. By developing their warrior potential, fusion leaders become strong and inspire others to be risk takers. They energize both themselves and the organization.

Personal Remembering

- What are your three worst failures? What did you learn from those experiences? Are you taking enough risks? If not, why?

- What is the one thing you most want to do in your organization but have not? What fear is holding you back?

- What sources of courage can you call on to take a risk or step through fear?

- Reach out to someone in your work or social life who puts you off. Build a bridge to that person. What did this experience teach you?

CHAPTER NINE

INTEGRITY

In the third century B.C., the emperor consolidated China into a unified empire for the first time. To commemorate the event, the emperor held a grand celebration. Attending the celebration was a spiritual master and three disciples.

As the celebration unfolded, the awestruck disciples asked about greatness. They could understand the greatness of the three heads of staff, one who had great knowledge of logistics, one of military tactics, and one of the dynamics of political and diplomatic relations. But the emperor had no such knowledge, nor noble birth. "How is it, then," they asked, "that he is emperor?"

The master smiled and explained. "Think of sunlight," said the master. "The sun nurtures and vitalizes the trees and flowers. It does so by giving away its light. But in the end, in which direction do they all grow? So it is with a master craftsman like the emperor. After placing individuals in positions that fully realize their potential, he secures harmony among them by giving them all credit for their distinctive achievements. And in the end, as the trees and flowers grow toward the giver, the sun, individuals grow toward the emperor with devotion."[1]

People grow toward the giver of energy, the giver of credit and affirmation. They flourish as persons when they receive affirmation. Human beings want to grow and feel pride in what they do, hence they admire and respond to a leader who honors their contributions.

Integrity is wholeness. Becoming whole and complete means that elements of the higher self—compassion, honesty, generosity to others—are developed and expressed, as in the case of the Chinese emperor. Being whole requires that the subtle and the strong forces in one's self be integrated. Moreover, integrity includes the spiritual notion of becoming one with the larger universe, of understanding one's connection with other people, organizations, communities, plants, and animals. Integrity knows the interdependence of things.

In a world far from equilibrium, the only stable platform of integrity exists within oneself. In an earlier era, when the world was more stable and less interdependent, organizations were like large machines, and individuals had little discretion to express their integrity—or lack of it. People performed fixed and self-contained roles. But when everything depends on everything else, when events are unpredictable and uncontrollable, and when people have great autonomy, the integrity of each person is essential. In a learning organization, change, decision making, customer satisfaction, and problem solving are everyone's responsibility. The integrity of the individual is the eye of the hurricane, the buoy that stands steady in the storm.

Integrity is represented by the archetype of the monarch, perhaps the most profound of our subtle-force resources.[2] Within each of us is the potential to behave as royalty toward our realm. We may bring to those around us prosperity or scarcity, happiness or suffering, enhancement or exploitation. It is the healthy and positive monarch energy that people admire and want to follow, just as the disciples admired the emperor in the opening story.

A manager stuck at a low level of integrity may act as a tyrant, as a rigid, selfish, controlling monarch who is hungry for attention and desperate for power, status, and personal honor. At his worst, this type of monarch is obsessed with "Me, Me, Me," or "See me, adore me." A selfish, vindictive, intolerant leader ultimately creates a kingdom of discouragement and scarcity. Fortunately, personal greed can be healed, and a despised ruler can be transformed into a beloved sovereign who behaves in the interests of others and the kingdom as a whole.

Serving the organization rather than exploiting it is the foundation for prosperity and harmony.

SERVANT LEADERSHIP

"He profits most who serves best."[3] The notion of servant leadership may have been sparked when Robert Greenleaf read Hermann Hesse's novel *Journey to the East*. The central figure of the novel is Leo.

> *Leo appears as a servant to a group of men on a journey.*
> *He performs the lowliest, most menial tasks to serve them,*
> *as well as cheering them with his good spirits and his songs.*
> *He has an extraordinary presence. He directs their way*
> *through the countryside, and does all he can to assist them*
> *as they travel. All goes wonderfully until Leo disappears.*
> *Leo is so important to the men that when he is gone, the*
> *journey falls into disarray. The men are unable to complete*
> *the journey without Leo.*
>
> *Years later, the narrator of the story is taken to the head-*
> *quarters of the order that sponsored the journey. There he*
> *meets Leo and discovers that he was not a lowly servant but*
> *the titular head of the order, a great leader.*[4]

Servant leadership is leadership upside down. Most of us have been raised in families, schools, and organizations in which leaders are authority figures who direct others and expect to be obeyed and served. Self-interest dominates. The servant leader goes beyond self-interest to develop others and give them opportunities for gaining material and psychological abundance. In Greenleaf's view, servant leaders display some of the following characteristics:

• *They are servants first.* The desire to serve others takes precedence over the desire to be in a formal leadership position. Such individuals move into leadership through service rather than from the need to exercise power and control. Servant leaders make a conscious choice to use their gifts in the cause of change and growth for individuals and the organization.

• *Servant leaders rely on foresight and vision.* They have an intuitive sense of the big picture, of where they and the organization are headed, and they can articulate a vision to others that gives inspiration and meaning to work.

• *Servant leaders inspire trust.* The spirit of giving is so unselfish that people trust the servant leader implicitly. The leader inspires confidence and respect for his or her values and judgment. Servant leaders operate out of deep wholeness and integrity.

• *Servant leaders listen first to affirm others.* One of their greatest gifts to others is listening, understanding fully the problems that are presented, removing their own agenda and needs from the listening process. Greenleaf refers to the prayer of St. Francis: "Lord, grant that I may not seek so much to be understood as to understand." The leader affirms her confidence in others. Unqualified acceptance enables others to experiment, grow, and be creative without fear.[5]

Dick Daft recalls a classic exemplar of servant leadership:

My department head created an environment that sup-
ported the growth of everyone, especially junior faculty
members. He broke down barriers between faculty sub-
groups to promote collaboration because it made research
and teaching more fun. He gave praise and credit. In the
faculty lounge or coffee room, or at a faculty meeting, he
spontaneously celebrated every person's success, whether in
publication or in the classroom, and soon everyone was
congratulating each other on personal achievements. He
led the way in donating book royalties to the department
as a way to finance activities that built a sense of commu-
nity. He shared information about the budget and other
administrative activities with anyone who would listen,
trusting the person to use the information wisely. He gave
away his hard-won insights into successful book publishing.
He initiated a Christmas party especially for secretarial
staff, with gifts tailored to their individual needs. His
giving created an extraordinary department and is the
truest example of servant leadership I have witnessed in
my career.

Mary Parker Follett years ago described the kind of leader
that motivated her. She captured the spirit of servant leadership.

The skillful leader then does not rely on personal force; he
controls his group not by dominating but by expressing it.
He stimulates what is best in us, he unifies and concen-
trates what we feel only gropingly and scatteringly, but he
never gets away from the current of which he and we are
both an integral part. He is a leader who gives form to the
inchoate energy in every man. The person who influences
me most is not he who does great deeds but he who makes
me feel I can do great deeds.[6]

Nourish the Unstated Needs of Others

In conventional management, people are conditioned to work hard by explicit opportunities to receive more money, status, advancement, and recognition. Servant leadership, however, nourishes subtle emotional and spiritual needs, creating a force for growth and change.

In *Managing from the Heart,* Hyler Bracey and others write that a servant leader has extraordinary power because he or she meets five unspoken employee requests. The inner person wants more than a steady paycheck. The unspoken requests are:

- Hear and understand me.
- Even if you disagree with me, please don't make me wrong.
- Acknowledge the greatness within me.
- Remember to look for my loving intentions.
- Tell me the truth with compassion.[7]

The servant leader addresses these subtle emotional and spiritual needs directly, and employees respond with love for their work and a full emotional commitment to solving problems and providing the highest service to customers. They grow toward the leader. The leader becomes the sun, a source of energy, as in the opening story.

Servant leaders hear, acknowledge, and honor others. They delegate outward and downward. Change can begin with the initiative of a single individual. Servant leaders have the courage to give to others. Greenleaf said that the very essence of leadership is going ahead to show the way, even without formal authority or position. "A servant leader ventures to say: I will go; come with me!"[8] The organization may not demand service to others; it may not even give permission. A leader tells the truth, takes the risk, and creates growth and change far beyond what formal expectations would warrant.

EXEMPLIFY VALUES

Those who lead from a thoughtful set of personal values provide the foundation for an enduring and prosperous corporate culture. A corporate culture can promote the growth and dignity of individuals, stand for honesty and integrity in everything the organization does, empower employees to freely inquire and solve problems, and affirm a direction for the company as a whole. But leading with high values is not always easy.

Levels of Leader Morality

Consider the following story:

> *Once upon a time, there was a young couple who, although very much in love, lived on different islands separated by an ocean bay. The boy was scheduled to leave on a long journey, and the girl felt she must see him one more time before he left. The only way from one island to the other was by ferryboat, so the girl went to the dock to ask the ferryboat captain to take her across. When he asked her for the fare, the girl admitted that she had no money. The ferryboat captain replied that money was not necessary. "I will take you to the other island if you stay with me tonight."*
>
> *The girl did not know what to do, so she went into the hills of her island to consult a wise hermit, whom we will call the first hermit. She related her story to him and asked his advice. He listened carefully to her story but said he could not tell her what to do, except to weigh the alternatives and*

sacrifices involved and come to a decision within her own heart.

The girl went down to the dock and accepted the ferryboat captain's offer.

The next day, when the girl arrived at the boy's island, the boy was there to meet her. After their embrace, the boy asked the girl how she got the fare for the crossing. When she explained what she had done, the boy pushed her away, saying, "We're through. Go away from me. I never want to see you again." Then he left her.

The girl was desolate and confused. She went into the hills of the boy's island, to search for another wise hermit who lived there. When she found the second hermit, she told him the story, asking what she could do now. The hermit replied there was nothing she could do but return home. He told her to make herself comfortable, to partake of his food, and he went down into the village to beg for her return fare. When he returned, she thanked him and asked, "How will I ever repay you?"

The hermit answered, "You owe me nothing. We owe this to each other. I am only happy to help." The girl then returned to her island.[9]

Before reading on, take a moment to rank the five characters—girl, boy, ferryboat captain, first hermit, second hermit—according to how much you like or admire them. Also think for a minute about why you like or dislike each character.

Although there is enormous variation in response to these characters, on average the second hermit is liked the most. The captain is liked least, with the first hermit, girl, and boy ranked somewhere in the middle. The characters are mirrors that can provide insights into yourself.

What does this story mean? People go through distinct stages of moral development.[10] The first stage is based on selfishness. People make decisions in order to obtain pleasure, security, power, possessions, or status, and they follow rules only to avoid punishment. The ferryboat captain represents the stage-one leader who is out for himself and doing whatever he can get away with.

The second stage is the adoption of society's norms and values. Good behavior is fulfilling the duties and obligations of the organization. People at this stage enforce laws and regulations. The boy represents stage two, subjecting the girl to his and society's values.

Stage three, the highest stage, reflects principles that transcend oneself and social rules. Behavior is motivated by the desire to develop and give to others. Leaders at stage three accept that individuals have different values, and they encourage each person's unique development. Their views on how best to serve the larger good are based on personal observation and reflection rather than on prevailing orthodoxy.

The first hermit is an empowering leader. He gives away control. The only way for the girl to grow, mature, and become a better person is to make decisions for herself. He treats the girl as a full adult. He accepts her choices unconditionally. The first hermit represents a style opposite to that of the boy, who is judgmental and wishes to control the girl's behavior to meet his needs and standards. If you disliked the first hermit, you may find it hard to empower others.

The second hermit exemplifies the servant leader. He demonstrates selflessness, generosity, brotherly love, and high moral character. He recognizes the intrinsic value of a human being and acts on that awareness. The second hermit serves others rather than grasping for himself. He represents the opposite of the ferryboat captain, who grabs for himself even if someone else gets hurt.

The important question is "Which level do you lead from?" It has been said that what people do not receive as children they spend the rest of their lives trying to get. Perhaps this is the source of the ferryboat captain's selfishness and the boy's need for control. Do you lead from these levels? If so, moving to the next level will take some effort. All of the potentials reflected by the characters are within each of us. Everyone has the potential to be selfish, to be controlling, to be vulnerable and make the wrong decision, to empower, and to serve. When the lower levels dominate, it takes more work to let the higher levels of leadership display themselves. Indeed, recognizing and acknowledging the boy, the girl, and the ferryboat captain within yourself is the starting point for growth toward becoming a leader who empowers and serves others.

Proclaim High Moral Standards

Fusion leaders are the first to demonstrate higher values. Such values make people want to follow you. In spite of the corporate realities of fear, greed, apathy, and divisiveness, true leaders trust their higher values and act accordingly. The conviction and confidence to stand up for one's beliefs are necessary in a chaotic world. People will respond.

"Humanity has every reason to place the proclaimers of high moral standards and values above the discoverers of objective truth," said Albert Einstein.[11] The proclaimers of high moral standards deserve an elevated place in organizations because they define the boundaries of life-affirming behavior. Such standards are the platform on which organizations are built. Discovers of objective truth work within a framework of values and standards. Proclaimers of high moral standards enable managers to act freely with the honesty and integrity they know to be correct.

Proclaiming high values communicates that people's worth is tied not to what they do but to who they are. It encourages everyone to bring their ethical and spiritual values to their work, and to do and become the best they are capable of. But the leader must find his or her own inner values first. To act otherwise will be seen as hypocritical.

"Statues of dragons cannot make rain; how can paintings of cakes satisfy hunger?" [Leaders] who have no real virtue within but outwardly rely on flowery cleverness are like leaky boats brightly painted—if you put mannequins in them and set them on dry ground they look fine, but once they go into the rivers and lakes, into the wind and the waves, are they not in danger? [12]

Build Honesty and Trust

Trust is the lifeblood of leader relationships. Think of each relationship you have—with spouse, child, parent, attorney, doctor, housekeeper, child care provider, landscaper, friend, boss, minister, subordinate, colleague. How does each relationship work when based on trust? How does it work when trust is missing? Trust enhances every relationship, permitting a free flow of information, caring, and shared activity.

Without trust, bad things happen. People keep secrets. True facts and feelings are not expressed. Suspicion and defensiveness arise. There is less communication and more control. Individuals protect themselves rather than cooperate. They have little desire for shared problem solving. Without trust, a leader is ineffective, and a company will never be able to change quickly in out-of-kilter conditions. Effective leaders trust others, earn trust from others, and trust themselves as well as the larger vision and forces that drive the organization.

Trust Grows out of Trustworthiness

There is a great hunger for honesty and trustworthiness. Employees want to trust their leaders. Virtually every survey about the qualities desired in leaders reports honesty and integrity at the top of the list. Kouzes and Posner surveyed thousands of managers about what they wanted in their leaders, and virtually every list was the same. The top three descriptors were *honest* (87 percent), *forward-looking* (71 percent), and *inspiring* (68 percent). At the bottom of the list were *independent* (5 percent) and *self-controlled* (5 percent). Kouzes and Posner concluded:

> *Honesty is absolutely essential to leadership. After all, if we are willing to follow someone, whether it be into battle or into the boardroom, we first want to assure ourselves that the person is worthy of our trust. We want to know that he or she is being truthful, ethical, and principled. We want to be fully confident in the integrity of our leaders.*[13]

How do you engender trust as a leader? Be bone honest. Delegate. Give up control. Encourage people to participate, and act on their suggestions. Accept ideas from others. Rely on others. Don't always have the right answer. Listen. Do away with burdensome policy and procedure manuals. Develop a shared vision with employees and let them carry it out. Focus your energy on the success of the group and not on yourself. Who can trust someone who focuses on his or her own gains at the expense of others?

Be open. Share information about the organization and yourself. Let people know you. Disclose what you really feel and believe about situations. Even when others disagree with you, they will admire your honesty and trust you. Openness means telling the truth, both good and bad. Grace Pastiak, the Tellabs executive referred to in Chapter Six, talked to her workers when the recession cut into orders. She told them publicly how bad things were. The employees decided that, to avoid layoffs, they would work a four-day week until orders picked up. Pastiak's openness indicated trust in workers, and they trusted in return, transforming a bad situation into a positive, bonding experience for the organization.[14]

Be absolutely honest, both with yourself and with others. Do what you say you will do, and when you say you will do it.

Some 70 percent of our communication is transmitted by what we do. People believe actions first, and immediately spot discrepancies between actions and words. As Kouzes and Posner say: "Leaders demonstrate what is important by how they spend their time, by the priorities on their agenda, by the questions they ask, and the people they see."[15]

A story about Gandhi illustrates absolute honesty:

> *A woman brought her son to see Gandhi because he was eating too much sugar. Despite her vigilance, the boy could not seem to give up sugar even though it was bad for him. The woman asked Gandhi if he would speak with the boy about this problem. Gandhi replied, "No, but bring him back in a week."*
>
> *In a week, the woman returned and once again petitioned Gandhi to speak with her son about his habit of eating sugar. Gandhi welcomed the boy and had a discussion with him about giving up sugar. The boy seemed to be affected by Gandhi's advice, and the woman thanked him deeply. As she turned to leave, she asked one final question: "Why did you see him today, but not last week?"*
>
> *Gandhi responded, "Because last week I was eating sugar."*[16]

Gandhi was honest and vulnerable. He admitted his own shortcomings and struggles, thereby engendering trust in others. The leader must go first in the game of trust.

If an organization is characterized by low levels of trust, leaders step up to change it. Can you find opportunities to be reliable and open? Can you take the initiative in trusting others and let them trust you in return?

V. Cheryl Womack, founder of VCW, Inc., in Kansas City, Missouri, shows her trust by giving people major responsibility for running the company and their own lives. She asks each employee to write a personal mission statement which they review annually and link to company goals. She tells them, "You have to take responsibility for your lives. There are no guarantees, only opportunities." She gives her employees substantial freedom, and challenges them to align their personal goals with those of the company. In return, they enjoy a share in the benefits their efforts bring. Some people aren't comfortable in this trust environment and leave within the first month. Among those who stay, turnover is minuscule.[17]

Bob Lengel learned an important lesson about trust from a group of his students.

> *The idea that trust grows out of trustworthiness was brought home to me in a graduate management class. The class had discussed the need to have trusting relationships in learning organizations. Just before the midterm exam, a student came to my office with two questions. "Are you going to trust us to take this exam without cheating, or are you going to separate us, make us clear our desks, and then look over our shoulders?" she asked. "How can you know, and how can we know, if we are trustworthy if you don't give us the chance to cheat?" I felt like cold water had been thrown in my face. I had been sending conflicting messages to the class. My actions spoke louder than my words.*
>
> *On exam day, I handed out the exam, told students they could not use notes or references of any kind, but they were free to pick up their belongings and find a comfortable place to take the exam. The only requirement was to return the completed test within three hours.*
>
> *In personal journals handed in the following week, almost everyone reported a deep reaction to the demonstration of trust. One student wrote that she had forgotten the theory I had asked about on the second question. She was working by herself with no one in sight. Her notebook was in the chair beside her. She had to face the challenge of*

whether she was trustworthy, and it troubled her deeply.
She did not cheat and lost thirty points on a hundred–
point exam because she was honest. Spending thirty points
to find she was worth trusting was far more important
than a better grade.

Trusting your vision for the organization, and trusting that people will move toward the vision, means having faith in the intangible, for there is no guarantee that things will work. Trusting subtle forces is what will enable you to give up traditional control. Where control has hitherto depended on close supervision, it can now come from the collective adherence to your organization's principles and vision. But for this shift to occur, you must have "faith in the process" as well as in concrete outcomes and measures.

Faith provides serenity in the face of uncertainty. Unexpected problems always arise, and it is faith that lets the leader trust the principles underlying the organization's forward momentum. There is no way to control everything in a chaotic world. The leader's role is to affirm values, vision, and people and then let go, having faith in the result.

Faith is more powerful than reason. Those raised to be scientific and rational in their approach to the world often eschew faith, believing only in things that can be measured and documented. That is the basis of rational management. But leadership draws from the higher understanding of the leader and the led.

GROWTH OF YOURSELF AND OTHERS

Self-awareness promotes moral leadership. Vaclav Havel, a playwright, dissident, and prisoner of the Soviet regime before becoming president of Czechoslovakia and then of the Czech Republic, said to the U.S. Congress: "Consciousness precedes being." After living so many years "pinned under a boulder," he came to understand that "the salvation of this human world lies nowhere else than in the human heart, in the human power to reflect, in human meekness, and in human responsibility."[18]

Leaders can increase their impact by addressing their own morality. Leader, know thyself. To change an organization's values, and ultimately the world, leaders take responsibility for their own level of moral development. If the second hermit is the character you most admired in the fable earlier in this chapter, can you take responsibility for bringing his traits of generosity, selflessness, and forbearance into your everyday life? Can you understand that the selfishness of the ferryboat captain exists within you, as does the judgmental boy? By admitting and accepting these less admirable qualities, you allow the fresh air and light of compassion to heal them, enabling higher values to emerge. This is the challenge each leader faces in the pursuit of integrity.

Leaders project their light or their shadow onto their world. They steer their course by their internal reality, by the demons and angels that live there. As Parker J. Palmer expressed it, "A leader is a person who must take special responsibility for what's going on inside him or herself, inside his or her consciousness, lest the act of leadership create more harm than good."[19] A leader projects values toward others, often unconsciously. Do a leader's actions and decisions demonstrate a commitment to the highest good for all concerned, or does the leader act from his or her own anger, greed, jealousy, insecurity, or fear of failure?

The way to avoid the latter course is to become conscious of your inner self and values. Self-awareness is sunlight. Bringing into the light one's true motives and values, even when selfish and negative, is healing, and provides the strength to act from a nobler place.

Self-awareness brings out higher potential in both the leader and the led. Becoming whole means uniting with your essential self, which enables you to touch the higher potential in others. Associates then trust the vision, love what they do, think independently, express their creativity, and maintain the highest standards of honesty. They and the organization thrive.

To Thine Own Self Be True

Palmer explained how leaders grow toward greatness by looking within and being true to what they find:

> *Great leadership comes from people who have made that downward journey through violence and terror, who have touched the deep place where we are in community with each other, and can help take others to that place. That is what great leadership is all about.*
>
> *Everywhere I look I see institutions that are depriving large numbers of people of their identity so that a few people can enhance theirs. . . .*
>
> *But if you are ever with people (or in an organization led by a person) who know "all the way down" who they are, whose identity doesn't depend on a role which might be taken away at any moment, you are with people and in settings which give you identity, which empower you to be someone. . . . The great spiritual gift that comes as one takes the inward journey is to know for certain that "who I am" does not depend on "what I do."*[20]

Many managers avoid this inner journey because it is difficult and threatening. But struggle is part of the leadership mantle. Leaders are the first to suffer. *Leaders step from the known into the unknown.* A leader path of growth, service, and empowerment is filled with doubt and uncertainty. Franklin D. Roosevelt, Gandhi, and Martin Luther King, Jr., all wrestled with inner torment. But they also embraced a higher path. The credibility essential for leadership is earned by developing one-self to match the values that people want to follow.

One effect of not looking inward is the "Sunday neurosis" that afflicts many managers. Without work to keep them busy, they look into a void on Sunday and realize the lack of meaningful content in their lives. Managers often bring work home to help distract them from this emptiness. Yet only by looking directly into the void can they be healed.

Remember, you can't engage the higher potential in others without first finding it in yourself. You can't change others; you can only change yourself. Changing yourself gives others a leadership guide and signals the freedom and opportunity for growth.

This chapter has been about personal integrity, which is an essential element in a world of disequilibrium, chaos, and interconnectedness. Integrity means wholeness. It means stepping outside narrow self-interest to serve others, acknowledging the interconnection of self, associates, family, organization, community, and world. Integrity means affirming and empowering others and setting high moral standards. We are one with each other and one with the universe. Helping others helps us. All living things respond to the light of the sun.

Several elements of fusion leadership integrity are summarized in Exhibit 9.1.

There are examples of leaders whose mission is to build a better organization and a better world. One is Isaac Tiggert, who founded Hard Rock Café with a partner. Frustrated by the separation of social classes in England, where a baker and banker could not meet in a restaurant to talk, he aspired to break that system. He personally hired every employee, and was proud of having twenty-five native languages represented among his staff. He trained poorly educated people in kindness, politeness, and classlessness. Everyone participated in the profits. Considerations of the heart and common courtesy overruled line authority. "Love all, serve all" became the guiding value.

Exhibit 9.1. Integrity

Conventional Strong-Force View	Fusion Leader Subtle View
• Maintain personal honesty	• Inspire trust
• Pursue self-interest	• Share information, power, resources
• Seek autonomy	• Seek interdependence
• Solve obvious problems	• Meet unstated needs
• Rise above others	• Serve others
• Develop personal career	• Affirm, build, mentor others
• Boast of great deeds	• Acknowledge others' great deeds
• Judge others	• Empower others, faith in others
• Go along with moral standards	• Set high moral standards
• Deepen insight into organization	• Deepen insight into self

All I did is put spirit and business together in that big mixing bowl and add love. I didn't care about anything but the people. Just cherish them, look after them, be sensitive to them and their lives. That important relationship with my staff is what made the Hard Rock, nothing else! It was an opportunity to blend spiritual life and business life.[21]

When our internal values are clear, we can live according to our code despite chaos, disagreement, and rapid change. Leaders who act from high moral values can lead others through destabilized and oppressive times while maintaining or enhancing others' self-worth and accomplishment. When people act from selfishness, greed, and fear, they try to take from the organization while denying the identity and needs of others. When leaders dig down deep and learn who they are, they can shift the focus toward serving and developing others.

Robert Greenleaf, who originated the notion of servant leadership, believed the greatest enemy to organizations and to society was fuzzy thinking on the part of good, intelligent, vital people who decide not to lead, not to serve. The real enemy is people who will not look inside, heal themselves, and thereby heal the organization. "In short, the enemy is strong natural servants who have the potential to lead but do not lead, or who choose to follow a non-servant."[22] They suffer. The organization suffers. Society suffers. Integrity starts with you.

Personal Remembering

■ If it is immoral to prevent those around you from growing to their fullest potential, are you being moral?

■ What are your deepest values? What are your company's primary values? What do you learn by comparing these?

■ A Hindu holy man said, "My life is my message, and my message is love." What message are you sending with your life?

■ Do your followers live in your shadow or in your light? What does this mean to you?

PART THREE

UNLOCKING SUBTLE FORCES THROUGH ORGANIZATIONAL FUSION

CHAPTER TEN

ORGANIZATIONAL FUSION

Tom and Diana were planning a vacation. Diana expressed reservations about going to the same resort, with the same golf, the same restaurants, and maybe even the same room they had experienced for the previous nine years. Tom liked the familiar and the routine, and cajoled her into cheering up and enjoying the time away from their busy careers. While in their room at the resort, the lights went out. Diana remembered seeing candles and matches in a kitchen drawer. Tom insisted on going to the car and getting a lantern-flashlight he kept for emergencies. When he returned, the living room was in a soft glow of candlelight. He blew out the candles and set the flashlight on its base to throw greater light into the room. "Now that takes care of it," he said. "We'll have plenty of light so long as the batteries last." Diana looked at him thoughtfully and said, "I think you've identified what's wrong with our marriage, what's wrong with our lives."

Tom insisted there was nothing wrong with their marriage or their lives, but for once, instead of arguing his

*point, he asked what she meant. Diana explained that the
flashlight was a metaphor for their lives, which were filled
with technology, efficiency, electricity, structure, cellular
phones, remote-control superficiality, and quick answers to
problems.*

*"The candlelight is missing from our lives," she said.
"Candlelight is softer, more personal, spiritual, sponta-
neous, deeper, less efficient, and easily extinguished. Candlelight illuminates relationships, while a flashlight enables
your company's work to get done. Candlelight represents
uncertainty, the flashlight represents certainty and routine,
just like our vacations here year after year."*

*As Diana talked, she became more resolute. She asked
that their lives not be run by business schedules and technology, and if they couldn't change this together, she would consider finding candlelight in her life in some other way. Tom
heard her, felt her resolve, and agreed to help bring candlelight back into their lives. He felt afraid of losing her, but he
also was afraid of the unknown world he would be entering.*[1]

Candlelight versus flashlight is a metaphor for people versus
technology, subtle forces versus strong forces. Candlelight
reaches through to the inner world, whereas flashlight shines
on the outer world. One candle can light a thousand other candles without diminishing its own light. Yet one candle can easily be extinguished.

The previous six chapters were about the subtle forces of individual leadership, which are represented by candlelight rather
than by flashlight. The subtle forces need initial protection
from the strong forces in order to burn brightly.

The change and uncertainty facing Tom are in some sense
facing many managers. The industrial age and its mass production mindset have left their residue in every organization.
The modern corporation, with its central authority, routine
practices, interchangeable parts, and enforced conformity,

showed that it could produce a huge quantity of standardized products and services. But people were routinized, too. A "leader" was a director and controller of assembly lines and those who kept them running.[2]

Command and control were antithetical to the human spirit. The most abundant yet least utilized resource was human creativity and ingenuity. The candle had been blown out. Flashlight technology dominated.

The industrial world now seems on the cusp of a new age in which the human spirit in organizations will be reborn. This will entail a massive shift in organizational form, culture, and leadership. And with this change may come the regeneration of vision, heart, courage, integrity, mindfulness, and deeper communication. This regeneration will be in harmony with personal subtle forces and will enable companies to change fluidly with an out-of-kilter environment. Change may become as natural as sunlight or rainfall.

Organizations today are caught in this struggle of transformation. The good news is that certain social innovations are facilitating fundamental yet rapid shifts within organizations. Opportunities are available to create organizational fusion on a large scale, to transform corporate culture and mindsets, to recapture the candlelight of subtle forces. In this chapter, we will explore the transition to a new organizational form. The remaining chapters will describe the new social technologies of organization-wide fusion and the principles that guide them. These last four chapters show how to unlock the spirit of change that will usher in a new and enduring way of doing business.

THE FUSION PARADOX

Organizational fusion grows from sustained organizational conversation across traditional boundaries. Organizational fusion is about breaking down barriers between people. It involves a shift from "I" to "We," from separated selves to community. The conversations it encourages enable a large number of participants to discover their subtle forces together.

Exhibit 10.1 revisits the fusion process outlined in Chapter One. Organizational fusion surmounts the boundaries of structure, hierarchy, and habit to integrate the interior voice of employees with the exterior needs of organization and environment.

Bringing together people for organizational fusion also creates personal fusion. Individuals achieve growth and identity through these relationships. People achieve their greatest learning and change together. Feedback from others is how we develop a self-concept—and learn about our skills and gifts. Conversations with people unlike ourselves help liberate us from limiting ideas. The more we engage in conversation and relationships across boundaries, the more we become whole as individuals.

Yet we find that managers often resist opportunities for such conversations—and the resulting fusion—because they fear losing their individual autonomy. Rugged individualism is their ideal. Relationships based on authentic conversation that builds on yearnings for common ground and individual expression strike them as too touchy-feely. But they are unlikely to break through to subtle forces until they take down these barriers.

A manager's conditioned ego may act like a trapped monkey. In India, monkeys are trapped by placing nuts in a pot with a narrow neck. The monkey inserts its hand to grasp the prize, but the full hand is too large to draw back through the opening. The monkey will not let go, despite being trapped. In much the same way, managers may hold onto position, status, security, and hierarchical structure even though they could enlarge their life and their productive powers by letting go. If they would only relax their grip on the externals they so prize, subtle creativity and ingenuity from the interior self would emerge, enabling them to enjoy the benefits of creative freedom and a

Exhibit 10.1
Organizational Fusion

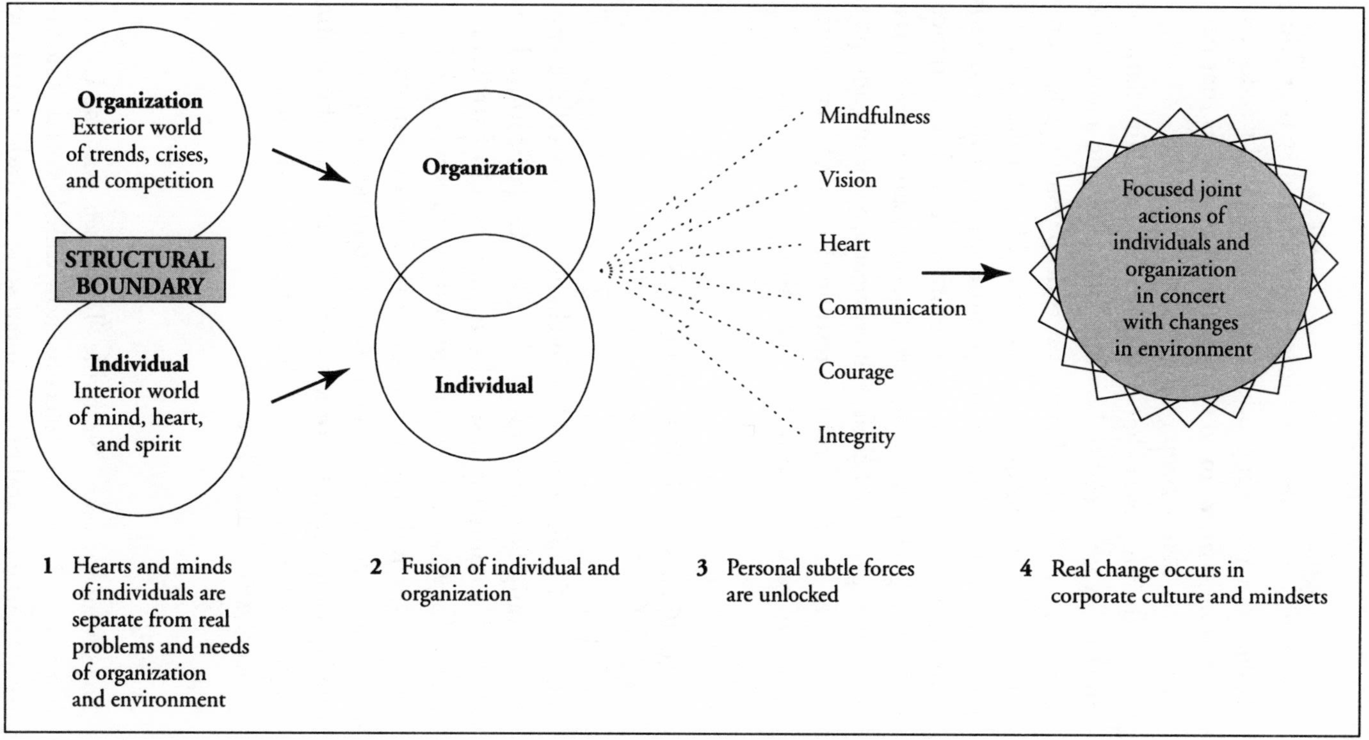

Organization
Exterior world
of trends, crises,
and competition

STRUCTURAL BOUNDARY

Individual
Interior world
of mind, heart,
and spirit

Organization

Individual

Mindfulness

Vision

Heart

Communication

Courage

Integrity

Focused joint
actions of
individuals and
organization
in concert
with changes
in environment

1 Hearts and minds
of individuals are
separate from real
problems and needs
of organization
and environment

2 Fusion of individual and
organization

3 Personal subtle forces
are unlocked

4 Real change occurs in
corporate culture and mindsets

shared vision. The feared loss of individuality is an illusion. Collaborative fusion produces connection and freedom at the same time—freedom to express the subtle forces that perhaps have never before been recognized.[3]

The fusion power that comes from joining in relationships must be experienced to be understood. Taking action to connect and serve with others answers deep yearnings for community and heightens one's appreciation of individual differences and gifts. Individuality is never more apparent than in a fusion community. When connected to others, people experience the joy of being who they really are. In conversation, they at last express their personal beliefs, values, creativity, vision, and passion. No longer are they forced to restrain their intelligence and creativity to conform with the mass production mindset.

UNLOCKING SUBTLE FORCES
IN AN ORGANIZATION

The new fusion approaches to change are powerful compared with change techniques of the past. Organizational fusion changes a company fast. The strong forces of structure and technology can be moderated and conditions established to nurture open dialogue, self-organization, dreams concerning corporate destiny, and opportunities to make a difference. People typically yearn to come together to increase the volume of their subtle voices. One of the companies that initiated such a process is Northern Telecom.

Nortel

For seventeen years, Nashville, Tennessee, was the U.S. headquarters of Northern Telecom, now called Nortel. The visibility, importance, and management style at headquarters created a very positive culture at the Nashville campus. People were proud to be with Nortel and had high morale, a strong identity, and a real sense of community. After the headquarters operation was moved in 1993, Nashville was downsized, and morale plummeted. The remnants included some twenty functional units, with each function reporting to a superior in another part of the world. Though based in the same city, the functions lacked a single boss or common identity. Approximately one thousand employees spread over four locations became fragmented and disgruntled, as reflected in low employee satisfaction scores.

The vice president of finance became sensitive to the low morale and wondered if something could be done. He contacted Bonnie Woodward, Director of Worldwide Customer Service and Order Management, who was known to have an interest in creating a positive culture and had a reputation as a successful leader. Together they established a Work Environmental and Revitalization Committee (WERC) to investigate ways to improve culture and morale. Woodward headed the committee, which explored a number of options, including an invitation for us to consult on the matter.

We saw a company in which managers spoke wistfully of employees' yearning for a greater sense of community, for involvement, for a renewed sense of belonging. The malaise was seen in the elevators, where people stayed silent rather than speak to each other. Most employees didn't know anyone outside their immediate work area and felt frustrated at the fragmentation, but didn't know how to change it. Some middle managers were thought to be blocking culture change by holding onto autocratic leadership styles. The questions for this company became "How can relationships among individuals, departments, and hierarchy levels be improved?" and "How can autocratic managers be persuaded of the need for change?"

The answer was a fusion event, which was made possible by the leadership of Woodward and WERC and the financial sponsorship of the finance vice president. The stated purpose of the event was to define a shared vision that would ensure Nortel Nashville's future, clarify its role in the larger corporation, create an open environment that fostered innovation and creativity, build a sense of community, and explore directions for personal and professional growth. Approximately sixty people, representing the full diversity of the Nashville campus, were invited to the retreat. They would offer a wide variety of perspectives and could become catalysts for change in their respective areas. The event, held at an off-campus site, lasted three days.

On the first day, participants were engaged in conversation that explored their common ground and shared history. Then the focus shifted to their current situation and the difficulties, challenges, and environmental changes they faced together. The second day was spent helping groups see their own responsibility for the state of affairs at the Nashville campus. Then a vision of the future was created that all participants could support. On the third day, specific activities or projects were identified that could solve the problems discussed on the first day and achieve the vision created on the second. Participants joined action teams that would work to implement these changes back on campus.

Retreat participants worked primarily at tables of eight employees drawn from different parts of the organization. This arrangement helped to break down barriers and promote conversation across all the units of Nortel Nashville. By the third day, the process of talking across departments, combined with the identification of present challenges and a shared dream for the future, released an explosion of energy. Leaders emerged everywhere. People were enthusiastic about what they were doing and could not wait to start implementing changes. The role of Nortel leadership and WERC at this point was to provide support so that action teams could follow through at their work sites.

The outcome of the retreat was nine action teams, as shown in Exhibit 10.2, a brochure distributed to announce a follow-up employee rally. All employees were invited to hear about the retreat and volunteer to serve on committees. The brochure also lists the members of the Work Environmental and Revitalization Committee, which coordinated the nine teams. Enthusiasm for the changes lasted several months, and some of the action committees were still active as we were writing this book in 1997. Perhaps most important, people are now greeting and talking to each other on the elevators!

The Call to Community

Why did an event like the one at Nortel have such impact, compared with conventional change efforts? Fusion breaks down barriers by means of guided conversations and thereby releases underlying subtle forces that have been suppressed in the traditional structure. In the case of Nortel, the future was shaped not by a randomly convened group of employees but by one that represented the whole system. A critical mass is needed at the fusion event for it to have impact at the work site.

Many leaders appeared from unexpected places. The most skeptical manager became an enthusiastic supporter of change. People from the repair facility, from finance and marketing, from almost every location began expressing their real feelings and asserting leadership. We saw the courage of new initiatives, authentic communication, genuine receptiveness to opposite views, enthusiasm for the shared vision, and unselfish service to the nine action projects. The subtle forces of leadership emerged in a short time across a broad spectrum of employees. A top-level Nortel person mentioned that for the first time, after hearing the wisdom and reasonableness of the conversations, he really wanted to let go of control. He saw that people really did care about the organization, and if trusted, they

Exhibit 10.2
Nortel Nashville Brochure: Report on Fusion Event

Shaping the Future of Nortel Nashville

National Guard Armory   **EMPLOYEE RALLY!**   September 26, 1996

Nashville Employees Searching and Working for a Better Future

The Work Environmental and Revitalization Committee (WERC) was formed as a result of concerns by the Nashville Leadership Council—among them that the Nashville locations "lacked a sense of community."

When concerns first surfaced seven months ago, the Leadership Council was aware that employees were not satisfied, but understanding what was at the core of the dissatisfaction proved difficult. WERC's job was to find out why.

Composed of Nortel Nashville employees representing various departments, WERC began

its task of exploring various ways to improve work relationships/effectiveness and job satisfaction among Nashville employees.

A three-day off-site meeting named, appropriately, "Future Search" was proposed.

With the help of Human Resources, WERC created a "suggested attendee list" for the session that represented employees from each division. The list was careful to achieve a balance among genders, races, ages and band levels.

During the three-day meeting, participants created a "mind map" that charted themes, trends, and issues in the

workplace. The ones that reflected the most concern became the basis for the formation of nine committees.

"The power and excitement that was generated at Future Search was phenomenal," said Bonnie Woodward, WERC chairperson. "People took ownership for these issues and embraced them."

Woodward does not see the Future Search team as another Employee Council or "Excellence" initiative. "We see the committee surviving leadership changes," said Woodward. "This is driven by employees for employees. It's truly up to us this time."

A New Paradigm

This diagram visualizes a new paradigm shaping the Nortel Nashville community. The mission is to define our future and begin to bring about a positive shift in our work environment. The Leadership Council sponsors WERC's efforts in building synergy amongst the Future Search Committees. Their responsibilities are to focus on their specific areas and explore opportunities to move us toward a shared vision and future.

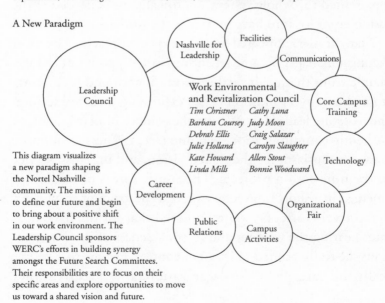

Facilities
Nashville for Leadership
Communications
Leadership Council
Work Environmental and Revitalization Council
Tim Christner   Cathy Luna
Barbara Coursey   Judy Moon
Debrah Ellis   Craig Salazar
Julie Holland   Carolyn Slaughter
Kate Howard   Allen Stout
Linda Mills   Bonnie Woodward
Core Campus Training
Technology
Career Development
Organizational Fair
Public Relations
Campus Activities

Exhibit 10.2
Nortel Nashville Brochure: Report on Fusion Event, cont'd

The Future Search Committees' Missions, Goals, and Members

Career Development—*Jason Hubbard,* Chair
To build the structure and provide the tools
that support Nashville campus employees in
their career development.

Burgess Oliver,   *Debbie Banks*
  Executive Sponsor   *Marin Ceri*
Allen Stout, WERC   *Teri Manghane*
  Committee Member   *Tony Van Atta*
Jill Austin
Nancy Price

Core Training—*Jill Austin,* Chair
Build a platform to deliver basic soft skills
training and diversity awareness to the
Nashville campus.

Alex Stillwell,   *Jeff Vinson*
  Executive Sponsor   *Rob Thompson*
Vance Riley   *Nancy Price*
Cheryl Patton
Linda Mills

Organizational Fair—*Teresa Galcy,* Chair
To plan an organizational fair at which all
employees have an opportunity to become
aware of the diverse organizations in Nashville
and to learn more about them.

Roger Schecter,   *Diana Douglas*
  Executive Sponsor   *Rich Kotler*
Doug Kasten,   *Andy Reynolds*
  Executive Sponsor
Jan Payne
Dick Rykwalder

Communications—*Tony Van Atta,* Chair
To foster an increased sense of community by
offering enhanced modes of communication
to involve employees.

Don Caldwell,   *Lina Mills*
  Executive Sponsor   *Kate Howard*
Judith Marr   *Carolyn Slaughter*
Judy Moon   *Robert Butters*
Rick Kotler   *Dick Rykwalder*
Jan Payne
Kelvin Pillow

Public Relations—*Michael Keef,* Chair
To offer employee support to the existing
public relations effort increasing PR for
Nortel Nashville.   *Don Caldwell*
Fran Scott,   *Judith Marr*
  Executive Director   *Thomas Fulton*
Alex Stillwell
Loretta Smith

Technology Awareness—*Monte Selfers,* Chair
To communicate with and provide education to
the Nashville campus on available technology and
reduce the fear of technology by making it fun!

Deborah Armstrong   *Johnny Brock*
Nancy Burkepile   *Diana Douglas*
Wilson Herndon

Campus Activities—*Kelvin Pillow,* Chair
To serve as a resource to the Employee Council
and Employee Activity Committee to increase
overall employee participation in planned activities.
To improve communications, structure and
deliverance of the groups' initiatives.

Sherman Frierson   *Mark Pierret*
Johnny Brock   *Craig Salazar*

Nashville for Leadership—*Bonnie Woodward,* Chair
Define the leadership competencies in order to
develop and implement an appropriate leadership
model for Nortel Nashville.
                                    Nancy Burkepile
Debbie Banks   *Debrah Ellis*
Tim Christner   *John Lebowitz*
Cathy Luna   *Bennie Smith*
Judy Moon   *Marilyn Trautman*
Allen Stout

Facilites—*Wendell Saerrell,* Chair
To guide and enhance the evolution of the
Nashville-area work environment while creating
an atmosphere that fosters teamwork,
communication and enthusiasm.

Jeff Eason,   *Kate Howard*
  Leadership Cncl. Sponsor   *Loretta Smith*
Kay Hollandsworth   *Teresa Galry*
Judy Moon
Monica Lesser

Reproduced by permission of Don Caldwell, Nortel Public Relations, Nashville, TN.

would act in its best interest. He saw people change in their potential to assume leadership responsibility, and he changed in his willingness to support and empower them.

The forces released by organizational fusion in the larger group created a new sense of community. This feeling illustrated the fusion paradox: when people allow themselves to become an intimate part of a large group, rather than losing autonomy or control they gain freedom to express who they truly are. Subtle forces expressed in an individual manifest as leadership. In the Nortel group, the subtle forces created an entire community of leaders.

Fusion into community is part of a significant trend. In the evolution of change management, there have been four distinct stages:

1. Outside experts were hired to solve company problems. This approach was based on *scientific management* that originated in the early 1900s and is still used by consultants today.

2. Employees solved problems. This is the way of *participative management,* which was introduced in the 1960s and continues into the 1990s.

3. Outside experts improved whole systems. As the *systems view* emerged, consultants realized that the interdependencies within large companies required changes that would affect the entire system. Thus experts engineered major innovations, such as the introduction of new computer-based systems or work processes, and the organization was left to deal with the consequent disruption among employees.

4. Employees participate in the improvement of whole systems. This emerging stage of change management is what we call organizational fusion. It is a large-scale collaborative process that breaks down barriers across the system and uses the collective intelligence of the workforce to create and implement needed changes. When fusion occurs, community results, and many employees become leaders. This is real empowerment.[4]

In this fourth stage, the expert's role is simply to help design a process that enables the organization to engage in fusion and change itself.

FUNDAMENTALS OF CHANGE

When a company group like Nortel undergoes significant change, the reason lies in the interior yearning of employees (Exhibit 3.1) rather than in the more obvious exterior pressures from the organization. Conversations are guided to help employees act from their desire for involvement, voice, community, impact, and worth. The yearning to express personal subtle forces is often unrecognized in top-down change programs, but it is the basis for organizational fusion that transforms people and organizations.

The Yearnings That Underlie Fusion Change

The whole thrust of organizational fusion is to unleash the natural ingenuity and inherent capability that have been suppressed in the traditional hierarchy. Fusion gives voice to interior yearnings. The process removes the organizational constraints that have prevented people from changing. Employees are no longer seen as a problem to be solved, and there is no longer an attempt to impose change from above. Instead, conditions are created in which individuals' inherent potential is released.

Our work in helping groups achieve fusion has shaped our thinking about the basic elements of personal and organizational changes. Other research that has guided our thinking is that of the American Quality Foundation; G. Clotaire Rapaille, founder of Archetype Studies, Inc.; and two AT&T managers, Marilyn R. Zuckerman and Lewis J. Hatala.[5] These researchers directly examine unconscious yearnings and potentials, as well as the settings that awaken rather than suppress them.

Latent potentials are uncovered by guided discussion and free-association exercises, which reveal participants' deepest feelings about change. Meditation and the telling of stories from childhood are also important tools.

In Chapter Three, we described how people were attracted to advertisements featuring open doors but disliked images of closed doors. If asked directly, consumers could not explain this difference. Their reactions were anchored in experiences stored in their unconscious. The researchers we have named developed methods that enabled subjects to touch unconscious feelings about change that had been formed during their childhood.

A number of key generalizations can be drawn from the research into latent feelings:

1. Americans dislike control and being controlled. Control represents thwarted opportunity, limitation, and rigidity.

2. They like the challenge of becoming the "best."

3. They like to work on breakthrough opportunities rather than incremental tasks. Something badly broken is more appealing than something in need of minor repair or improvement.

4. Caring and emotional involvement propel them forward into change.

5. They have a preference for action over analysis.

6. They are motivated by their personal dreams for the future—and demotivated when such dreams are blocked.

Again drawing on common images from the childhoods of respondents, researchers found that successful improvement in the lives of Americans tends to involve four distinct elements, which appear below. These elements are important for changing people in adulthood and for changing organizations.

1. *Failure or crisis.* In childhood, this could be getting a low grade on an assignment or trying to ride a bicycle and falling down. Crisis or failure is a key element that opens people to substantive change.

2. *A vision for the future.* The vision is a personal dream of what can be, what the child really wants. Perhaps the dream is to get an A on an assignment, receive the approval of a teacher, or learn to ride a bike. Typically, in successful change experiences, a mentor or coach helps the child work through and come to terms with failure, awaken the dream, and then begin steps toward achieving that dream.

3. *Challenge.* Achieving one's dream is hard work. Many obstacles have to be overcome. The child learning to ride a bike may fall down repeatedly, or the student may have to redo an assignment several times. But struggle energizes people and challenges them to overcome all odds. They benefit from a mentor or coach during this period of personal improvement.

4. *Feedback in the form of celebration.* Once the challenge has been surmounted and the dream achieved, feedback is essential. Perhaps Mom and Dad take the child for an ice cream cone after she has learned to ride the bike, or have a special dinner to honor the successful science project. Celebration crystallizes the success and brings closure, enabling the individual to refocus on the next activity. And when things don't work, feedback helps the person face the reality of failure and begin the struggle for improvement again.

The research findings that support a fusion approach to change are summarized in Exhibit 10.3. The conventional view is based on personal ego and traditional structure, which maintain that failure is bad, control is good, people are the problem that management must fix, employees change because they are forced to do so, and individuals prefer the easy path. The view on which fusion change is based is the opposite in every respect, appealing to the unconscious yearnings that represent people's highest motivation.

Effective change leaders create a sense of urgency and crisis that makes people face reality and opens them to change. They awaken and articulate the shared vision, mentoring and coaching employees to take on the challenge. They provide support during the struggle. Finally, as the organization successfully embraces change, the leader takes time to celebrate, rewarding individuals for their struggle and preparing them for the next battle.

The Fusion Mindset Shift

Many participants came to the Nortel event skeptical and defensive. Managers didn't want to change themselves and didn't believe that a single event could bring about culture change. But

Exhibit 10.3. Attitudes to Individual Change

Conventional Strong-Force View	Fusion Leader Subtle View
• Failure or crisis signifies bad management	• Failure or crisis awakens people to action
• Breakdown is bad	• Breakdown triggers breakthrough
• Control is good	• People hate to be controlled
• Change is needed to fix people and the problems they create	• Change happens when people are emotionally involved in the process
• People change when forced to do so	• People change to further their personal dream
• People are supposed to change	• People change when cared about by a mentor or coach
• Change must be planned	• Change is the outcome of experiment and risk taking
• People prefer the easy, familiar path	• People are at their best when challenged by difficulty
• Leaders cause organizations to change	• Leaders modify conditions that prevent change

the fusion process is larger than any individual, and no person can control it. As more people participate in the conversations, they are drawn into a whole larger than themselves, which melts the ego defenses that resist change. A mindset shift occurs.

Most managers are convinced of the rightness of their own way of doing business and believe strongly that *other* parts of the organization need changing. That's why managers are willing to attend an event—to help others change. They often operate on the assumption that their job is to design goals for their colleagues, control tasks with as little dependence on others as possible, keep their personal thoughts and feelings separate from others except as absolutely needed, and encourage rationality and objectivity, thereby protecting people from negative emotions.[6]

This management paradigm is overturned in a fusion event. During such an event, participants flood the system with personal viewpoints and information; thus everyone is involved in the decision process. Free and informed choice occurs among participants, and emotional commitment is generated for implementation of changes. The entire fusion event circumvents resistance, so that implementation of change is achieved easily and fast.

At Nortel, several managers seemed in denial about their own need to change, preferring to blame others. But as they became involved in personal conversation and heard issues surface from around the organization, they began to see their own part in the problem. In a fusion event, denial is often followed by confusion and frustration, perhaps even anger at the widely differing concerns and beliefs being expressed in the room. The mountain of problems seems so huge as to be insurmountable. This triggers a crisis of hopelessness. But gradually, through the creation of a joint vision and identification with action teams, renewal occurs. Participants search for hope, a candle lit in the dark. They see that they are in this situation together, and they create a shared dream for the future. Gathered on this common ground, they accept the challenge to make real change happen, and a flood of enthusiasm is released. Everything and everyone come together in a unity of sorts, in community. Resistance melts as everyone participates in the design and implementation of significant change initiatives and projects.

By the end of a fusion event such as Nortel's, managers and other participants have changed their minds. They have suddenly realized that every important problem can be solved, and that the group has the power to make real impact. People who started out withdrawn or skeptical or defensive often become leaders. A collective mindset shift occurs that moves a company toward partnership and empowerment and away from command and control. The subtle forces are free. Community, the secret of organizational fusion, emerges. This is a change that people must go through together.

Personal Remembering

- Are you traveling through life by candlelight or flashlight? Explore what this means to you.

- Tell a story about a key event or milestone in which you underwent personal change. How does your experience support or contradict the ideas about change in this chapter?

- What would you most like to change about yourself? What would you most like to change about your organization? What insight do you gain by comparing these desired changes?

- What does being in community mean to you? Does your organization reflect this level of community? Why?

CHAPTER ELEVEN

FUSION TECHNOLOGIES AND EVENTS

"Good morning," said the fox.

"Good morning," the little prince responded politely. "Who are you? You are very pretty to look at."

"I am a fox," the fox said.

"Come and play with me," proposed the little prince. "I am so unhappy."

"I cannot play with you," the fox said. "I am not tamed."

"What does that mean—'tame'?"

"It is an act too often neglected," said the fox. "It means to establish ties."

"To establish ties?"

"Just that," said the fox. "To me, you are still nothing more than a little boy who is just like a hundred thousand other little boys, and I have no need of you. And you, on your part, have no need of me. To you, I am nothing more than a fox like a hundred thousand other foxes. But if you tame me, then we shall need each other. To me, you will be unique in all the world. To you, I shall be unique in all the world. . ."

"I am beginning to understand," said the little prince.

"My life is very monotonous," said the fox. "But if you tame me, it will be as if the sun came to shine on my life. I shall know the sound of a step that will be different from all the others. Other steps send me hurrying back underneath the ground. Yours will call me, like music, out of my burrow. . . Please—tame me!"

"I want to very much," the little prince replied. "But I have not much time. I have friends to discover, and a great many things to understand."

"One only understands the things that one tames," said the fox. "Men have no more time to understand anything. They buy things all ready-made at the shops. But there is no shop anywhere where one can buy friendship, and so men have no friends any more. If you want a friend, tame me. . ."

"What must I do to tame you?" asked the little prince.

"You must be very patient," replied the fox. "First you will sit down at a little distance from me—like that—in the grass. I shall look at you out of the corner of my eye, and you will say nothing. Words are the source of misunderstandings. But you will sit a little closer to me, every day. . ."

The next day the little prince came back.

"It would have been better to come back at the same hour," said the fox. "If, for example, you come at four o'clock in the afternoon, then at three I shall begin to be happy. I shall feel happier and happier as the hour advances. At four o'clock I shall already be worrying and jumping about. I shall show you how happy I am!"[1]

The little prince is learning about relationships, about the sustained conversation that builds emotional ties. He's taking his first steps toward community, toward building a fusion-based relationship. He is starting to move from "I" to "We." Connecting with another takes time, and a comfortable place, but for both the fox and the little prince, it yielded great satisfaction.

The tie between the little prince and the fox occurred through conversation and is a metaphor for what happens to organizational participants in a fusion event. At a fusion event, managers learn about relationship ties and build a culture on those ties rather than on a formal control structure. They may start in denial about the need for ties or for a new organizational mindset ("I'm too busy for this sort of thing"), but end up in renewal that transforms the company's culture. A fusion event reduces structural and ego barriers between people, thereby freeing subtle forces such as vision, courage, and heart. The event provides the growing field for these capabilities in each manager.

In this chapter, we will describe how to design the paradigm shift away from conventional management toward fusion leadership.

THE FUSION MICROCOSM AND FUSION TECHNOLOGIES

A fusion event contains a microcosm of the organization. In a few cases, the entire organization may participate, but usually 100 percent participation in a single event is not possible. The principle of the microcosm is illustrated in Exhibit 11.1. Representatives from all parts of the organization, and often key stakeholders from outside the organization, join together to engage in sustained, guided conversation. Accessing the viewpoints of all groups in an organization could take months under normal circumstances; in a fusion event, it happens in three days. The acceleration of change in the microcosm is remarkable, and creates a critical mass for fusion that can sustain itself back at the organization.

The microcosm also serves as a petri dish in which a new culture strain is created. The microcosm embodies the new qualities of culture and behavior the organization is trying to

Exhibit 11.1
The Function of the Microcosm

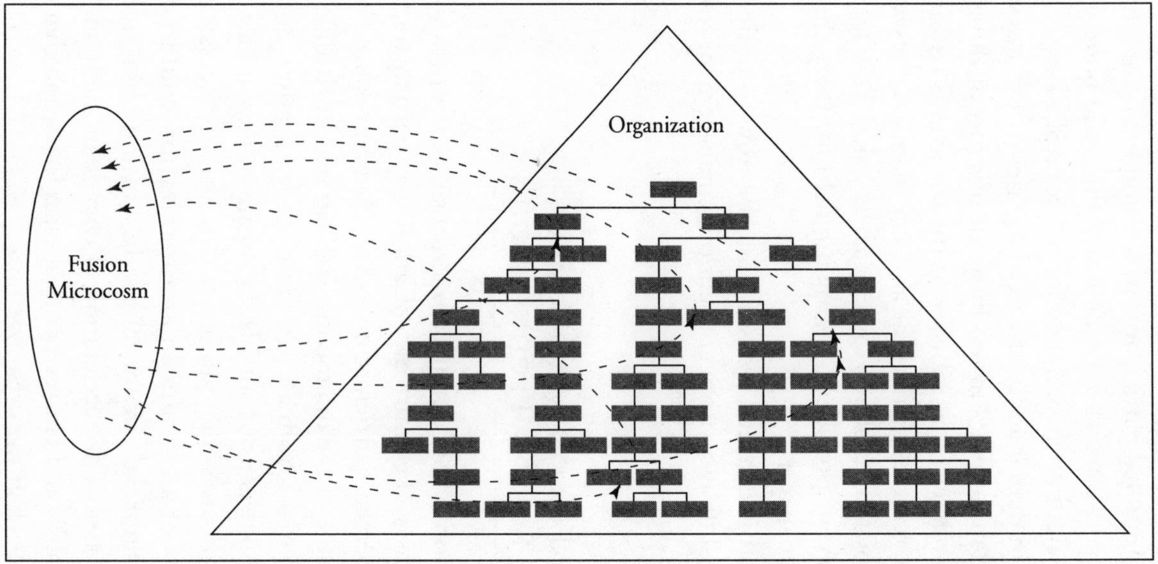

Organization

Fusion
Microcosm

achieve. Participants experience, often for the first time, true empowerment, concern for each other across boundaries, a sense of the issues facing the entire system, and a shared dream for the future. The microcosm becomes a true community, and the culture grown there is transplanted back to the organization where it takes root and can transform the whole system.

What kind of microcosm event can create fusion and actually transform an organization? In recent years, a number of approaches have been developed for large groups, each of which has its advantages and reported successes.[2] In our own experiments with large-group interventions, we have found four general technologies that work exceedingly well. Exhibit 11.2 shows these fusion technologies and the conventional approaches they replace.

Dialogue

Dialogue is a form of communication that was used in ancient Greek philosophical discourse as a platform for democracy and by Native American groups as a form of interpersonal communication. The roots of *dialogue* are *dia* and *logos,* which in combination can be thought of as "stream of meaning." The shared meaning that people in dialogue develop becomes the glue that holds them together.[3] Participants in a dialogue may be stakeholders who do not have a good relationship, who are polar opposites, or who have been unable to engage in substantive conversation. By talking authentically to one another, they discover common issues and common dreams on which they can build a new future.

In our dialogues, people are guided to open up to one another and suspend their tightly defended assumptions and views. The structure slows down the conversation, making it unlike traditional discussion or problem solving. Whereas discussion involves batting things back and forth and problem

Exhibit 11.2
Fusion Event Technologies

Technology	Design	Purpose	Replaces
Dialogue	 ● 12–30 people (circle of individuals)	Promote relationships, shared meaning, empowerment, new future, appreciative inquiry, collective thinking	Sensitivity training (T-groups), personal growth workshops
Future Search	 ○ 40–80 people (tables)	Foster information exchange and action among stakeholders; shared vision; whole system change	Conventional strategic planning, outside consultants/experts, top-down change
Whole-Scale Change	○ 100–500 people  (tables)	Reconstruct whole organization (similar to future search, only bigger)	Conventional strategic planning, reengineering, restructuring, work flow and system changes
Leadership Enactment	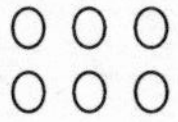 ○ 15–50 people (tables)	Nurture identity as a leader; awaken subtle potentials of vision, heart, courage, etc.	Conventional leadership training, empowerment instruction, classroom-based activities

● Individuals
○ Tables

solving strives to home in on a specific solution, dialogue meanders among people and feelings without direction before reaching closure. A statement does not require a verbal response, but calls for listening and reflection. Dialogue seeks breadth and diversity rather than focus on a single answer. The participants do not attack each other; the emphasis is on authentic conversation. Dialogue asks people to listen without judgment, reflect on their own thoughts and feelings, respect differences, seek a deeper level of understanding, release control of outcomes, and work to identify underlying and unstated assumptions.

What does a dialogue look like? There are various formats. The single large circle is one. Another is "café dialogue," in which people move among a number of small groups. Our dialogues typically include up to twenty-five people from the same organization. They sit in a circle, and the discussion is guided by two facilitators. The introductory conversation is designed to build mutual trust and common ground. We encourage "appreciative inquiry" rather than expressions of difference, dislike, or conflict.[4] Participants come to appreciate one another as a result of discussing such things as the time they felt most excited and fulfilled in their work, what they value most about themselves, how they would heighten the vitality of their organization, or a memorable communication experience. This sharing does not all have to take place in the large circle. Sometimes people will subdivide into smaller cafés for discussions and then report back to the larger group. Establishing a sense of community among all participants is a necessary focus.

As the group becomes comfortable in conversation about issues that are personal and emotional, a new culture begins to form. Old assumptions about group activity are replaced with new beliefs and intentions that are shared by group members.[5] Each person is recognized and accepted as a whole person, free to express his or her truth, even if that takes the form of a negative feeling or an unconventional belief. As group members hear one another and fuse into community, each individual experiences greater freedom to be who he or she really is.

A dialogue event helps participants change their mental models, their view of other people and the group as a whole. After some struggle, they give up their need to control the group, and an egalitarian microcosm is formed in which growth is possible. People listen, detach from their narrow assumptions, and empower one another. They accept others as they are rather than trying to fix them.

Striking results occur as people talk about what is truly on their minds. The group dialogue becomes an open forum on matters they urgently care about—both personal and work-related. As they get into their most personal concerns, the sense of community grows rapidly.

As the dialogue evolves over two or three days, various mindset shifts typically occur. One is that participants start to think of the group as a whole. In the everyday work world, people tend to be focused on themselves, their own group, and their personal interests. In a dialogue, they are guided to think of the needs of the whole system that is represented in the room. This helps them understand their part in a bigger picture.

Another mental shift is to take personal responsibility for the whole. Participants empower themselves to make sure the dialogue accomplishes something meaningful. In this setting— unlike that of a traditional organization, where it is expected that direction will come from the top—the dialogue facilitators take a low profile, and participants must gradually take responsibility for group success. They have no one but themselves to turn to. Thus they learn to empower themselves, take initiative, make suggestions, and introduce ideas that will deepen and broaden the conversation. The newly acquired habits of considering the whole and empowering oneself can then be transplanted to the larger organization.

As the dialogue group becomes a community, another interesting change occurs: participants take on the unresolved tasks of the organization. All having a stake in the organization, they identify dissatisfactions and discuss their shared dream about what the organization could become. They typically discuss barriers to achieving that dream, and they may organize themselves into action teams to begin removing such barriers. Thus the dialogue starts out with a primary focus on relationships and community building, but in our experience, participants often use their newfound community to address shared concerns.

Dialogue is a substantial improvement over standard agenda-based meetings and problem-solving discussions. It also differs from sensitivity training groups, which were popular in the 1970s and still have a following. In sensitivity training, people are encouraged to criticize one another in order to break through ego defenses. By contrast, dialogue creates a feeling of safety, common ground, and mutual trust, through which people learn to appreciate each other, push back the strong forces, and act from the subtle ones.

Future Search

Future search is one the most powerful means of creating fusion.[6] Our image for future search, as illustrated in Exhibit 11.2, is eight round tables. These tables represent eight stakeholder groups—for example, management, marketing, production, finance, customers, suppliers—that share an issue or problem, such as the creation of a new strategic plan, reengineering, total quality, empowerment, or a new corporate culture. However, the group at each table is mixed—a microcosm of the whole. Rather than each stakeholder group staying separate, it is distributed among the tables so that diverse stakeholders can hear each other and build a future together. This mixing of participants for the sake of maximum diversity is the key element of future search. Indeed, people can be rotated among tables two or three times to ensure the widest discussion and the greatest reduction of barriers. Ideally, stakeholders from outside the focal organization will also be included. For example, if quality customer service is an issue, it is important to have customers in the room so that employees can hear their frustrations firsthand.

The future-search conversation over two or three days breaks down barriers and improves social integration and community among the forty to eighty people present. Participants express their frustrations as well as their dreams, producing common ground and outcomes in which everyone has a stake.

The future search typically consists of a set sequence of activities. It begins with a process in which people are connected to each other via their shared history. Then difficulties, frustrations, and the bigger trends in the environment are identified so that participants become aware of the complexity facing them. At this point, they are guided to take personal responsibility for the solution of the issues that concern them. A shared dream for the future is created, and participants split into action teams that will work to achieve it. The entire event typically takes place over three days, and by the end, everyone is enormously motivated. A critical mass has been formed, and individuals carry the momentum back to the workplace, becoming warriors and evangelists for the new culture, strategic plan, reengineered procedures, or whatever improvement the future search focused on.

The power of future search lies in its ability to achieve collaboration and fusion among diverse parts of the system. People commit to action plans they care about, and they will work hard for several months to implement those plans. Future search can give an enormous boost to project management, for example. Instead of a project creeping along over many months or years, all stakeholders can gather together in one room, surface all barriers to progress, jointly create a desired future, and implement the changes in a fraction of the time normally required. Similarly, the creation of a strategic plan by means of future search is a bottom-up process that involves all participants. Everyone understands the total plan and will work to implement it.

Future search represents a paradigm shift in thinking that replaces conventional strategic planning, consultant experts, or top-down implementation of reengineering, quality programs, and the like. Typically, consulting firms that are hired to help with strategic planning search for problems and opportunities, surveying both the external environment and selected employees. This work is then pulled together in a written document and presented to top management. We observed one such strategic plan developed for a successful financial services firm in the northeastern United States at a cost of $500,000. Soon thereafter, the president who commissioned the study left the firm. No one else was associated with the plan, so it sat in a drawer. Employees who had given their time in interviews and surveys were irritated because nothing resulted from their effort. Other employees were angry about the waste of half a million dollars. The plan produced no benefit because no one was emotionally involved in it, and it represented the view of outside consultants rather than of those who knew the bank. A future search would have both created and implemented the strategic plan in short order—and for a fraction of the cost.

The workout process developed at General Electric has characteristics similar to those of future search. People are brought together from diverse departments and work in crossfunctional teams to solve shared problems. Participants have an opportunity to connect with each other, identify the problems, create an ideal solution, and then start implementation by obtaining the approval of top management.

Whole-Scale Change

Another major innovation in facilitating rapid organizational change is *whole-scale* or *real time strategic change,* which was developed to meet the needs of large corporations. It grew from work with Ford Motor Company, where thousands of employees had to be taught to think in terms of a new, more empowering culture. Working with fifty to one hundred people per event was simply too slow. Kathie Dannemiller and her associates developed techniques that brought together up to two thousand people at one time.[7]

A fusion event of this scope requires enormous planning and logistical support. The plan schedules every activity to the minute. All participants typically meet in one large hall, although for some multifaceted issues, parts of the room may temporarily focus on different tasks. For example, a whole-scale event dealing with reengineering might involve four major work processes. During the problem-solving phase, these would be tackled in different parts of the room.

Whole-scale events follow the previously described stages of getting people connected, surfacing the underlying dissatisfaction, creating a preferred future, and then taking action steps to fix the problems and achieve that future. The design is such that each table is a microcosm of the whole system, as is each portion of the room. Thus participants are forced to think and conceptualize in terms of the needs of the whole and not just their specific departments. During the dissatisfaction phase of the event, problems are communicated to the entire group via speaker panels. For example, it is not possible to have a customer sitting at every table, so a panel of customers may address the group as a whole, describing their pain and frustration in dealing with the company and why they have taken their business elsewhere.

The power of such a large gathering is that the organization can literally be redesigned on the spot. In one, two, three, or four successive conferences over several weeks, large segments of the organization can focus on the strategic plan, then the redesign of work processes to achieve that plan, the organization structure to best manage the work, and the support systems and cultural norms that will sustain the new organization. In some cases, companies have shut down, redesigned themselves using the whole-scale process, and emerged in new forms in just a few weeks or months. The experience of such an event is astonishing, with enormous energy and commitment developed by the critical mass in the room. Watching hundreds of people transform together is like witnessing a miracle. After this occurs, the organization cannot return to the limiting, controlling, isolating bureaucracy that ignored the needs of employees, customers, and suppliers.

Leadership Enactment

Leadership enactment, in the version we have developed, uses techniques from dialogue, future search, and leadership training to help participants discover and awaken their own subtle potentials for vision, communication, courage, heart, mindfulness, and integrity. The leadership seminar becomes a microcosm of an empowered organization, with individuals enacting their own potentials. Fusing with others, participants identify their concerns, issues, and areas of needed personal and organizational growth. The facilitator guides them away from overreliance on the rational ego with stories, music, videos, self-reflection, fusion, and dialogue. As trust and community are created, the workshop becomes a place where people get in touch with their own dreams (vision), their fears and ways of overcoming them (courage), ways of sending symbolic messages about values and vision and discerning the underlying yearnings of others (communication), thought processes based on deeper creativity, with a perspective from "outside the box" (mindfulness), positive emotions such as fun, bliss, and enthusiasm (heart), and fundamental honesty and the impulse to serve the people they lead (integrity).

During the course of a four- or five-day seminar, participants also receive feedback about themselves, both from other people and through personality questionnaires. Often for the first time, individuals find true leadership resources within themselves. Armed with confidence and their newly discovered leadership gifts, managers are equipped to become change leaders back in their organization.

The power of leadership enactment is that it changes the identity of participants. By getting in touch with their subtle forces of leadership, they begin to think of themselves as leaders and take personal responsibility for changing their company. In addition, they learn to use fusion to touch the subtle force in others, awakening leadership potential in ever-widening circles.

Leadership enactment is the foundation of the leadership development program at the Owen Graduate School of Management, Vanderbilt University. Elements of fusion are also present in leadership programs such as those at the Center for Creative Leadership, the Pecos River Learning Center, the Covey Leadership Center, and in other programs that focus on developing the leader within rather than on helping managers operate conceptually and rationally.[8]

Leadership enactment differs substantially from traditional classroom training. In the classroom, the teacher is above the pupil and provides information and ideas oriented to cognitive learning. By contrast, the facilitator in leadership enactment helps people discover their own leader potentials through guided conversation with others. The facilitator often acts as an equal in discussions and exercises. The fusion that is created during the workshop lasts for months afterward. Participants may make lifelong friends who become part of a leadership support system. When a manager attends as a lone company representative, fusion unlocks the personal resources that enable him or her to become a champion for change back home. And when a number of employees from a single organization attend together, they fuse to create a band of warriors committed to transformation.

EXAMPLES OF FUSION EVENTS

In the previous chapter, we described a future search at Nortel. Here we will share examples of fusion events for a medical center, a government organization, and a utility company.

A Medical Center Future Search

The organization was a large academic medical center at a Midwestern university. The center included a university hospital, a medical school, and about 800 physicians who participated in teaching, research, and patient care. Because of its outstanding reputation, the center was successful and profitable, despite weak relationships across specialties and with referring physicians in the surrounding city. As managed care entered the region, the environment became destabilized and uncertain. Center administrators felt vulnerable and wanted to make changes to keep up with managed care. One initiative was to form a separate medical group of some 450 doctors who would focus on providing responsive clinical care. A governing board of 36 physicians was elected by the members of this group. We were invited to facilitate a fusion event of the board members and a few other stakeholders.

Better relationship ties were needed among the group members themselves, as well as with patients, referring doctors, and other health care organizations. Board members wanted to create a strategic plan. The chief medical officer stressed the need for the board to come together as a working team, and for the new medical group to be seen as a separate, patient-responsive entity in the medical center complex. The group needed to create an organization that would survive in an era of managed health care and respond quickly to changing health needs in the region.

We arranged a one-day planning meeting with the executive committee of the board, during which we listened to their needs and introduced fusion technology ideas. The committee decided on 64 retreat participants—36 board members along with other stakeholders—who would form eight mixed conversation groups at the event. Six stakeholder groups were academic physicians' specialties, one group was senior administrators, and another was nursing administrators.

A big culture problem was the mindset of rugged individualism among academic physicians and their strong identification with their own specialties. The extreme case was surgeons, who reputedly had little respect for other specialists or for administrators. They just wanted to practice medicine, and they had great power because of the revenues they generated for the medical center. However, all doctors were feeling the discomfort of health care changes.

At the start of this future search, connections across boundaries were formed through the development of a common history. Participants then constructed a large chart of the trends and events affecting the medical group. The chart revealed a world of unimagined complexity that felt overwhelming to many.

The next day began with an analysis of key trends, and then participants discussed their activities in response to the trends. This triggered a small breakthrough. The surgeons publicly admitted that they did not behave for the good of the larger system, and they apologized. Other physicians also expressed regret for contributing to a negative culture, and several individuals owned up and took responsibility for their stovepipe mentality.

Next, mixed groups worked on "ideal future" scenarios, in which hopes and dreams began to surface. This was more "idealistic" than participants expected. A vision of the future emerged that was shared by all the diverse stakeholders. People pulled together. By the end of the second day, the participants were bonding as a community and were optimistic about their joint future. They communicated honestly, and one-time antagonists toasted each other over drinks at dinner.

The third day was spent defining personal and group action plans to achieve the desired future. Consensus emerged on five problem areas that were seen as needing immediate action: contracting, quality improvement, culture change, physician collegiality, and incentives/goals. Participants assigned themselves to one of the five action teams.

A big surprise for everyone was the enthusiastic commitment to the action teams, especially to the two "soft" topics of culture and collegiality. These two teams committed themselves to producing specific proposals for change and implementing those proposals by agreed deadlines.

By the third day, many individual leaders had emerged. The large-group fusion process also created personal fusion for many participants, unlocking their subtle forces. A nurse drew a picture of a shattered Waterford crystal vase—her image of medical center fragmentation. She also drew a beautiful unbroken vase representing its future. Several surgeons stepped forward to apologize for previous isolating behavior, held out an olive branch to nurses whom they had not treated with respect, and took the lead on the five action teams. Other participants succeeded in quieting the autocratic president of the medical center when he made an effort to control the activities. Individuals stepped forward to articulate their vision for the future and help build community in the medical center.

At the close of the event, members of the culture action team asserted their leadership by asking the roomful of participants to sign on, literally, to a proposed new medical center credo: "We provide excellence in health care for all of our patients. We treat patients and each other as we wish to be treated. We continuously evaluate and improve our performance."

This team later led the development of a basic value pledge for the center's several thousand employees. The pledge, which would appear on every identification badge, declared:

I will give our patients and their needs my highest priority.
I will take responsibility for finding a solution to any
problem or complaint that a patient or family member
may have. I will do my part to ensure the success of the
Medical Center. OUR PATIENTS COME FIRST.

For many academic physicians, living out these expressed values involved a sea change in personal mindset and behavior. Three of the five action teams (contracting, quality, incentives) merged with standing committees on those issues that subsequently made real progress toward new structures and systems. The most visible impact was on the soft side. One specialty department announced three weeks after the event that it would see all patients referred by other specialties on the day of the referral. This was a breakthrough, because many physicians routinely scheduled referrals days or weeks in advance so that they had blocks of time for research. This breakthrough precipitated other changes that improved physician-to-physician collaboration and communication.

September 18, three months after the June retreat, was the target date for implementing the new culture. A large outdoor picnic and celebration were planned. Prior to the kickoff date, one hundred employees at a time attended four-hour meetings where implementation of the new culture and values was explained. The most striking event on September 18 was the signing by all attendees of six-by-eight-foot sheets that would hang on the walls inside the medical building. Physicians, administrators, and other employees walked through an entryway, read the new credo and basic value pledge, and signed their names on the sheets. The leadership provided by the collegiality and culture action teams inspired enormous progress in changing culture and working relationships.

The chief medical officer was delighted. He said several times over the ensuing weeks that the future search produced an outcome beyond what he had dared imagine. He was incredibly pleased and surprised with the event that produced the changes he witnessed.

A Government Dialogue

The group of thirty managers brought together for a dialogue were in the worst mental and emotional shape we had ever seen in the course of our work. They were part of the civilian management contingent at a military base that was in decline. Their job was to make personnel cuts and to maintain work stability during the rapid turnover of military forces. They were sent to the dialogue to explore how employee involvement and empowerment could improve quality and productivity in the face of shrinking resources.

The dialogue was to last three full days. Beginning on a modest personal level, we asked the participants to talk about their position in their family's birth order and its impact on them as children and later as adults and managers. The group seemed uncomfortable, and by the end of the first morning, the atmosphere was one of denial and confusion. Participants disagreed with each other over trivial issues, resented being away from work, and resisted the whole idea of dialogue. As the group became more and more vocal, the room was filled with frustration and anger. Nearly everyone complained about government cutbacks, the unrealistic expectations placed on them, the frequent changes in goals as military officers succeeded each other, and the constraints of resource limitations and bureaucratic regulation. At the end of the first day, everyone seemed discouraged.

The following morning saw more of the same, so we confronted the managers on their state of mind. We pointed out that they sounded like powerless victims. They denied it. We pointed out that they exhibited the thought patterns of passive employees. They denied it.

As they began to hear what we were saying, we asked them straight out: "Why don't you quit? If things are so bad and you are the victims of this onslaught, why don't you have the courage to leave?" As this question soaked in, the atmosphere in the room shifted. People began to speak directly about their own hopelessness and frustration, admitting to feelings of powerlessness and a desire to take back their power. They stared into their own emptiness, and they did not have a solution.

As the discussion continued on the second day, participants began to identify things they might do. They divided into smaller groups to identify specific problems and ways to resolve them. They also talked about an overall vision that would hold them together. Excitement and enthusiasm replaced the previous feeling of powerlessness. On the third day, a volunteer called the base commander and arranged an appointment for the following week, when the group in its entirety would ask his support for the changes it contemplated. The changes were all achievable, despite the declining resources and government bureaucracy. One of the facilitators attended the meeting with the commander, who was delighted with the group's initiative. He approved everything that was requested, including the creation of a middle manager forum. These middle managers had decided that the larger system did not always support them, so they would support each other.

In a dialogue, we take a low profile as facilitators. Once fusion occurred among the civilian managers, leaders started to emerge. The personal fusion and unlocking of subtle forces were striking in a group that started so dispirited, hopeless, and powerless. As the group moved toward its desired future, it became self-organizing. We were able to become observers as it proceeded toward its goal of creating initiatives for the base commander to approve. Two leaders helped organize the larger group, and several others took responsibility for small groups and specific initiatives. Everyone made contact with some elements of heart, vision, courage, communication, mindfulness, or integrity, and participated vigorously in the dialogue. The organizational fusion in the room engendered personal fusion for individuals, creating a roomful of leaders.

We met with this group two months later, and they were proud of their progress. By finding their own power, they were able to give power away to others through greater employee involvement. The forum was still active, and the managers were proposing more changes under the aegis of the base commander.

PECO Energy Whole-Scale Event

The human resources department at PECO Energy initiated a transformation of itself from a controlling repository of administrative policies and procedures to a value-added work group that consulted with and supported line activities. This entailed a redesign of work processes and a mindset shift from user-*un*friendliness to sensitive service—all during a period in which the electrical power industry was going through the chaos of deregulation.

The whole-scale event was initiated by William Kaschub, vice president of HR, and was facilitated by Paul Tolchinsky and Sylvia James of Dannenmiller Tyson Associates.[9] A planning team of HR professionals and line managers benchmarked the best practices of outstanding HR departments in other companies before designing the whole-scale process.

What they came up with was a series of four events: a visioning event, a process redesign event, an organizational design event, and a checkpoint event. These were held over a period of six months, with approximately two hundred PECO employees at each event, representing every stakeholder viewpoint. Several HR employees attended every event, and invited employees from all other departments attended as participation cascaded throughout the company with each subsequent event.

At the visioning event, participants developed a mission and vision statement for the human resources department. In the second event, five HR work processes were reengineered to fit the vision created at the first event. These were selection and staffing, job pricing, career planning, workforce planning, and policy development and deployment. The purpose of the organizational design event was to decide who should perform the newly designed work processes. The major decision was which activities should be done by line employees and managers and which by the HR department. Participants designed a new organizational structure, transferring many human resource tasks to the line divisions. Finally, the checkpoint event reviewed the progress of HR's redesign effort and ensured continued momentum and alignment of employees and managers across the company. A preliminary plan for an HR call center was presented, which implemented the new culture of service. The call center gave instant access to line managers for human resource information and services.

During the four events, roughly eight hundred PECO employees were engaged in determining the new course of HR. The call center facilitated the movement of tasks away from HR, enabling that department's staff to become consultants to the business units. The function of HR was redefined, thanks to the initiative of many leaders in both HR and line departments. The line departments went through a mindset shift also, accepting much of the responsibility for human resources. In addition, leaders emerged to implement new information systems and other technologies. Over a few months, changes took place that cut deep into the organization, enhanced the impact of human resource activities, and empowered employees with leadership responsibility. The changes also promoted a diverse work force, individual accountability, and continuous improvement in individuals and work teams while creating an environment of teamwork, openness, trust, respect, integrity, continuous learning, and customer focus.[10]

The PECO event, like the others described here, represents a level of transformation considered impossible a few years ago. Cultural transformation—change in the mindsets and shared norms of employees—occurred through organizational fusion. And the release of subtle forces and leadership capacities was brought about through personal fusion.

One theme in all types of fusion events is that organizational and personal fusion reinforce each other. Individuals discover their own wholeness in a fusion relationship with others. And organizational fusion needs the leadership and enthusiasm of participants to transform the larger system. Fusion is accomplished through conversation across traditional boundaries that meets people's yearnings to be part of something larger than themselves, to face reality and new challenges, to create a shared future together, and to take action that serves others and the organization. Fusion leaders understand how to orchestrate fusion to achieve bursts of motivation and change. Fusion leadership is about managing both personal and organizational fusion. We describe the principles underlying fusion in the next chapter.

Personal Remembering

- If you were to propose a dialogue in your organization, what would be the reaction? How would you respond?

- When things go wrong, where do you look first for the cause—in others or in yourself? Why?

- In your family, where are you in the birth order? What impact has this had on you as a child, as an adult, and as a potential fusion leader?

- What has been your greatest frustration with management retreats? Did real fusion occur? Why?

CHAPTER TWELVE

FUSION PRINCIPLES

A washerman in India took his clients' clothes to the river each day, washed and dried them, then took them back to his clients, using his donkeys to carry the load. One day, he found a lioness that a hunter had killed, but the hunter had left alive the cub that had been in her womb. The washerman nursed the cub back to health. As the cub grew, it played with the donkeys, lived with the donkeys, and soon believed itself to be a donkey. The lion ate with the donkeys, even learned to bray like a donkey. The washerman trained the lion to do donkey work, loading clothes on its back for transport to and from the river.

One day, a big lion came and saw the donkeys and thought what a nice meal they would make. Then he saw the young lion and was surprised. "What is this? How is it possible for a lion to be side-by-side with these donkeys? Lions eat donkeys." The big lion charged the riverbank. The donkeys and young lion were scared and ran away. But the lion caught the young lion, who said, "Oh, please, don't eat me, Mr. Lion. Please let me go back to my brothers and sisters." And the big lion said, "Are you crazy? You aren't a donkey, you're a lion."

"No, no, no," the young lion said, "I am a donkey.
I work for the washerman. I carry the laundry. I am
certainly a donkey." The big lion said, "Look at my face.
What do you see?" And the young lion said, "I see a lion."
Then the big lion held the young lion over the river water
to see his reflection. "Now look at your face. What do you
see?" And he said, "It's the same face." And then the lion
said, "Now open your mouth and roar." And the young
lion opened its mouth and roared.[1]

In that moment, the young lion discovered its potential to be
a lion. In a world where strong-force hierarchies have socialized
employees to be donkeys, can conditions be systematically created that will unlock their potential to become lions? Can organizations or leaders find ways to show young lions their true
potential and how to go beyond the limits of their domesticat-
ing experiences? What are the principles of fusion that unlock
the subtle forces of the lion within us?

This chapter summarizes the elements that can be incorpo-
rated into a fusion event to ignite both personal and organizational fusion. It explains the fundamental fusion processes that
need to be present, describes the formula for achieving organizational fusion, and enumerates the outcomes that can be expected when subtle forces are awakened in a critical mass of
employees. The journey from separation to community, from
hierarchy to fusion, from donkey to lion can be mapped out in
advance of fusion technology events. Fusion can be achieved
by any leader or organization willing to try.

WHY DOES FUSION WORK?

In Chapter One we described a few examples of the frustration
and failure associated with change implementation. We proposed that the reason for implementation difficulty is an overly

narrow perspective on change dynamics. Conventional change strategies have focused on technical knowledge and skill acquisition for individuals and on formal structures, strategies, and work processes for organizations. Changing the objective world of individuals and organizations is the underlying goal. The subtle voices of the interior world of caring, dreams, and other subtle forces have been ignored, and as a consequence, conventional change strategies contain only one-half of the necessary conversation. Conventional change strategies have been directed toward the donkey that is expected to do as it is told. Too often, corporate training programs, TQM, and reengineering efforts are exercises for which there is little employee enthusiasm and ownership. The lion within people is not awakened.

In this book we have argued that organizational fusion has the potential to bring the subtle voices of the interior world into balance with the strong voices of the exterior world. Fusion works because it merges these two voices, unlocking commitment and motivation for real change.

Exhibit 12.1 illustrates a framework for how fusion events compare to traditional change efforts.[2] The primary focus of a change program can be the individual (I) or the collective (We). Change can also focus on the interior, subjective world of individuals and collectives or on the exterior, objective world of these entities.

The four cells in Exhibit 12.1 cover the range of foci of change programs. Cells one and two are the interior and exterior worlds of individuals (described in Chapter Three). The interior world of individuals includes mind, heart, and spirit and is the source of the subtle forces of mindfulness, vision, heart, communication, courage, and integrity. The exterior of individuals is the conditioned self, which has learned to operate in the external world, often to the exclusion of internal potentials.

Cells three and four pertain to the organizational whole. The interior world of the organization in cell three includes

Exhibit 12.1
Comparison of Fusion to Conventional Change Approaches

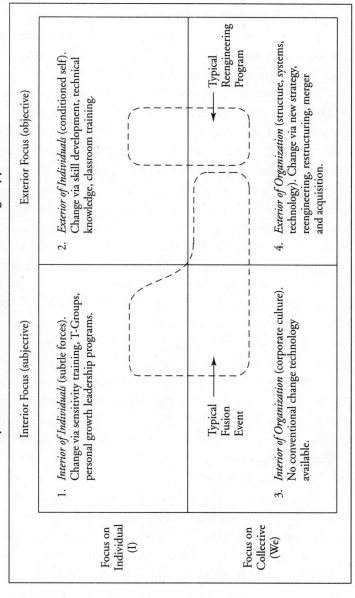

Interior Focus (subjective)

Exterior Focus (objective)

Focus on Individual (I)

1. *Interior of Individuals* (subtle forces). Change via sensitivity training, T-Groups, personal growth leadership programs.

2. *Exterior of Individuals* (conditioned self). Change via skill development, technical knowledge, classroom training.

Typical Reengineering Program

Focus on Collective (We)

Typical Fusion Event

3. *Interior of Organization* (corporate culture). No conventional change technology available.

4. *Exterior of Organization* (structure, systems, technology). Change via new strategy, reengineering, restructuring, merger and acquisition.

the subjective and intangible elements that people must work out together in collectives. If people are going to work together, they must find shared norms, assumptions, a future, values, mindsets, and understandings about which they agree—which comprise corporate culture. Cell four represents the traditional objective elements of organization that deal with the external world, including its structure, systems, technology, and work flow.

Developing individuals in corporate training programs is typically done via knowledge and skill acquisition during classroom training, which is in cell two. Cell two training programs are typically successful within their limited scope. Programs designed to generate self-knowledge, such as sensitivity training or personal growth leadership programs, are in cell one. Cell one development programs are often disappointing because individuals may change, but the program gives little weight to the organizational system in which individuals must act with others. This weakness is evident when a manager is sent to a leadership program, has an inspiring and enlightening experience, and then is frustrated on his return because the organization hasn't changed. Organizational strong forces socialize him back to the old way, blocking the use of his newly acquired self-knowledge. In cell three, conventional attempts to transform corporate culture and the organization's interior values and mindsets have generally failed. In cell four, change in the exterior of organizations is typically accomplished with new strategies, reengineering, restructuring, or mergers, all of which are designed to alter the objective part of the organization.

The comparison of a fusion event with a typical large-scale change program, such as reengineering, is illustrated by the shaded areas in Exhibit 12.1. Conventional change programs occur on the right side of the chart. Reengineering or a strategy-making retreat focus on the objective, outer world of the organization. These programs often include substantial individual skill training in the area of new work processes and technology. Thus, a reengineering program trains individuals in the classroom to fit the organization's new strategy and work process.

We believe that fusion avoids frustration and disappointment with implementation because the interior worlds of individual and organization are also embraced. Fusion events bring together the interior voice of individuals, acting together in a collective, to address the exterior world of strategy and structure. By expanding the focus of change programs to include the interior aspects of individual and organization, fusion ignites the enthusiasm and commitment of employees. Fusion events work because individuals are energized to achieve change for the organization and for themselves. With fusion designs, for the first time, organizations can actually change corporate culture while also changing structure and systems. When the subtle forces are unlocked during fusion, organizational change becomes attractive and exciting to employees rather than something to resist.

How Does Fusion Work?

A fusion event is an extraordinary experience, in which participants typically discover a new world of authenticity, relationship ties, freedom from conventional control, shared vision, emotional involvement, and creative solutions to long-standing problems. Fusion events are the best tools social science can offer organizations that are seeking to keep up with their environments. A fusion event can be the big lion that shows the young lion how to believe in itself. Such events enable a conventional organization to create a critical mass of motivation and enthusiasm to propel individual and cultural change. The unfolding of these dramatic changes over several months, rather than the normal period of several years, often seems miraculous.

We consider the most important principles underlying organizational fusion to be the following:

Microcosm of the Whole. The fusion event includes a representative microcosm of the relevant organizational system, including all groups with a stake in the issues under discussion. During the event, each section or table also represents a microcosm of the whole. A maximum mix of participants is assigned to each table during most activities. No one can safely hide behind the walls of his or her department or function. Face-to-face conversation across the whole system breaks open narrow mindsets. Each department or level hears and absorbs the needs and aspirations of all others. The microcosm also constructs the ideal culture the larger organization is trying to achieve. Within the petri dish of the microcosm, "me" is converted into "we," then transported back to the larger organizational system. People become change agents for new initiatives and the new, improved culture. Just as important is the sense of safety created in the microcosm. The microcosm is a laboratory in which new behaviors can be tried, and in which people can speak from the heart because their defenses have been dropped. Without the immediate pressures of daily work, personal and organizational fusion can develop quickly.

Removal of Familiar Structure. The fusion event is egalitarian. People sit in circles, and titles and reporting relationships count for little. Individuals and groups manage themselves. Participants speak for themselves. Everyone is on an equal footing. Every voice is heard, every voice matters. Each person's hope, frustration, problem, and need are expressed and become part of the larger consensus. This is often participants' first experience in a nonhierarchical structure, which is the one most suited to an out-of-kilter environment. In the fusion setting, people open up, facing themselves, each other, and a larger

reality. They see how they fit into the larger picture and feel free
to experiment with new behaviors that capture their inner
yearnings for impact, connection, and responsibility.

Surrender of Control. With thirty to five hundred people
moving through facilitated activities, conventional managers
must give up control. The critical mass creates a powerful fusion force that draws people in. The individual's frame of reference is merged into that of the organizational whole. The
process is seductive and fun. Passion and enthusiasm replace
skepticism and fear as people feel themselves becoming an important part of something larger than themselves, something
they had wanted but hadn't realized they wanted. Giving up
control feels good, and has the surprising result that other people assume responsibility and take action. The assumption
about the need for strong-force hierarchical control can be challenged and broken in this setting. The power of collaboration
reveals its worth.

The Wisdom of the Group. A fusion event brings together
the life and work experiences of many people, who know infi-
nitely more about the organization and its situation than do
outside experts, consultants, or facilitators. This intelligence is
simply awakened, surfaced, consolidated, and transformed into
the wisdom that can create a new future and remove barriers
to that future. The use of participants' wisdom is what makes
the event—and later the organization—unstoppable. The delu-
sion that a single manager or group has the wisdom needed to
create a future and solve organizational problems is soon rejected. A collective wisdom has been there all along, simply
waiting to be unlocked and applied.

Subtle-Force Yearnings. Most people yearn to express their
interior selves in their work, to release the subtle forces that

enable the essential self to fuse with the conditioned self. The fusion event provides a habitat for these yearnings. People can express their frustrations, dreams, and problems, and state the outcomes they desire. They can work on what they care about, and care for each other. The fusion event goes around their ego defensiveness and resistance. The water behind the dam is free to flow to the ocean. Fundamental questions of meaning and existence, which are rooted in fundamental shared longings, can be openly discussed. Collective inquiry replaces false assumptions with a deeper truth about who people really are and what they wish to achieve together. Participants can express their dreams for the organization's future and find ways toward an attainable shared dream. Rather than fighting for small scraps of time, as at the office, they have abundant time to make previously avoided inquiries into things that really count.

Changes to Both Culture and System. The fusion event changes mindsets that shape corporate culture. Culture is the foundation on which other change occurs. As many failed change programs attest, new computer technology, work relationships, reengineering, and quality programs will not endure unless culture also changes. Conversely, changes in corporate culture will not endure unless teams also change elements such as strategy, structure, and systems. The social and the technical, culture and organization (Exhibit 12.1) must change together. One reinforces the other. Thus the fusion event uses changes in culture to change the technical and organizational systems, and vice versa.

Employee-Generated Change. Employees move toward change, in themselves and in their organization, under the following conditions:

- When there is a crisis that demands action
- When they are free of external control

- When they are emotionally involved in the process
- When the changes are steps toward achievement of their dream
- When they have an opportunity for action that will fix things
- When they receive feedback on what they have done

All of these elements are present in organizational fusion events. Employees get to deal with their own frustrations and things they care about, and they are treated as equals by management. People are the solution. Everyone takes equal responsibility. Donkeys get to become lions. Engaging people to make changes rather than trying to change them is a key to the success of fusion technologies.

THE FORMULA FOR ORGANIZATIONAL FUSION

Our experience and that of other social scientists suggest that massive organizational change can begin during a two-to-three-day fusion event if it includes the right conversations and activities. These critical elements of design are summarized below in a formula.[3] They can be a part of any fusion event, whether dialogue, future search, whole-scale change, or some other approach. So long as the elements in the formula are present, successful change is bound to occur.

$$\text{Organizational Fusion} = \text{Microcosm} \times \text{Connection} \times \text{Dissatisfaction} \times \text{Vision} \times \text{Action}$$

In a fusion event, the first step is to make sure that all parts of the relevant system are represented. When the gathering is not a true microcosm—for example, when all the attendees are middle managers—minds are unlikely to be changed, because there is no interplay of perspectives. The microcosm must be present not only in the room but at each table. Organizational fusion occurs through guided conversation across traditional boundaries. Without diversity, the potential for fusion is diminished.

During the event, the first step is to help people *connect*, and this requires establishing common ground. Participants get to know one another as human beings despite differences at work. They develop rapport and enjoy working at a table together. Without this step, the subsequent steps in a fusion event lack a foundation. Activities such as exploring the past foster this connection. Its development is an important step toward psychological safety, which encourages the release of subtle forces.

The next element is *dissatisfaction.* A sense of urgency or crisis must be present if substantive change is to take place. Participants, opening themselves to the views of other stakeholders, must together face the truth of unhappy people, rampant conflicts, slow production, inefficient work flow, angry customers, bad strategy, or whatever else isn't working. Every person's dissatisfaction and frustration will be heard. This reality is a basis for common ground. Once all of the dissatisfaction is out on the table, the group is ready to consider doing things differently.

Vision for the future is the fourth element in the fusion formula, and has the greatest capacity to touch people. Participants create a future they want to achieve together. They can do this verbally or through pictures, model making, or skits. This is a right-brain activity, engaging heart and spirit. Without the articulation of a vision that pulls everyone together, action teams will not persist as long with their initiatives. For example, an experiment that had people work in teams on a series of problems without an overarching vision found that the teams lost motivation fairly quickly and experienced unhealthy conflict. Other teams facing the same tasks, but who worked toward a shared vision, maintained higher motivation for a longer period of time, with less conflict.[4] Creating a shared vision produces high dividends that continue to flow after the fusion event is over and the participants have returned to their work.

Finally, a fusion event must include clearly defined *action steps*—activities, initiatives, and projects that will implement changes, remove barriers, and achieve the vision. Participants commit to specific action steps and start implementation before they leave the conference. Action teams draw up schedules, lists of activities, and deadlines for each part of their respective change projects. Each action feeds the change process with an opportunity for success and celebration.

The formula for organizational fusion creates personal fusion, too, transforming managers into leaders. The fusion elements overwhelm the resistance of skeptical individuals. When employees experience each of the five equation elements together, change is inevitable. Guided conversations will have a positive outcome. It is hard to fail. A fusion event harnesses the best within each person, and builds a critical mass to energize a chain reaction that is difficult to stop.

FUSION OUTCOMES

Lasting outcomes for individuals who attend a fusion event include emotional bonding and a new mindset. A paradigm shift occurs when people unite and express their subtle potentials for leadership, when they become aware of the issues of the larger organization, when they see how the donkey of narrowness and rigidity can be replaced by the lion of collaboration and organizational flexibility. Indeed, lasting change is impossible unless conversations explode the old, limited viewpoint and reveal the promise of a new fusion-based culture. As the dust clears after an event, participants head back to the organization changed in significant ways:

1.   *The mindset of each participant has expanded.* Each person has seen the complexity of the entire organization and cannot retreat back into the limited perspective of his or her own job or department. Each has felt empowerment and partnership in the fusion event. The donkeys see themselves as lions. People are conscious of others' needs, of the whole system, and of the possibilities of a new future. Each level and function can see and feel the complexity and yearnings experienced by all others. Everyone is able to make decisions that respect the needs of the whole system as well as those of their own part.

2.   *Each person is imprinted with the enduring vision of the organization's future and his/her place in it.* Each participant's dream has become part of a larger vision. This positively charged future pulls people toward it, releasing spirit and enthusiasm over the long term for the accomplishment of action plans for improvement. The vision provides shared purpose, meaning in day-to-day work, hope that invigorates the subtle forces, and the challenge to do one's best. It contributes to the sense of community as employees pursue the ideal future together.

3.   *Emotional connections are deeper than ever before.* Boundaries between departments and levels are significantly reduced, and there is an appreciation of fellow employees that stretches across the organization. The ties that have been created provide the basis for an enduring corporate culture in which partnership and empowerment are key values. Individuals feel a new sense of community, of organizational wholeness. Workers in all parts of the organization feel included and share in commitment and consensus. Managers who in the past have zealously defended the hierarchy can for the first time relax and give up control, enjoying the expression by others of personal accountability.

4.   *Each person is now a leader, taking personal responsibility for the success of the organization.* Empowerment takes hold, often

for the first time. Participants now see themselves as leaders responsible for change and able to act from the subtle forces of vision, heart, courage, communication, mindfulness, and integrity. They accept responsibility for realizing their own yearnings and contributing their gifts toward a shared future. Employees no longer expect all change to be initiated by bosses or other departments, and are less prone to blame others for failure. They own up to their feelings, shortcomings, and frustrations, and are forgiving of their own imperfections as well as those of the organization. The new mindset of responsibility enables them to lead the charge for change.

5.   *A shift has occurred from the paradigm of hierarchical control to one of partnership.* Participants have experienced the microcosm of emergent self-organization and now see how ill-suited the strong hierarchical structure is to a changing environment. They finally understand how to give away power—and how to accept it. The shift occurs simultaneously at the upper and lower levels of the organization. The fusion idea is transplanted from the microcosm to the larger organization and continues to grow over time. The fusion event has planted seeds that will quickly crack the asphalt of traditional structure and control.

6.   *Action has become the overriding imperative.* The entire fusion process is designed to implement change, to trigger immediate action rather than initiate new rounds of analysis, data-gathering, or theorizing. Attention at the fusion event is focused on the subtle forces, on the experience of work, and on organizational systems. Participants buy in because of their emotional involvement. They change behavior together, becoming a fighting force for implementing change back on the job. Fusion harnesses the organization's inner and outer resources for action—to fix, to achieve. Unlike a consultant's report or a research proposal, the fusion event makes implementation of change a done deal.

Personal Remembering

■ Is there a lion hidden within you beneath the donkey surface? Why don't you free the lion? Could you do it if others did it too?

■ What gives life to your organization? What are you contributing to this life force?

■ Relationships are at the core of fusion. If you could ask three questions of coworkers before joining a new organization, what would they be? What do your questions say about you?

■ Tell a story about your best experience with community. What lesson does this story have for you as a leader?

CHAPTER THIRTEEN

FINAL WORDS ABOUT FUSION LEADERSHIP

Ahbleza is a Sioux warrior, son of a chief and perhaps soon to be chief himself. He is contemplating marriage to Hayatawin, the proud-walking woman. Life's tethers are compounding for him. Ahbleza is happy, but there is something lacking.

In his sleep he hears Wanagi, the medicine man, his friend, who is like a father to him, calling. He arises, loads a pipe, and goes to Wanagi's lodge. The medicine man refuses the pipe, lighting his own instead. They sit, not speaking.

Ahbleza finally talks of his many worldly concerns: worries about the coming of winter, about how many horses to pay for the bride, about others' expectations of a future chief. He speaks of his father's influence over him, about going on one more hunt before settling down alongside a woman, and about how he usually handles barriers by going around them instead of removing them.

Wanagi sits, not answering. His face reflects the dancing light from the fire. After a second pipeful, he speaks one

*phrase, Walpani iciya wo (Throw out everything). The
phrase could be interpreted many ways, but Ahbleza, ever
the warrior, decides to take it as a command. Start again.
Regard yourself as a newborn. Renew yourself completely.
He begins immediately.*

*Let the people see a man who tests himself, he grits, one
who throws off everything he accumulates—including any
thoughts other persons have given him that were originally
not his own. He gives away all his robes and the hides used
for lodge covering. He gives away his horses, making
himself foot-going; then he gives away his final pair of
moccasins. He gives away his lances, bows, knives, every
weapon he owns except his hands. He gives until nothing
exists for him but his person. And then he discards from his
mind whoever or whatever outside of himself influences him.*

*Finally, wearing only a loincloth, he leads his one
remaining horse, his favorite, and ties it at the last lodge
in the long line of lodges—a gift for the crippled boy whose
family has nothing. "Until he walks, this horse will carry
your son gently," he tells the mother.*

*Then Ahbleza turns and walks to the other side of the
knoll. He unties the string at his waist, the loin cover falls to
the ground. "I will live with my bareness, out of view, until
I know I am truly loyal to myself. Only then will I dare to
walk as a chief." He walks away onto the plains, alone.*[1]

Ahbleza's act means he will lead from his inner strength, not
from his material acquisitions or external position. He has
learned that holding on to the external can be harder work than
letting go. Ahbleza can't know his interior self when attached
to the external world. He discovered freedom in his detach-
ment, and the personal power that comes from not being
owned by his external position or possessions. This is a symbolic act—shedding his possessions is like shedding the exte-

rior behaviors, habits, and approvals that limit him. This is an act of personal accountability. No one but himself can be responsible for his interior growth as a man and as a leader. Not surprisingly, Ahbleza went on to become a great chief.

Leadership, as presented in this book, is about two things: the individual and the collective. Individual leadership grows from *personal fusion,* which develops within you the subtle forces that attract other people as followers. Personal fusion is a call to wholeness, the integration of the essential, interior self and the conditioned, exterior self, which together offer a grand warehouse of resources for leadership. Personal leadership calls on both the monk (self-awareness) and the warrior (action), both Gandhi and Patton. Personal fusion is embodied in Ahbleza, who can walk away naked yet also lead his tribe into war.

The collective is about the organization as a whole. *Organizational fusion* is about releasing subtle forces in a large group in order to build relationships, connections, community, and a positive culture and value system. This interior aspect of the organization can then be integrated with the exterior and strong-force elements of work-flow design, organizational structure, systems and technologies, policies and procedures, and expectations of bosses.

The scarcity of fusion leaders and the painful slowness of change in corporations reflect lingering industrial-age values of separation and control. Subtle forces such as imagination and ingenuity have been drowned out by the strong forces of rationality, efficiency, and the bottom line. Vision, integrity, courage, heart, and mindfulness all come from within, yet corporations typically insist that employees pay attention only to external pressures.

Ahbleza knew the importance of subtle forces and inner strength, so he temporarily walked away from external possessions and expectations. By bringing these opposing forces into balance, he became a great chief. Suppressed subtle forces explain why managers and employees often become dependent, perhaps frozen into decision paralysis, unaware of their own vision, unable to see the big picture, acting like donkeys rather than lions and never discovering their inner leadership treasure chest. The treasure chest can be opened with fusion events and fusion leadership. The treasure is within you, within your organization.

Are you ready to accept the challenge? The chaos and uncertainty of an out-of-kilter world are natural conditions for change, for nothing is certain. The challenge in becoming a fusion leader, in learning to make all things possible, is to stop trying to control that which defies control. The subtle forces are released, not controlled. Control suppresses them. The path of the fusion leader offers the potential of boundless freedom with purpose and meaning.

DROP YOUR TOOLS

Personal or organizational transformation is as much about letting go of old habits and attachments as it is about acquiring new behaviors. There is something about the human ego that attaches to the external things that got us where we are, and we often don't let go even under dire threat.

In 1949, thirteen wildland firefighters lost their lives at Mann Gulch, and in 1994, fourteen more firefighters lost their lives under similar conditions at South Canyon. In both cases, these 23 men and four women were overrun by exploding fires when their retreat was slowed because they failed to drop the heavy tools they were carrying. By keeping their tools, they lost valuable distance they could have covered more quickly if they had been lighter. All 27 perished within sight of safe areas.

The reluctance to drop one's tools when threat intensifies
is not just a problem for firefighters. Navy Seamen sometimes
refuse orders to remove their heavy steel-toed shoes when they
are forced to abandon a sinking ship, and they drown or
punch holes in life rafts as a result. Fighter pilots in a dis-
abled aircraft sometimes refuse orders to eject, preferring
instead the "cocoon of oxygen" still present in the cockpit.[2]

Similarly, airlines know that checked baggage can be far safer than carry-ons, because in an emergency, passengers clog the aisles trying to recover bags before exiting to safety.

Dropping your tools is a metaphor for unlearning, detaching from, and leaving behind the old way when responding to a crisis. The old way of organizing and controlling is about strong forces that are external to people. The old way is a bag of heavy tools that, if held on to, threatens the life of an organization.

Dropping tools is also a metaphor for giving up ego. Ego is attached to material, financial, and external possessions, including one's position in the hierarchy, the boss's approval, and traditional control. When ego is attached to the old way, there is little room for subtle potentials such as vision, courage, heart, and communication to awaken and express themselves.

Each leader has to become free in his or her own way. While at Ameritech, Bob Knowling was part of a team charged with introducing system changes that would better address employees' hearts and minds. It could have been fun.

But it wasn't happening. We weren't being bold. We were
still operating like bureaucrats. It was as if we'd been
neutered. We had all of this room to play in, we had all this
air cover from the chairman, but the only bold initiatives
were coming from external consultants—and they were
getting frustrated with our change team.

*Finally, one of the consultants asked me, "What are
you afraid of?" I'll never forget that conversation. I said,
"What do you mean?" He said, "You have great instincts,
but when the chairman does something dumb, you look the
other way. When a business unit leader has an operating
style that is totally different from the change model, you
won't call him on the carpet. Do you want a job so bad
that you're willing to accept what you know is wrong?"*

*Man, that was heavy to wear. He finally said, "You're
not free." It took some time for all that to soak in. Then
I decided, "What's the worst thing that could happen to
me? I could lose my job. But if I lose my job because I've
developed into a world-class change agent, there ought to be
about a dozen companies out there ready to pick me up."*

*I realized that I couldn't live in fear. Whether or not I
changed the company, I knew I would change myself. I'd
have new skills and capabilities. I'd be a very valuable
commodity.*[3]

Knowling dropped his attachment to his job. He was free.
But why is dropping tools to become free so hard? One reason
may be denial. You may not be willing to acknowledge the
depth of the emergency facing you or your organization. Perhaps the crisis has not yet persuaded you that new ways of leading and organizing are urgently needed. Perhaps you believe
that controlling things with the old tools is still the best way.
Perhaps you don't know how to drop your tools, having been
conditioned by a lifetime of structure and control. Perhaps
change would be to admit failure, which the ego dislikes above
all. Perhaps you hold on to familiar tools, even when the situation becomes desperate, because the unfamiliar alternative also
looks desperate. The unknown world of extended conversation,
shared dreaming, and the engagement of creativity, ingenuity,
and passion may seem so strange as to be unreal. Perhaps it's

better to stick with what you know than to try something so different. After all, your personal identity may be inextricably linked to your current position and way of doing things.

However, change won't occur within yourself or within your part of the organization without your initiative. And until you are in touch with your own subtle forces—the interior "I"— you will not see, appreciate, or know how to release the subtle forces in others. Personal fusion is an essential first step, and it can be achieved either by your own efforts or by collaboration with others in a fusion event.

Organizational fusion, too, demands appropriate leadership initiative. Indeed, moving forward toward fusion-based organizing requires far greater leadership than was ever demanded under traditional control structures. Fusion events do not replace leadership but extend it. A fusion event creates a team of horses that suddenly accelerates from a trot to a gallop. The demands on the driver multiply.

IS IT TIME TO ACT?

"Five, four, three, two, one, zero," says the television announcer, and on the television screen a building shakes and then begins to fall inward on itself, leaving the surrounding buildings unharmed. A series of small explosions at key structural points brought the building down in a few seconds. If traditional salvage technology—the wrecking ball—had been used, the demolition would have taken months. Similarly, a fusion event can topple a rigid structure and culture in a few weeks, as opposed to the years that would be required by the wrecking ball of a traditional consultant's reports loaded with top-down recommendations. A fusion event can implode the old culture, implementing change unbelievably fast.

At what point are you or your organization ready to drop your tools? When is it time to implode the old culture and seek safety in a fusion approach? Is your company ready to begin? Are you ready to lead change? Your answers to the following questions will indicate where you stand:

1. Do you believe that the leader needs to change first in order to change the organization?

2. Do you see the need to unlock your own subtle forces for leadership via personal fusion as a resource for leading change in your organization?

3. Can you take the risk of initiating substantive change in your part of the organization?

4. Do you see among employees widespread knowledge of and enthusiasm for the organization's mission and its future?

5. Do employees feel part of a community where collaboration seems natural? Is rugged individualism in balance with people building relationships across traditional boundaries for the sake of the company's larger purpose?

6. Do middle managers display subtle forces of leadership? Do they use elements of vision, communication, courage, heart, integrity, and mindfulness change things? Do middle-and lower-level managers take personal responsibility for moving the company forward?

7. Are employees feeling a sense of ownership? Do they buy into their tasks, teams, vision, and organization? Is work more than a job?

8. Are the right people in the right places? Are individuals in positions that excite them and enable them to express themselves?

9. Is meaningful conversation common? Can people listen to each other without defensiveness? Are conflicting views welcomed? Is broad understanding reached before decisions are implemented?

10. Is change seen as the organization's real work? Is change implemented quickly? Is there a critical mass of people working to change things? Is change sponsored in many places at once?

11. Do you and other leaders consider that success depends equally on people and performance, on subtle and strong forces, on soft and hard factors, on social and technical systems?

12. Does a whole-organization viewpoint dominate? Are employees attuned to the environment of customers and competition, and do they work within the big picture rather than fight for their limited viewpoints?

13. Is the organization flooded with information and authority? Do people know what they need to know and have authority to make choices to produce results? Do midlevel managers pass along information and resources to empower others?

14. Do employees take risks to explore new and uncertain territory? Are people more interested in trying things than in analyzing things?

15. Does everyone share in success? Does your organization celebrate it? Does everyone receive feedback about how he or she has contributed to the whole?

16. Does your organization feel flat and flexible, and do systems free people to act?

If you answered yes to the first three questions and no to several others, there is high potential for real change through fusion. It is time to drop some of your organization's tools. The shift is possible if you are ready to let go of the old ways, ready to drop your own tools. In an out-of-kilter world, a fusion leader initiates culture change by bridging boundaries with conversation, engaging individual initiative and team collaboration, and facilitating the pursuit of a common vision.

Fusion Is Not an Event

The emphasis in this book has been on achieving personal and organizational fusion through fusion technologies. Dialogue, future search, and whole-scale change are powerful technologies that can jump-start individuals and organizations seeking a new direction. However, in working with companies, we find that disproportionate emphasis is given to the three-day event because of its incredible power. The event is not the solution, not the end of the change process. It is simply a new beginning. Problems are not "fixed" by the event. The fusion event has to be carefully blended into the larger strategic context of the organization. Leaders who believe an event will solve their problems are mistaken. More leadership is required after the event than before. New initiatives have to be kept moving. A fusion event accelerates a lot of action, but the real work is done back on the job, where change must be sustained.

To be sustainable, fusion must become a way of living, a way of leading, a way of behaving, an enduring approach and value that underlies corporate culture. Fusion is about transcending traditional boundaries in the organization and within yourself. A fusion event, with its trained facilitators, simply allows the airplane to get off the ground. You and your organization will have to fly the airplane and, more important, land it.

Another metaphor may further illuminate the nature of a fusion event. Although the briquettes in your barbecue cook best when separated in checkerboard fashion, they cannot be lit that way. They pass their heat from one to the other only if they are touching. The fastest way to light briquettes is to put them in a pile, apply lighter fluid, and start a fire. The heat is transmitted through the adjoining briquettes, and the whole pile is quickly ignited. A fusion event brings people together in a "pile" so they can all ignite their subtle forces at the same time. After they have gone from cold to hot, they can return to their various places in the organization, prepared for the longer-term work ahead.

The best fusion practices are those initiated by managers themselves, either without an event or subsequent to an event, when the new way of thinking needs to be reinforced. Fusion principles can be easily applied in day-to-day management. Here are some examples:

- One operations vice president in a financial services firm changed the way all-hands meetings were held in his operations area. In previous meetings, the 150 people sat in rows facing the front of an auditorium. For a day and a half, they were treated to a succession of panels, videos, and invited speakers. During question periods, the audience stayed largely silent. Communication was all one-way, a huge number of employees sitting passively, doing as they were told, offering not a voice, not a question, not a challenge, nor a hope for the future.

  After the vice president had learned the principles of fusion, he reorganized the meeting along fusion lines. People sat in groups of eight to ten at round tables, each table containing a crossfunctional mix. After a panel presentation on, say, safety or consolidation of computer resources, participants at each table briefly discussed the issues presented. The small groups were instructed to have each person "discuss what you heard." This produced a lively exchange and deeper understanding, because each person heard something different. The format gave all participants a sense of empowerment and enabled them to find their voices. Conversations across traditional boundaries were mind-expanding and exciting. Each group was then invited to ask the panel one question that it considered of great importance, and excellent questions were asked. The use of round tables was instrumental in breaking down

barriers across functions and between top and bottom.
The small-group conversations enabled everyone to feel
involved.

- A similar approach was used by the provost of a small
  state university. When important meetings were held that
  involved faculty, administration, and sometimes students,
  attendees would congregate with their own kind. The
  provost organized round tables and seating assignments
  that mixed these groups. The discussions following talks
  that he and others gave were transformative. Teachers, administrators, and students heard each other—often for
  what seemed like the first time. Mindsets broadened, involvement heightened, and discussions continued far beyond the meeting. This small, single element of fusion,
  of getting the briquettes to touch one another and generate heat together, started a shift in perspective and behavior that affected all corners of the university.

- Another application of fusion thinking can be seen at
  McDevitt Street Bovis, a large construction manager. The
  parties involved in each construction project are brought
  together beforehand for a daylong facilitated meeting. The
  meeting enables potentially antagonistic parties to smooth
  work flow throughout the project, increase cooperation,
  reduce lawsuits, and often beat the deadlines. In a typical
  meeting, the facilitators divide the room into three
  groups—the building owner, the architect and engineer,
  and Bovis representatives. The three groups find common
  ground when they discover that their goals for the project
  are similar. All three want the project completed on time
  and under budget, and they want to satisfy the people who
  will use the building. They also want their relationships
  to extend beyond the current project. On this common

ground, the parties are willing to make concessions and
work together beyond formal contract commitments.

A typical meeting goes by without any of the participants even referring to the formal contract. A performance
agreement is worked out on the human level, and it therefore carries the force of personal commitment. Since Bovis
started using this approach, working relationships among
parties have improved, as have the buildings, and legal fees
have plummeted. Bovis has never been to court in connection with any of the hundred or so projects for which it
has held this kind of fusion meeting beforehand.[4]

- Consider the problem of trying to meld two companies
  together after a merger. MasterBrand Industries needed
  to integrate two companies into one home improvement/
  hardware manufacturer that reflected a unified vision.
  The answer was to bring together seventy-five key managers from the two companies for a three-day meeting.
  They formed crossfunctional advocate teams that broke
  down vertical walls between departments, and managers
  individually became catalysts for remaking the Master-
  Brand culture. The managers were initially skeptical, but
  they went along with their boss, who gave each a copy
  of *Oh, The Places You'll Go,* by Dr. Seuss. The book became a prized symbol of the group's pioneering efforts
  and achievements.[5]

- Another great day-to-day application of fusion technology
  is for project management teams. In a technology hardware company, new product teams included participants
  from around the organization, headed by a single project
  leader. The projects faced enormous problems of coordination and were beset by slow progress resulting from se-
  quential activities and partial commitment by participants.

The technology vice president decided to try a different approach. When a new device was about to be launched into production, he brought all the players into a room for two days of guided conversation. The major stakeholders all participated, and the implementation of the new product was reduced by a year. Why? Because each employee bought into the project, and people worked in parallel. Project participants were excited and enthusiastic about their impact. Resistance to change was easily overcome, and mindset changes occurred quickly during crossfunctional discussions. Engineers, for example, came to appreciate the need for collaboration with production and marketing. Top-down management pressure was not needed in the face of this bottom-up arousal of subtle forces of leadership.

Fusion conversations can be designed by any leader in any setting. A fusion microcosm, even if only in a single department, can begin to transform the entire organization.

WHY TAKE ACTION?

Why act to change your organization? Why change yourself? Why take on a long-term struggle? Why should you care? Isn't conventional management good enough? Well, conventional management *may* be good enough. But if it is not, then who better to take on this responsibility than you?

The essential point of this book is that management confusion and organizational resistance will continue until leaders find models that are more congruent with human nature. Is the assembly-line approach to management congruent with human nature? Or do the deep, powerful, and intimate forces within people—vision, mindfulness, heart, integrity, courage—form a more natural culture for organizational success?

Your organization is operating in a world unlike the world of twenty or even ten years ago. For most companies, the world is permanently out-of-kilter, and stability is impossible. Today's world presents surprises and stresses daily and hourly. The ideal organization is focused on change, growth, experimentation, bottom-up learning, and relationships. This is far from the world of formal long-range planning, predictable outcomes, and top-down directives that enforce efficiency, stability, and incremental change.

When uncontrolled, weeds dominate the flower garden. When unrestrained, the strong forces of traditional structure overwhelm personal subtle forces. The leader's task is to awaken subtle forces and yearnings. There are numerous potential change leaders in your organization, but many catalyzers, risk takers, and champions of change are in a dormant state. You can't awaken them by decree. These flowers require fertilizer, water, good soil, and occasional weeding. Each flower will grow by itself if you cut back the weeds.

Can you be like Ahbleza and drop your attachment to today's structure and possessions? Can you drop the tools that are not appropriate for this emergency? The answer is within you, within your people, within your organization. Both personal fusion and organizational fusion are about turning inward to manage outward. Fusion leadership is about releasing all the ingenuity available to your organization. Sustainable fusion may seem like a hard road, but actually it is the easiest road. Letting go is easier than holding on. Why continue to seek control over that which defies control? Why continue along the path of stress, confusion, and fear? The fusion path offers spiritual freedom and a renewed sense of meaning. If you drop your out-of-date attachments and tools and enable others to do likewise, changes will soon appear. In an out-of-kilter world, do you have any other choice?

If you light the fusion candle, fires of change will soon burn throughout your organization. Try to imagine people's minds, hearts, and spirits set free, each committed to your company's highest purpose. But this liberation won't even begin without leadership. Can you be like Ahbleza and shed the clothes of formal structure and control? Collaborative fusion won't happen without your leadership. Do you have the vision, courage, and integrity to begin?

Personal Remembering

- If you retired today, what would your coworkers say about you? What do you wish they would say?

- A Baha'i holy man said, "When the most important work is before us, let the important work go." What is the most important work facing you?

- Who is the richest person in the world—the one who has the most possessions or the one who has the fewest desires? Why?

- What are you holding onto in your organizational life that is the most difficult to let go of? How would it feel to let go?

NOTES

CHAPTER ONE

1. Barry Oshry, *Seeing Systems: Unlocking the Mysteries of Organizational Life* (San Francisco: Berrett-Koehler, 1996).
2. For an overview of the new sciences approach, see Margaret J. Wheatley, *Leadership and the New Science: Learning About Organization from an Orderly Universe* (San Francisco: Berrett-Koehler, 1994); Margaret J. Wheatley and Myron Kellner-Rogers, *A Simpler Way* (San Francisco: Berrett-Koehler, 1996); Jeffrey Goldstein, *The Unshackled Organization* (Portland, Ore.: Productivity Press, 1994); Ralph D. Stacey, *Complexity and Creativity in Organizations* (San Francisco: Berrett-Koehler, 1996).
3. This quote is attributed to Abraham Maslow.
4. This basic idea can be found in a number of sources, among them Aristotle, *The Nicomachean Ethics,* trans. by H. Rackham (Cambridge, Mass.: Harvard University Press, 1982); Saint Thomas Aquinas, *Summa Theologica,* trans. by brothers of the English Dominican Province, rev. by Daniel J. Sullivan (Chicago: Encyclopaedia Britannica, 1952); Alasdair MacIntyre, *After Virtue: A Study in Moral Theory* (Notre Dame, Ind.: University of Notre Dame Press, 1984); Stephen Covey, *The Seven Habits of Highly Effective People: Powerful Lessons in Personal Change,* (New York: Fireside Books/Simon & Schuster, 1990).

5. James L. Lundy, *Lead, Follow, or Get out of the Way: Leadership Strategies for the Thoroughly Modern Manager* (San Diego: Slawson Communications, 1986); James M. Kouzes and Barry Z. Posner, *Credibility: How Leaders Gain and Lose It, Why People Demand It* (San Francisco: Jossey-Bass, 1993); Constance H. Buchanan, *Choosing to Lead: Women and the Crisis of American Values* (Boston: Beacon Press, 1996); Jay A. Conger, Rabindra N. Kanungo, and Associates, *Charismatic Leadership: The Elusive Factor in Organizational Effectiveness* (San Francisco: Jossey-Bass, 1988).

6. John Southerst, "First, We Dump the Bosses," *Canadian Business,* April 1992, pp. 46–51.

CHAPTER TWO

1. Based on Sogyal Rinpoche, *The Tibetan Book of Living and Dying* (San Francisco: Harper San Francisco, 1993), p. 34.
2. "Schools of Tomorrow," *Time,* September 12, 1960, p. 74.
3. Sogyal, *Tibetan Book of Living and Dying,* p. 21.
4. Based on ideas in Wheatley, *Leadership and the New Science;* Wheatley and Kellner-Rogers, *A Simpler Way;* Goldstein, *Unshackled Organization;* Stacey, *Complexity and Creativity in Organizations.*
5. Personal communication from George Starcher and Dorothy Marcic, 1994.
6. The distinction between transactional and transformational leaders was first articulated by James MacGregor Burns in *Leadership* (New York: HarperCollins, 1978).
7. David K. Hurst, *Crisis & Renewal: Meeting the Challenge of Organizational Change* (Boston: Harvard Business School Press, 1995).

CHAPTER THREE

1. Sogyal, *Tibetan Book of Living and Dying,* p. 41.
2. Stratford Sherman, "Leaders Learn to Heed the Voice Within," *Fortune,* 22 August 1994, pp. 92–100; "How Tomorrow's Best Leaders Are Learning Their Stuff," *Fortune,* 27 November 1995, pp. 90–94 and 100–102; Genevieve Capowski, "Anatomy of a Leader: Where Are the Leaders of Tomorrow?" *Management Review,* March 1994, pp. 10–17.

3. Based on the idea of the *conditioned self* and the *essential self* in Susan M. Campbell, *From Chaos to Confidence: Survival Strategies for the New Workplace* (New York: Simon & Schuster, 1995): 110–14.

4. Marilyn R. Zuckerman and Lewis J. Hatala, *Incredibly American: Releasing the Heart of Quality* (Milwaukee: ASQC Quality Press, 1992), p. 36.

5. Robert Bly and William Booth, *A Little Book on the Human Shadow* (San Francisco: Harper San Francisco, 1992). Thanks to Cliff Barry and Shadow Work Seminars for this example.

6. Abraham Zaleznik, *The Managerial Mystique: Restoring Leadership in Business* (New York: HarperCollins, 1989).

7. Sogyal, *Tibetan Book of Living and Dying*, p. 134.

8. Mort Meyerson, "Everything I Thought I Knew About Leadership Is Wrong," *Fast Company*, April-May 1996, pp. 71–75 and 78–80.

9. Leon Alligood, "The Horse Whisperer," *Nashville Banner*, 2 July 1997, p. A1.

10. Lundy, *Lead, Follow, or Get out of the Way*; Kouzes and Posner, *Credibility*.

11. William Faulkner, "The Bear," in *Go Down Moses, and Other Stories* (New York: Random House, 1942).

12. "The Stuff Americans Are Made of: The Personal Quality Improvement Process of the American Quality Foundation," Research Report (Milwaukee: ASQC, 1994).

CHAPTER FOUR

1. We have heard this story from a number of sources.

2. Based on the allegory of the cave in Book 7 of *Plato's Republic*, trans. by B. Jowett (New York: Modern Library, 1982).

3. Elliott Jaques, "The Development of Intellectual Capacity: A Discussion of Stratified Systems Theory," *Journal of Applied Behavioral Science* 22:4 (1986): 361–83; Alexander Ross, "The Long View of Leadership," *Canadian Business*, May 1992, pp. 46–51.

4. Edward O. Welles, "The Shape of Things to Come," *Inc.*, February 1992, pp. 66–69, 72.

5. Ellen J. Langer, *Mindfulness* (Reading, Mass.: Addison-Wesley, 1989).

6. Langer, *Mindfulness*, p. 4.

7. Bernard M. Bass, *New Paradigm Leadership: An Inquiry into Transformational Leadership* (Alexandria, Va.: U.S. Army Research Institute for the Behavioral and Social Sciences, 1996).

8. James Gleick, *Genius: The Life and Science of Richard Feynman* (New York: Pantheon Books, 1992).

9. Ian Mitroff, *Break-Away Thinking: How to Challenge Your Business Assumptions (and Why You Should)* (New York: Wiley, 1988).

10. Joel Arthur Barker, *Future Edge: Discovering the New Paradigms of Success* (New York: Morrow, 1992).

11. Peter F. Drucker, "The Discipline of Innovation," *Harvard Business Review* (May-June 1985): 66–72.

12. Barker, *Future Edge.*

13. Bruno Bettelheim, *The Uses of Enchantment: The Meaning and Importance of Fairy Tales* (London: Penguin, 1991), pp. 99–100.

14. Noel M. Tichy and Stratford Sherman, *Control Your Destiny or Someone Else Will* (New York: Doubleday, 1993); Stanley Bing, "Executive Shelf Life," *Esquire,* June 1992, pp. 69–70.

15. Joseph Campbell, *The Hero with a Thousand Faces,* 2nd ed. (Princeton, N.J.: Princeton University Press, 1968), p. 89.

CHAPTER FIVE

1. The essence of this story came from a talk heard by one of the authors at a community spiritual service in Santa Fe, New Mexico.

2. Jon R. Katzenbach and the RCL Team, *Real Change Leaders: How You Can Create Growth and High Performance at Your Company* (New York: Times Business, 1995), p. 64.

3. Peter M. Senge, *The Fifth Discipline: The Art and Practice of the Learning Organization* (New York: Doubleday Currency, 1990), p. 208.

4. Inspired by William Poundstone, *The Recursive Universe: Cosmic Complexity and the Limits of Scientific Knowledge* (New York: William Morrow, 1985), pp. 90–91.

5. John Sculley with John A. Byrne, *Odyssey: Pepsi to Apple—A Journey of Adventure, Ideas, and the Future* (New York: HarperCollins, 1987).

6. Kouzes and Posner, *Leadership Challenge,* p. 99.

7. B. Thomas, *Walt Disney: An American Tradition* (New York: Simon & Schuster, 1976), pp. 246–47.

8. James C. Collins and Jerry I. Porras, "Organizational Vision and Visionary Organizations," *California Management Review,* Fall 1991, pp. 30–52.

9. George Land and Beth Jarman, *Breakpoint and Beyond: Mastering the Future—Today* (New York: HarperBusiness, 1992), p. 12.

10. Kouzes and Posner, *Leadership Challenge,* p. 89.

11. Land and Jarman, *Breakpoint and Beyond,* p. 128.

12. John Kotter, *The Leadership Factor* (New York: Free Press, 1988).

13. Kouzes and Posner, *Leadership Challenge,* p. 82; Alan Farnham, "State Your Values, Hold the Hot Air," *Fortune,* 19 April 1993, pp. 117–24.

14. Katzenbach, *Real Change Leaders,* pp. 68–70.

15. Richard L. Daft, *Management,* 4th ed. (Fort Worth, Tex.: Dryden Press, 1997), p. 218.

16. James C. Collins and Jerry I. Porras, "Organizational Vision and Visionary Organizations," *California Management Review,* Fall 1991, 30–52.

17. Kouzes and Posner, *Leadership Challenge,* p. 98.

18. John Kotter, *A Force for Change: How Leadership Differs from Management* (New York: Free Press, 1990), p. 37.

19. Roger Thompson, "There's No Place Like Home Depot," *Nation's Business,* February 1992, pp. 30–33.

20. For further information on using mental imagery to create vision, see William P. Anthony, Robert H. Bennett, III, E. Nick Maddox, and Walter J. Wheatley, "Picturing the Future: Using Mental Imagery to Enrich Strategic Environmental Assessment," *Academy of Management Executive* 7:2 (1993): 43–56; Burt Nanus, *Visionary Leadership: Creating a Compelling Sense of Direction for Your Organization* (San Francisco: Jossey-Bass, 1992), pp. 33–35.

CHAPTER SIX

1. Robert Moore and Douglas Gillette, *King, Warrior, Magician, Lover: Rediscovering the Archetypes of the Mature Masculine* (San Francisco: Harper San Francisco, 1990).

2. Thomas Cleary, trans., *Zen Lessons: The Art of Leadership* (Boston: Shambhala, 1989), p. 28.

3. Warren Bennis, *On Becoming a Leader* (Reading, Mass.: Addison-Wesley, 1989).

4. "Come from the Heart," by Richard Leigh and Susanna Clark, EMI April Music Inc./GSC Music/Lion Hearted Music, 1987.

5. Kouzes and Posner, *Leadership Challenge,* p. 270.

6. Judy B. Rosener, "Ways Women Lead," *Harvard Business Review* (November-December 1990): 119–25, 120.

7. John Holusha, "Grace Pastiak's *Web of Inclusion,*" *New York Times,* 5 May 1991, Sec. 3, pp. 1, 6.

8. V. S. Verson Jones, trans., *Aesop's Fables* (New York: Avenal Books/Crown, 1912), p. 18.

9. *Leadership: A Forum Issues Special Report* (Boston, Mass.: Forum Corp., 1990).

10. Inspired by Alfie Kohn, *No Contest: The Case Against Competition* (Boston: Houghton Mifflin, 1986), p. 94.

11. A. K. Ramanujan, ed., *Folktales from India: A Selection of Oral Tales from Twenty-Two Languages* (New York: Pantheon Books, 1991), p. 3.

12. William H. Peace, "The Hard Work of Being a Soft Manager," *Harvard Business Review* (November-December 1991): 40–47.

13. Doug Boyd, *Mystics, Magicians, and Medicine People: Tales of a Wanderer* (New York: Paragon House, 1989), p. 60.

14. Joshua Hyatt, "The Odyssey of an *Excellent* Man," *Inc.,* February 1989, pp. 63–69; "Mapping the Entrepreneurial Mind," *Inc.,* August 1991, pp. 26–31.

15. Lao Tzu, *Tao Te Ching,* chap. 43. There are numerous translations of the *Tao Te Ching.* This quote comes from *The Essential Tao: An Initiation into the Heart of Taoism Through the Authentic Tao Te Ching and the Inner Teachings of Chuang Tzu,* trans. by Thomas Cleary (San Francisco: Harper San Francisco, 1991), p. 35.

16. Danaan Parry, *Warriors of the Heart* (Bainbridge Island, Wash.: Earth-stewards Network Publications, 1989), pp. 7–10.

CHAPTER SEVEN

1. "The Sound of the Forest," from W. Chan Kim and Renee A. Mauborgne, "Parables of Leadership," *Harvard Business Review* (July-August 1992): 123–28, 124.

2. Stephen R. Covey, *Principle-Centered Leadership* (New York: Simon & Schuster, 1991), pp. 111–112.

3. Monci Jo Williams, "America's Best Salesmen," *Fortune,* 26 October 1987, pp. 122–34, 128.

4. Joseph Jaworsky, *Synchronicity: The Inner Path of Leadership* (San Francisco: Berrett-Koehler, 1996), p. 182.

5. Thomas J. Peters and Nancy K. Austin, *A Passion for Excellence: The Leadership Difference* (New York: Random House, 1985).

6. Linda Smircich and Gareth Morgan, "Leadership: The Management of Meaning," *Journal of Applied Behavioral Science* 18:3 (1982): 257–73.

7. Tichy and Sherman, *Control Your Destiny or Someone Else Will,* p. 65.

8. Kotter, *A Force for Change,* p. 51.

9. Roger Smith, "The U.S. Must Do as GM Has Done," *Fortune,* 13 February 1989, pp. 70–73.

10. This point was made in Thomas J. Peters, "Symbols, Patterns, and Settings: An Optimistic Case for Getting Things Done," *Organizational Dynamics* (Autumn 1978): 3–22; "Management Systems: The Language of Organizational Character and Competence," *Organizational Dynamics* (Summer 1980): 3–26.

11. David Armstrong, *Managing by Storying Around: A New Method of Leadership* (New York: Doubleday Currency, 1992), p. 5.

12. J. Martin and M. Powers, "Organizational Stories: More Vivid and Persuasive than Quantitative Data," in *Psychological Foundations of Organizational Behavior,* ed. B. M. Staw (Glenview, Ill.: Scott, Foresman, 1982), pp. 161–68.

13. Pat Apel, *Nine Great American Myths: Ways We Confuse the American Dream with the Christian Faith* (Brentwood, Tenn.: Wolgemuth & Hyatt, 1991).

14. Armstrong, *Managing by Storying Around,* p. 51.

15. Susan Benner, "Culture Shock," *Inc.,* August 1985, pp. 73–82.

16. Nancy K. Austin, "Wacky Management Ideas That Work," *Working Woman,* November 1991, pp. 42–44.

17. Maryann Keller, "Slash, Burn, and So Long," *Canadian Business,* June 1994, pp. 36–47.

18. Peters, "Management Systems."

19. Kouzes and Posner, *Leadership Challenge,* p. 202.

20. David C. Limerick, "Managers of Meaning: From Bob Geldof's Band Aid to Australian CEOs," *Organizational Dynamics* 19:4 (Spring 1990): 22–33, 30.

21. Robert H. Lengel and Richard L. Daft, "The Selection of Communication Media as an Executive Skill," *Academy of Management Executive* 2:3 (1988): 225–32.

22. Mary Young and James E. Post, "Managing to Communicate, Communicating to Manage: How Leading Companies Communicate with Employees," *Organizational Dynamics* 22:1 (Summer 1993): 31–43, 37.

23. "Enforcing a No-Memo Policy," *Small Business Report,* July 1988, pp. 26–27

24. Tichy and Sherman, *Control Your Destiny or Someone Else Will,* p. 62.

25. Nancy K. Austin, "Just Do It," *Incentive,* September 1996, p. 26.

26. These images were reported in David Limerick and Bert Cunnington, *Managing the New Organization: A Blueprint for Networks and Strategic Alliances* (San Francisco: Jossey-Bass, 1993), pp. 200–204.

CHAPTER EIGHT

1. We have heard this story from a number of sources.
2. Moore and Gillette, *King, Warrior, Magician, Lover.*
3. Robert Bly, *Iron John: A Book About Men* (New York: Vintage Books, 1992).
4. Lester Korn, *The Success Profile: A Leading Headhunter Tells You How to Get to the Top* (New York: Simon & Schuster, 1988), p. 142.
5. "Even They Eat Humble Pie," *Inc.,* October 1992, p. 80; Daft, *Management,* p. 199.
6. Jerry B. Harvey, *The Abilene Paradox and Other Meditations on Management* (San Francisco: New Lexington Press, 1988), pp. 13–15.
7. Pat Riley, *The Winner Within: A Life Plan for Team Players* (New York: Putnam, 1993), pp. 239–42.
8. Harvey, *Abilene Paradox,* p. 63.
9. M. Scott Peck, *The Road Less Traveled: A New Psychology of Love, Traditional Values, and Spiritual Growth* (New York: Touchstone/Simon & Schuster, 1978), p. 294.
10. Sam Walton with John Huey, *Sam Walton: Made in America* (New York: Doubleday, 1992), p. 39.
11. Cleary, *Zen Lessons,* p. 43.
12. Kahlil Gibran, *The Prophet* (New York: Knopf, 1987), p. 58.
13. Campbell, *Hero with a Thousand Faces,* p. 91.
14. David Green, "Learning from Losing a Customer," *Harvard Business Review* (May-June 1989): 54–58.
15. Barker, *Future Edge.*
16. Clarissa Pinkola Estes, *Women Who Run with the Wolves: Myths and Stories of the Wild Woman Archetype* (New York: Ballantine, 1992), p. 120.
17. Stephen E. Ambrose, *Band of Brothers* (New York: Simon & Schuster, 1992), pp. 182–98.
18. This information was given to the authors by a personal friend of the King family.
19. Joseph Campbell, ed., *Myths, Dreams, and Religion* (New York: NAL/Dutton, 1970), p. 245.
20. Musashi Miyamoto, *The Book of Five Rings,* trans. by Thomas Cleary (Boston: Shambhala, 1993).

CHAPTER NINE

1. Kim and Mauborgne, "Parables of Leadership," p. 128.
2. This discussion is based on Moore and Gillette, *King, Warrior, Magician, Lover.*

3. Motto of Rotary International.

4. Robert K. Greenleaf, *Servant Leadership: A Journey into the Nature of Legitimate Power and Greatness* (Mahwah, N.J.: Paulist Press, 1977), p. 7.

5. Greenleaf, *Servant Leadership,* and Chris Lee and Ron Zemke, "The Search for Spirit in the Workplace," *Training* (June 1993): 21–27.

6. Quoted in David K. Hurst, "Thoroughly Modern—Mary Parker Follett," *Business Quarterly* 56:4 (Spring 1992): 55–58, 58.

7. Hyler Bracey, Jack Rosenblum, Aubrey Sanford, and Roy Trueblood, *Managing from the Heart* (New York: Dell, 1993), p. 192.

8. Greenleaf, *Servant Leadership,* p. 15.

9. David A. Whetten and Kim S. Cameron, *Developing Management Skills,* 2nd ed. (New York: HarperCollins College), pp. 66–67.

10. L. Kohlberg, "Moral Stages and Moralization: The Cognitive-Development Approach," in *Moral Development and Behavior: Theory, Research, and Social Issues,* ed. T. Likona (Austin, Tex.: Holt, Rinehart and Winston, 1976), pp. 31–53.

11. Quoted in Michael Crichton, *Travels* (New York: Knopf), p. 375.

12. Cleary, *Zen Lessons,* p. 106.

13. Kouzes and Posner, *Credibility,* pp. 14, 255.

14. Holusha, "Grace Pastiak's *Web of Inclusion.*"

15. Kouzes and Posner, "The Credibility Factor: What Followers Expect from Their Leaders," *Management Review,* January 1990, pp. 21–33, 33.

16. We heard this story from a number of personal sources.

17. Charles Burck, "Succeeding with Tough Love," *Fortune,* 29 November 1993, p. 188.

18. Parker J. Palmer, *Leading from Within: Reflections on Spirituality and Leadership* (Indianapolis: Indiana Office for Campus Ministries, 1990), p. 2.

19. Palmer, *Leading from Within,* p. 5.

20. Palmer, *Leading from Within,* pp. 7, 11–12.

21. Jack Hawley, *Reawakening the Spirit in Work: The Power of Dharmic Management* (San Francisco: Berrett-Koehler, 1993), p. 77.

22. Greenleaf, *Servant Leadership,* p. 45.

CHAPTER TEN

1. Inspired by Michael Jones, *Creating an Imaginative Life* (Berkeley, Calif.: Conari Press, 1995), p. 166.

2. Dee W. Hock, "Institutions in the Age of Mindcrafting." Paper presented at the Bionomics Annual Conference, San Francisco, 22 October 1994.

3. M. Scott Peck, *The Different Drum: Community Making and Peace* (New York: Simon & Schuster, 1987).

4. Marvin R. Weisbord, *Productive Workplaces: Organizing and Managing for Dignity, Meaning, and Community* (San Francisco: Jossey-Bass, 1987).

5. This discussion is based on Zuckerman and Hatala, *Incredibly American;* "The Stuff Americans Are Made of"; and G. Clotaire Rapaille, *Decoding the American Mind* (New York: Penguin/Viking, 1993).

6. Chris Argyris, *On Organizational Learning* (Cambridge, Mass.: Blackwell, 1993).

CHAPTER ELEVEN

1. Antoine de Saint-Exupéry, *The Little Prince,* trans. by Katherine Woods (Orlando: Harcourt Brace, 1971), pp. 78–84.

2. An overview of these approaches can be found in Barbara Benedict Bunker and Billie T. Alban, "Editors' Introduction: The Large Group Introduction—A New Social Innovation?" *Journal of Applied Behavioral Science* 28:4 (December 1992): 473–479; and Nancy M. Dixon, "The Hallway of Learning," *Organizational Dynamics* (Spring 1997): 23–34.

3. David Bohm, *On Dialogue* (Ojai, Calif.: David Bohm Seminars, 1989).

4. Suresh Srivastva, David L. Cooperrider, and Associates, *Appreciative Management and Leadership: The Power of Positive Thought and Action in Organizations* (San Francisco: Jossey-Bass, 1990).

5. William N. Isaacs, "Taking Flight: Dialogue, Collective Thinking, and Organizational Learning," *Organizational Dynamics* (Autumn 1993): 24–39.

6. Marvin R. Weisbord and Sandra Janoff, *Future Search: An Action Guide to Finding Common Ground in Organizations and Communities* (San Francisco: Berrett-Koehler, 1995).

7. The whole-scale technology is not fully described in a single publication, but one approach can be found in Robert W. Jacobs, *Real Time Strategic Change* (San Francisco: Berrett-Koehler, 1994).

8. Jay A. Conger, *Learning to Lead: The Art of Transforming Managers into Leaders* (San Francisco: Jossey-Bass, 1992).

9. William J. Kaschub, "PECO Energy's Employees Redesign HR: The Large-Scale Interactive Approach." Unpublished manuscript, PECO Energy, 1996.

10. Kaschub, "PECO Energy's Employees Redesign HR."

CHAPTER TWELVE

1. We have heard many versions of this story. For two of them, see Jay A. Conger & Associates, *Spirit at Work: Discovering the Spirituality in Leadership* (San Francisco: Jossey-Bass, 1994), pp. 206–8; and Solané Verraine-Kress, "The Lion's Road: An Interview with Gangaji," *Crosswinds,* November 1994, p. 30.
2. This discussion was inspired by a conversation with Tim Dalmau of Dalmau and Associates and by Ken Wilber, *The Eye of Spirit: An Integral Vision for a World Gone Slightly Mad* (Boston: Shambhala, 1997), Chapter One.
3. This formula was inspired by Richard Beckhard, *Organizational Development: Strategies and Models* (Reading, Mass.: Addison-Wesley, 1969).
4. Based on Ronald Lippett, "Future Before You Plan," in *NTL Managers Handbook*, ed. Roger A. Ritvo and Alice G. Sargent (Arlington, Va.: NTL Institute, 1983), pp. 374–381.

CHAPTER THIRTEEN

1. Hawley, *Reawakening the Spirit in Work,* pp. 117–18.
2. Karl E. Weick, "Drop Your Tools: An Allegory for Organizational Studies," *Administrative Science Quarterly* 41 (June 1996): 301–13.
3. Noel Tichy, "Bob Knowling's Change Manual," *Fast Company,* April-May 1997, pp. 76–82, 78.
4. Thomas Petzinger, Jr., "Bovis Team Helps Builders Construct a Solid Foundation," *Wall Street Journal,* 21 March 1997, p. B1.
5. Patrick Flanagan, "The ABCs of Changing Corporate Culture," *Management Review,* July 1995, pp. 57–61.

INDEX

THE AUTHORS

RICHARD L. DAFT holds the Ralph Owen chair and is director of the Center for Change Leadership in the Owen Graduate School of Management, Vanderbilt University, Nashville, Tennessee. His specialty is the study of organizational change and leadership. Daft received his M.B.A. and his Ph.D. in organization theory from the University of Chicago. He has authored or coauthored many scientific articles and several books, including his worldwide best-selling textbooks *Organization Theory and Design,* 6th ed. (West, 1998), and *Management,* 4th ed. (Dryden, 1997).

Managers from hundreds of companies have been involved in Daft's courses on leadership and change, and he has acted as a consultant to dozens of companies and not-for-profit organizations.

ROBERT H. LENGEL is associate dean for executive education and founder and director of the Center for Professional Excellence at the University of Texas at San Antonio. He earned his B.S. in aerospace engineering at Pennsylvania State University, his M.S. and M.B.A. degrees from Rensselaer Polytechnic Institute, and his Ph.D. in business administration from Texas A&M.

Lengel has spoken before many groups, taught thousands of students, and has introduced managers from more than one hundred companies to the scientific and philosophical principles behind change in corporate America. He has developed and conducted corporate training programs and engaged in consulting and research for many corporate clients, including the military, public and private schools, energy companies, aerospace companies, theme parks, retailers, and telecommunications companies. He has also published numerous scientific articles.

Berrett-Koehler Publishers

ERRETT-KOEHLER is an independent publisher of books, periodicals, and other publications at the leading edge of new thinking and innovative practice on work, business, management, leadership, stewardship, career development, human resources, entrepreneurship, and global sustainability.

Since the company's founding in 1992, we have been committed to supporting the movement toward a more enlightened world of work by publishing books, periodicals, and other publications that help us to integrate our values with our work and work lives, and to create more humane and effective organizations.

We have chosen to focus on the areas of work, business, and organizations, because these are central elements in many people's lives today. Furthermore, the work world is going through tumultuous changes, from the decline of job security to the rise of new structures for organizing people and work. We believe that change is needed at all levels— individual, organizational, community, and global—and our publications address each of these levels.

We seek to create new lenses for understanding organizations, to legitimize topics that people care deeply about but that current business orthodoxy censors or considers secondary to bottom-line concerns, and to uncover new meaning, means, and ends for our work and work lives.

See next page for other books from Berrett-Koehler Publishers

Other leading-edge business books from Berrett-Koehler Publishers

Leadership and the New Science
Learning about Organization from an Orderly Universe

Margaret J. Wheatley

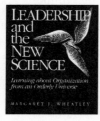

OUR UNDERSTANDING of the universe is being radically altered by the "New Science"—the revolutionary discoveries in quantum physics, chaos theory, and evolutionary biology that are overturning the prevailing models of science. Now, in this pioneering book, Wheatley shows how the new science provides equally powerful insights for changing how we design, lead, manage, and view organizations.

Paperback, 172 pages, 3/94 • ISBN 1-881052-44-3 CIP
Item no. 52443-236 $15.95
Hardcover, 9/92 • ISBN 1-881052-01-X CIP • **Item no. 5201X-236 $24.95**

A Simpler Way
Margaret J. Wheatley and Myron Kellner-Rogers

A SIMPLER WAY is the widely awaited new book from Margaret J. Wheatley, author of the bestselling *Leadership and the New Science.* Here, Wheatley and Kellner-Rogers draw on the work of scientists, philosophers, poets, novelists, spiritual teachers, colleagues, audiences, and each other in search of new ways of understanding life and how organizing activities occur. *A Simpler Way* presents a profoundly different world view that changes how we live our lives and create organizations that thrive.

Hardcover, 168 pages, 9/96 • ISBN 1-881052-95-8 CIP
Item no. 52958-236 $27.95

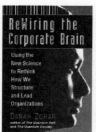

Rewiring the Corporate Brain
Using the New Science to Rethink How We Structure and Lead Organizations

Danah Zohar

DRAWING ON a solid background in the new sciences, *Rewiring the Corporate Brain* details the ways in which organizational structures mirror the organization of the human brain, shows how to utilize the capacity of the whole corporate brain, and describes a fundamentally new conceptual model for transformational change to the structure and leadership of organizations.

Hardcover, 250 pages, 11/97 • ISBN 1-57675-022-1 CIP
Item no. 50221-236 $27.95

Available at your favorite bookstore, or call (800) 929-2929

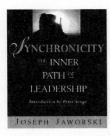

Synchronicity: The Inner Path of Leadership

Joseph Jaworski

SYNCHRONICITY is an inspirational guide to developing the most essential leadership capacity for our time: the ability to collectively shape our future. Joseph Jaworski tells the remarkable story of his journey to an understanding of the deep issues of leadership. It is a personal journey that encourages and enlightens all of us wrestling with the profound changes required in public and institutional leadership, and in our individual lives, for the 21st century.

Hardcover, 228 pages, 6/96 • ISBN 1-881052-94-X CIP
Item no. 5294X-236 $24.95

Imaginization

New Mindsets for Seeing, Organizing, and Managing

Gareth Morgan

"**I**MAGINIZATION" is a way of thinking and organizing. It is a key managerial skill that will help you develop your creative potential, and find innovative solutions to difficult problems. It answers the call for more creative forms of organization and management. *Imaginization* shows how to put this approach into practice.

Paperback, 350 pages, 8/97 • ISBN 1-57675-026-4 CIP
Item no. 50264-236 $19.95

Complexity and Creativity in Organizations

Ralph Stacey

THE MOST COMPREHENSIVE and thorough book yet written on how the new science of complexity can be applied to organizations, *Complexity and Creativity in Organizations* invites you to explore how this new science might provide us with more useful frameworks for making sense of life in organizations. Ralph Stacey shows how creative futures emerge from spontaneously self-organizing processes of complex learning.

Hardcover, 320 pages, 5/96 • ISBN: 1-881052-89-3 CIP
Item no. 52893-236 $34.95

Available at your favorite bookstore, or call (800) 929-2929

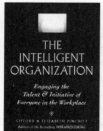